Screen

Consciousness

Consciousness Literature the & Arts 04

General Editor:
Daniel Meyer-Dinkgräfe

Editorial Board:
Anna Bonshek, John Danvers,
William S. Haney II, Amy Ione,
Arthur Versluis, Christopher Webster

Screen Consciousness

Cinema, Mind and World

EDITED BY

ROBERT PEPPERELL AND
MICHAEL PUNT

Amsterdam - New York, NY 2006

Cover Design: Aart Jan Bergshoeff

The paper on which this book is printed meets the requirements of "ISO 9706:1994, Information and documentation - Paper for documents - Requirements for permanence".

ISBN-10: 90-420-2016-4
ISBN-13: 978-90-420-2016-0
ISSN: 1573-2193
©Editions Rodopi B.V., Amsterdam - New York, NY 2006
Printed in the Netherlands

Contents

Acknowledgements

In the course of the preparation of this book there have been many people who have helped us with their generosity, thoughts and time, not least Daniel Meyer-Dinkgräfe. The conference he convened in Aberystwyth in 2005* provided the first public airing for some of the ideas that have since been developed here, and gave us confidence that what we were doing was interesting. Ours is a high risk academic field and only develops through the intellectual support of others. The conference offered a timely opportunity to test the rigour of our approach and respond to the kindly advice and interventions.

In the same vein we would also like to thank Roy Ascott, Martha Blassnigg, Amy Ione, and Stephen Thompson for their thoughts and help in developing this idea from its original suggestion to a substantial representation of our shared thoughts. The task of production was not without its problems and we are all extremely grateful to Aparna Sharma for her patient copy editing of this book, a task made more complex by the diversity of linguistic backgrounds and disciplines from which the contributors come. And to Andy Prior who, against formidable odds, solved our formatting problem as all hope of understanding the unwieldy word-processor was fading. This project also received academic support from the School of Art, Media and Design at the University of Wales, Newport and the School of Computing, Communications and Electronics at the University of Plymouth.

Finally, as mentioned at the outset, this book emerged from an earlier collaboration between the editors that led to the publication of *The Postdigital Membrane,* and in a sense this work is an extension of that project. That book was dedicated to Daisy Pepperell and in the spirit of history and symmetry — dogs that seem to have barked throughout this collection — we would like to dedicate this book to her sister, Emily.

Robert Pepperell
Michael Punt

March 2006

*The International Conference on Consciousness, Theatre, Literature and the Arts

Contributors

Martha Blassnigg is a Cultural Anthropologist and Film and Media Theorist with a background in documentary filmmaking and film restoration, currently undertaking research at the School of Art, Media and Design at the University of Wales, Newport, in which she examines how the historically determined concept of the angel and its philosophical implications become connected to the perception of cinematographic technology. She is also participating in a number of collaborations at Trans-Technology Research at the University of Plymouth and is a reviewer for *Leonardo Reviews*. Previously, her research at the University of Amsterdam with a specialisation in ethnographic documentary film led her to an empirical study in which she conducted ethnographic fieldwork in Vienna on the subject of clairvoyance between 1997-2000. Her Masters thesis at the University of Amsterdam, *Seeing Angels and the Spiritual in Film: An Interdisciplinary Study of a Sensuous Experience* compared cinema technology with the metaphysical phenomenon of appearances, and was accompanied by her documentary film, *Shapes of Light* (2000). In her latest documentary film, *Lotte Hahn* (2004) a portrait of her grandmother's artistic and personal life, she treats the subject of personal memory in its relation to time and space.

Amy Ione is Director of The Diatrope Institute, a Northern California-based organization that disseminates information relating art, science and Visual Studies. Her articles on innovation in art, science, and technology have been published in books and journals of several disciplines including *The Journal of the History of Neuroscience, Trends in Cognitive Science, Journal of Consciousness Studies* and *The Encyclopedia of Creativity*. Her accomplishments as an internationally exhibited artist include a commission from the city of San Francisco to do artwork for the 33rd Annual Civic Art Fair (1986). She recently completed her fourth book, *Visualizing Innovation: Art, Science, Technology and Visual Studies*, which was published in 2005.

Sybille Lammes is working as an Assistant Professor at Utrecht University. Her area of work is broad and encompasses both old and new popular media. What binds all her research is her interest in the interrelationships between media and techno-science, in particular focusing on how social categories are shaped and contested in this equation. How does popular culture function as a space of negotiation, where imaginable techno-scientific developments are related to social questions of ethnicity, gender and class? She has published on the relationships between science and science fiction (*EASST Review*) and has written chapters on the subject of science fiction and early imaginations of technologies in *Mediated Identities* (2001) and *Mapping the Margins: Identity Politics and the Media* (2003). Recently she has conducted research on videogames that invite players to colonise, conquer and map new territories, while along the way increasing their resources and technological knowledge. This resulted in a contribution to the well-received book *Level Up: Digital Games Research Conference* (2003).

Angela Ndalianis is Head of the Cinema Studies Programme at the University of Melbourne. Her research areas focus on contemporary cinema and its convergence with entertainment forms such as theme parks, comic books and computer games. She is also interested in the history of entertainment media and the technologies that drive them, and her book *Neo-Baroque Aesthetics and Contemporary Entertainment* (2004) explores this theme through a comparison of c17[th] and late c20[th]/early 21st baroque culture. She has published articles in a number of journals and has contributed to the anthologies, *On a Silver Platter: CD-Roms and the Promises of a New Technology* (1999), *MetaMorphing: Visual Transformation and the Culture of Quick Change* (2000), *Rethinking Media Change* (2003) and *Hop on Pop: the Politics and Pleasures of Popular Cultures* (2002). She is currently completing a book about the history of the theme park, its origins and its impact on contemporary urban spaces.

Robert Pepperell is an artist and writer. He studied at the Slade School of Art and went onto work with a number of influential multimedia collaborations including Hex, Coldcut and Hexstatic. As well as producing experimental computer art and computer games he has published several interactive CD-ROMs and exhibited numerous digital installations including at the Glasgow Gallery of Modern Art, the ICA, the Barbican Gallery, and the Millennium Dome, London. His book *The Posthuman Condition* was first published in 1995 and its new edition in 2003 contained the subtitle, *Consciousness beyond the brain*. His second book *The Postdigital Membrane* was in collaboration with Michael Punt, published in 2000. He has spoken and lectured widely on art, philosophy and new technology. He currently teaches at the University of Plymouth and University of Wales, Newport. He is Associate Editor for *Leonardo Reviews*, the journal of the International Society for Arts, Sciences and Technology (ISAST).

Michael Punt is Editor in Chief of *Leonardo Reviews,* a member of the Leonardo/ISAST Advisory Board, and the MIT/*Leonardo* Book Series Committee. He gained his PhD at the University of Amsterdam and is now a Reader in Art and Technology at the University of Plymouth, where he leads Trans-Technology Research in the School of Computing, Communications and Electronics. He has made 15 films and published over fifty articles on cinema and digital media in the last decade. His recent publications include a book-length study on early cinema, *Early Cinema and the Technological Imaginary* (2000) and articles on cinema history and digital technology for *The Velvet Light Trap, Leonardo, Design Issues* and *Convergence.* Between 1996 and 2000 he was a regular contributor to *Skrien,* a Dutch journal of film and television criticism, where he wrote a monthly column on cinema, art and the internet. His most recent book, in collaboration with Robert Pepperell, *The Postdigital Membrane: Imagination, Technology and Desire,* was published by Intellect Books in 2000.

Patricia Pisters is Professor of Film at the Department of Media and Culture, University of Amsterdam. She has published among others *Micropolitics of Media Culture: Reading the Rhizomes of Deleuze and Guattari* (2001) and *The Matrix of Visual Culture: Working with Deleuze in Film Theory* (2003). Currently she is teaching on Maghreb and non-western cinema and conducting a research project on Transnational Media, Imagined Communities and Intercultural Values for which she co-edited a book entitled, *Shooting the Family: Transnational Media and Intercultural Values* (2005). Within the Amsterdam School of Cultural Analysis (ASCA) she is starting an interdisciplinary project between film scholars and neurobiologists, called 'The Rhizotorium.'

Susan Stuart is a Senior Lecturer in Philosophy in the Faculty of Arts at the University of Glasgow. She teaches in the Humanities Advanced Technology and Information Institute (HATII) and in the Department of Philosophy. Her research interests are in the philosophy of mind, Kant's epistemology, questions of ontology, and idealism and technology. She has published on the application of Kant's transcendental psychology to contemporary issues in cognitive science, deception, theories of mind and autism, the conditions for conscious agency, the ontology of digital objects, and on teaching philosophy in cyberspace. She is currently engaged in research on the binding problem and how information that is stored across the brain is integrated into one unitary conscious experience, the self as neither body nor mind but active agency, and applying Dilthey's *Geisteswissenschaften* to the information user in their context. She is the Regional Director of the European Computing and Philosophy Association, and has recently been appointed to the American Philosophical Association's committee for Philosophy and Computing.

Pia Tikka is a researcher in the Graduate School of Audiovisual Media, Elomedia, at the University of Art and Design Helsinki. Her background is in Film, Cinematography and Graphic Design. She has directed long feature films; *Daughters of Yemanjá* (1996) and *Sand Bride* (1998), and worked in a range of feature film productions, including films by director Mika Kaurismäki since 1989. Currently Pia Tikka's enactive cinema project, *Obsession* is being exhibited in the Museum of Contemporary Art, Kiasma, Helsinki. It functions as a laboratory for her practice-based doctoral research into the emotive-cognitive dynamics of cinema.

Introduction

The idea for this collection of essays originally came from Robert Pepperell and was a consequence of our extended reflection on various collaborations that we have worked on together, as well as a number of individual projects that have occupied us over the past decade. One of the key questions framing the initial discussions about this book concerned the shaping of an overarching research structure that would embrace a wide range of disciplines while maintaining the necessary rigour to make it valuable to a community comprising certain sorts of artists, technologists and theorists. In addition, much of our time and energy as editors were directed towards thinking about the way discussions concerning technology might be opened up by an alternative to the dominant materialist approach. As long-standing practitioners in various arts, we realised this was an intuitive move that had to be made if art was to be more than just a banal exposition of the technological surpluses of the latest invention to hit the streets. Having worked on various projects with analogue and electronic technologies, and also having critically examined the interaction of art and science, we were both very aware that simply exploring the latest technologies for their creative applications inevitably led sooner or later to an artistic cul-de-sac. More often than not it seemed to us that new technologies were divisive: on the one hand gathering an uncritical and enthusiastic band of supporters anxious to work at the leading edge of science and technology to the exclusion of history, and on the other an entrenched band of reactionary traditionalists refusing to acknowledge that even something as apparently useful and basic as drawing — what Ingres called the probity of art — was essentially a form defined by a technology. In the 1980s and 1990s both of us had experienced at first-hand the futility of this polemic in relation to electronic media, and in various ways we have offered more inclusive perspectives. Pepperell's *The Posthuman Condition* was an intervention intended to realign our perception of what it means to be a human by situating that very concept in an ecology of ideas and matter quite particular to the prevailing technological environment of the late twentieth century. Punt's research into late nineteenth century technology and the emergence of cinema, published in a series of articles between 1995 and 2000, culminated in *Early Cinema and the Technological Imaginary*. Punt's claim was that if the determining impact of an imagined relationship between the user and the device was factored in, quite crucial outstanding questions concerning the use of technology could be answered. In the case of cinema for example, neither economic determinism nor a realist imperative could fully account for why moving image technologies became so unexpectedly popular, or for that matter became an entertainment at all. From these two independent studies a number of shared preoccupations emerged, including a recognition that the transcendental and the material needed to be reconciled, in a way that critically and creatively embraced the undoubted materiality of technology without prescribing the users' scope for action.

In 2000 we jointly published *The Postdigital Membrane: Imagination, Technology and Desire*, a book that resulted from several years of shared thought and discussion. In it we began to identify a nexus of interests that, although not immediately concerned with art and technology, appeared to be dealing with something of the same structural problem, that is, reconciling apparently mutually exclusive concepts that our daily, lived experience confirmed could quite happily coexist without causing too much damage. Drawing on a wide range of examples we argued that the apparent exclusivity of many ideas derived from an arbitrary dualism, which even postmodern plurality did not dissolve. What was called for was the conceptual model of the *membrane* — an interface between differential pressures in which there is no stable state, save the one that the act of observation imposes. In this, of course we were drawing heavily on quite generalist ideas in popular theoretical physics, Consciousness Studies, philosophy and cultural analysis. *The Postdigital Membrane* was by no means a conclusive theory that addressed our initial problem, nor was it ever intended to be. It did however offer a rhetorical strategy that was an alternative to either the polemical antagonism or the liberal pluralism dominating art/science debates at the time. Whether the ways in which the materiality of prevailing science and technology and the transcendental aspirations of artists are understood has changed five years on is open to question, but it is certainly noticeable that the current vogue for 'transdisciplinarity' was foreshadowed in that book, and in much that we have both published and spoken about since. As we survey the intellectual landscape at the borders between art, science and technology we realise the overlap is less symptomatic of publishing or funding imperatives than of the increasing permeability of fragile disciplinary boundaries, something the membrane metaphor we adopted was to help us account for. This anthology is a concrete manifestation of this increasing permeability, which moves first by drawing together a number of discrete topics in which there is a synergy between art, science and technology, and then by identifying certain levels of coherence in what at first sight — certainly to the twentieth century observer — might appear to be an random series of essays.

In the processes of developing the anthology we had the advantage of our work with *Leonardo* extending over virtually the whole period of our collaboration. As a journal devoted to the interface between art, science and technology, which has been published for the better part of forty years, we were able to track the fashions in the debates, and more especially our various editorial roles in *Leonardo Reviews* also positioned us well to analyse the publishing trends in the field. Quite soon it became evident that in the past decade a preoccupation with the mind and its external manifestation had captured the intellectual imagination more than any other single topic. This seemed to be true whether we were looking at contemporary discussions about art and technology or at some of the earliest thoughts people had about cinema. Overarching nearly a century of reflection on creativity, culture and technology, the cinema and its relationship to the mind seemed to be an ever-present concern. Despite the visibility of the topic of representation and legibility informed by psychoanalytic, materialist or realist discourses, underlying all the literature seemed to be the perplexing (human) questions of how we know what we know, and in particular how we can be certain about something even when we know it is an illusion. The cinema seemed to provide a perfect illustration of the condition that we became fascinated with. From the literature it is obvious that this was something that had touched many philosophical speculations along with scientific evidence drawn from human physiology, especially inasmuch as it draws our attention to the way in which the mind, body and world are interacting and integrating. These last two topics — philosophy and body (in the broadest sense of the term) — converged, or at least it seemed so from publishing trends, in a developing area called 'Consciousness Studies'. The past decade or so has witnessed the struggle to assert a 'Science of Consciousness', as evidence by a number of initiatives including the work at the Noetic Institute, the Center for Consciousness Studies at the University of Arizona, a number of galvanatic conferences including Arizona's own biennial *Toward a Science of Consciousness, The*

Swiss Biennial on Science, Technics + Aesthetics organised by René Stettler at the Neue Galerie, Lucerne, *Consciousness Reframed (*now hosted by the University of Plymouth), journals such as the *Journal of Consciousness Studies*, and *Leonardo,* and of course more recently the series that includes this book under the editorship of Daniel Meyer-Dinkgräfe at the University of Aberystwyth. The emergence of this new field in the mid-1990s was marked by a deliberate and self-conscious attempt to pool insights from heterogeneous disciplines and to impose a materialist rationale upon them. The fact that this attempt has, by general consent, failed is less the fault of its eclectic methodology than the erroneous assumption that consciousness is amenable to materialist descriptions. The dynamism of Consciousness Studies seems to be generated not by a smooth convergence towards scientific goals but by a positive and respectful incorporation of incompatible, and often irrational, outcomes and approaches.

Quite early on it seemed to us that the topic of Consciousness Studies would inevitably form one of the threads that would weave its way through any attempt to think about modern technology in relation to is human use and cultural meanings. Consequently, as we discussed the kinds of contributors who would make this volume valuable to those people interested in the question, we were faced with several problems: first, how could we draw together the necessary range of appropriate specialisms to reflect our own idea of what might be important in advancing our case without inviting unproductive dissonance? Second, how could we make complex and inevitably abstract material concrete and manageable to the non-specialist (which to some extent included ourselves)? And finally, how could we ensure the resulting volume made a genuine contribution to new knowledge, rather than simply rehearsing contradictory positions? One strategy we adopted was to seek to interpose Consciousness Studies between film and mind, where for cultural theorists psychoanalysis had traditionally stood. This was more than simply updating Film Studies or nodding in the direction of cognitive film theory. The authors included here are in their own ways struggling to reconcile the oncoming rush of new data from science and technology with the rich knowledge gained from the long view of history, philosophy and art. Film, with all its sentient, sensuous and social qualities, provided a common reference point between all these forces, and Consciousness Studies provided the intellectual impetus to revisit familiar problems with fresh insights.

Since the contributions shaped the ultimate intellectual thrust of the collection, the title caused us much discussion and heartache. We used the term 'cinema' tentatively, although in some ways it is the most obvious, given the number of our contributors who employ it and given the way in which institutions provide a significant interpretative context for technologies. This is especially so as it evokes Gilles Deleuze's work, which forms one of the key philosophical interventions in the period that concerned us. At one point we wondered if 'film' might be the better term since it reverberated with our earlier thoughts in *The Postdigital Membrane* in a way that grounded them in materiality more than we had managed in that book. Only after we had read all the contributions did the term 'screen' seem to chime with the discussions of 'reality' that threaded through the various chapters. The screen, we thought was an object that was apparently implanted firmly in reality, yet frequently cited as a site of illusion and a metaphor for the internal workings of the mind. We noticed that all the authors regarded the concept of reality with a certain amount of scepticism. We should not have been surprised because if there is one topic of discussion that characterises the current debates in the science of consciousness it is the issue of radical constructivism. Prior to the socio-political theory in the humanities concerning who owns reality, Consciousness Studies, as we understand it here, is driven by a lack of agreement about where it might be in the first place, and in particular how it might be related to the mind and the world. We preferred to allude to this complexity by the use of the concept 'world', less contested than reality, and more inclusive of the multiple inconsistencies we were trying to manage. In the end the phrase 'Screen Consciousness' offered us a poetic summary of a series of speculations that we understood were firmly grounded in the happy coexistence of doubt and certainty.

At times, as the various chapters arrived in our inboxes, we felt like astronomers collecting data from slightly unfamiliar instruments, each mapping a different sector of the academic galaxy. From practitioners of art history, philosophy, technology studies, and film theory came material that both confirmed the enormity and complexity of what is 'out there', and at the same time reinforcing the potential for underlying pattern and harmony. It is a truism that one cannot see connections without at the same time seeing differences, and the diversity of ideas and approaches seemed, paradoxically, to strengthen our conviction that the papers represented a collective and coordinated shift in our understanding of contemporary ideas. Several authors, for example, use the potency of the spectator-film relation to argue for a relocation of the burden of mind away from the head (where it has long been sited) and into the material of the world itself. While as editors we were to some extent bound to inflect the data we received by pre-selecting certain kinds of input, as astronomers must, we also wanted to leave room for the unexpected in the hope this would generate ideas that were new to us, and hopefully to our reader.

Finally, after identifying the authors and persuading them to join us in this speculation we were faced with the task of sequencing the contributions, and decided that it would be impossible to construct a linear trajectory through what is essentially a partially mapped intel-lectual land mass. We decided to try and create a route such as an explorer might, hacking just enough undergrowth away either side to make a path and placing little markers from time to time so that should we need to retreat and take a slightly different turn we would not have to go back to the start. As a consequence we have opened this anthology with Amy Ione's essay in which she locates the artist in the current discussion of Consciousness Studies. She situates our concern with 'the complex conundrum of consciousness' in a recent history of the divide between science and the humanities, and further situates that in the emergence of the idea of science. As she reminds us, the term *scientist* is fairly recent and was "as pleasing as the word 'electrocution' and, in the mid-nineteenth century, must have sounded very un-English." Yet within half a century it took on the patina of an antique as scientific claims to truth and reality appeared to be axio-matic. The chief stumbling block that this poses for Ione is not the hegemony but the distortion of history, especially as it concerns the general involvement of the arts in scientific research. In a brief over-view she argues that the proximity of art and science as praxis can be historicised in such a way that it seems that art in fact led scientific method. One of the keys to this seems to be the bracketing of emotion and questions of spirituality in scientific research and depositing them into the arts, but as she points out, in even an extreme case of so called emotive arts, such as the paintings and drawings by van Gogh, the intentions and methods of the artist can be adequately accounted for in rational terms. Yet the terrain of reconciliation between these two falsely divided fields of action is in the study of human consciousness in which the artist's vision can no longer be attributed to some divine gift but must be understood in the spectrum of all human awareness. Whether creativity is typically human or an aberration it can only be understood as continuous with our various ways of knowing the world and in this respect art is crucial to the study of consciousness. Ione's chapter, then, cuts to the very issue at the heart of this anthology: the arbitrary and historical nature of disciplinary boundaries and the potential within Consciousness Studies for fruitful re-engagement.

Angela Ndalianis' chapter inverts Ione's historical strategy by beginning with the present catching up with the future, and in doing so picks up the theme of continuity in a 'bootstrap' version of the world as its own best model. Focusing on theme park design and architecture she identifies the coalition of the spiritual past and the transcendent future in the material and semi-material manifestations of post-electronic entertainment. The theme park, amusement arcade and games environment collapse history in a utopian version of the past as an obtainable present. Not surprisingly consciousness shifting media such as film, radio and television provide real world points of reference, but more recently technology and science itself, as for example at EPCOT, have been used to bind the real and the imagined into a coherent whole. Ndalianis' point however is that there are significant examples where the imagined provides the navigational markers for the material, as for example in Gehry's architecture and in the way that robots appear in the context of entertainment. The particular pointlessness of the robot such as *Aibo*, for example, allows it to develop an intelligence based on adaptive learning. Moreover robots that appear in films (and even star in them) become indistinguishable from human stars and in this respect, suggests Ndalianis, may satisfy the Turing test. In the closure of the gap between the real and the fictional, the investment of technology with a soul in a Christian culture for example, is no longer a blasphemy but an inevitability. One that heralds a further collapse as mutually exclusive belief systems converge on the idea that consciousness is not necessarily a property of the human body.

Ndalianis' conclusion makes a necessary move to situate science, technology and entertainment at the core of our ethical and practical understanding of our environment. Sybille Lammes develops this theme of the interrelation between science and belief systems following some well established, but often overlooked, discussion in the field of Science and Technology Studies (STS). One of the methodological orthodoxies of STS aims to show how techno-science (as she calls it) is the outcome of a network of determining forces (actors) shaping our perception of the real. Drawing on actor-network theory, and in particular the work of Bruno Latour, she argues that the asymmetrical relations for example, between faith and science, are paradoxical in that they are thought to share some common ground while at the same time are regarded as mutually exclusive. She unravels some of the implications of this concept in another context in which belief and knowledge are in perpetual contradiction; namely the cinema. In a close textual analysis of the film *The Island of Lost Souls* (1932) directed by Erle C. Kenton, and based on H.G.Wells' novella *The Island of Dr. Moreau,* Lammes argues that Moreau's scientific practice in isolation cleanses the inherent contradictions that face the perceiver. In so doing the film argues for a kind of science informed by Christian belief. In her reading, the film (and the novella) can be understood as a theological and ethical discussion mediating between wild nature and western culture, and directly addresses such pressing cultural issues (in 1932) as evolution, eugenics and the meaning of science and technology. As with Ndalianis' contribution the core factor, the one that enables Moreau to act as a translator between two contradictory positions, is a particular imbrication of technology and pleasure in popular cinema.

Michael Punt attempts to account for the special place of moving image technology in our understanding of consciousness by historically situating it in an emerging Modernist set of preoccupations in the face of the collapse of some of the certainties that classical physics offered. Punt argues that popular film works with on-screen and off-screen emotions to both show and tell the spiritual world. In doing so it offers a strange out of body experience in which bodily desire remains ever present. This, he asserts, was as true at the end of the nineteenth century as it is today. By tracing the relationship between science and telepathy and insisting on observation as a property of consciousness and not the material world, he shows the divergence of spiritual matters from direct scientific discussion and their relocation in the interaction between technology and entertainment. This led to the forceful expulsion of the force of mind from legitimate scientific research. In some areas however, it became clear that the sorts of challenges to materialism that telepathy offered could not be ignored. Most notably these were in research into human perception. Art and the cinema were key actors in the development of a coherent approach to understanding reality as a consequence of temporary interrelationships (as for example in the cinematograph where each image derives its meaning from its immediate literal and technological context). Although the cinematograph along with other forms of pictorial representation was very rapidly reinstated in the dominant materialist ideology, elsewhere in the sciences and the arts new methodologies were developed which responded to the dubiousness of the certainty that underpinned this worldview. In his conclusion, Punt draws attention to the art historian Aby Warburg whose radical approach to understanding art was symptomatic of the most insightful minds at work at the close of the nineteenth century and yet whose time (intellectually) has only just arrived. One reason why he thinks this is so is because only with the coalition of non-classical physics and a direct concern with consciousness can the alternative to a realist hegemony as an explanatory form be advanced.

Martha Blassnigg also addresses the asymmetrical treatment of science and faith in relation to the nature of human consciousness, and pivoting on the cinema as a perceptual paradox she draws on her research with clairvoyants and both nineteenth and twentieth century philosophers to support a view of reality as a distribution of perceptions. Recognising the special place of film in the previous contributions, she turns our attention to the dominant critical reaction to representation. She points out realism has almost exclusively informed Film Studies, in spite of the evidence that at the time of its popularisation an equally popular philosophy of thought and perception was being developed by Henri Bergson, which was to some extent informed by the cinematograph and such things as clairvoyance and spirit photography. Bergson's thoughts were cast into the shadows, at least as far as film was concerned, and perhaps would have remained there but for Gilles Deleuze' unexpected realisation that the cinema can show both behaviour and spiritual life. In a triangulation of Bergson, Deleuze and Edgar Morin she forces film to yield to a plural relationship with matter that is much more even-handed than either psychoanalytic or cognitive film theory. This opens the way for a discussion of clairvoyant perception informed by her own field research in which she is able to develop a holistic response to the concept of the real. The senses as single entities, she argues, are always integrated and never act in isolation so that in this way she regards the mind as a product of our own senses *in action*. This leads her to the analogy of the kaleidoscope (rather than a telescope) to describe the clairvoyant experience. She conceptualises a continuity between senses and consciousness that is consistent with Deleuze' use of Bergson in which to a significant extent the film *becomes* the viewer — or more contentiously — the viewer's consciousness.

Patricia Pisters more fully positions Deleuze at the crossroads of consciousness and cinema, reminding us on the way of Deleuze' antipathy to psychoanalysis and linguistics, she uses his return to biology — more especially molecular biology. The biological liberates us from the preconception of the humanities and acknowledges the universal chaos so that we may bind with it in a state as undifferentiated as the material of our brain. Only when we try to differentiate the chaos and impose order, as for example by taking opinions and stands do we need philosophy, art and science to recover the lost chaos. From this assertion Pisters asks what problems do film, philosophy and science have in common. She argues that film provides a particular illusion in which many of the paradoxes of Consciousness Studies and neuro-science are mirrored. Rather like the previous arguments, hers is a bootstrap version of reality drawn in this case from biological phenomena observable in brain activity such as mirror-neurons. Images touch the brain directly in the sense that the material of the bio-matter appears to be affected by the spiritual of the image. Deleuze's work on cinema (*Cinema 1* and *Cinema 2*) elaborates this as an effect of cinema — time and movement, which functions independently of any concept of representation. Pisters continues with an analysis of a number of film texts which exemplify and illustrate the correlation between cinema and the sensation of insight. She concludes her essay, as Deleuze does, by examining the impact of technological and social evolution on the psychomechanics of cinema in which animation affects the brain in the same way as other forms of life.

So much for screening mind, film and reality, discussed in the previous contributions relative to a number of established theories and histories of technology and perception. In the last three contributions there is a direct attempt to reconcile this version of the cinema — the film between chaos and life — with the sort of discussion of Consciousness Studies that we have all been allied with. Pia Tikka's essay *Cinema as Externalization of Consciousness* opens this last section deep in the heart of contemporary Consciousness Studies with an essay that like many of the previous contributions is also driven by the idea that higher-level conscious cognition emerges from mostly unconscious biological functions. At times, she argues, this process is revealed in certain forms of production and she regards filmmaking as a relevant model of the mind at work. In a study of Eisenstein's film practice, chosen because of his particular interpretation of the concept of embodiment that is close to much current thinking on the topic, she systematically shows how the concept of cinematic consciousness as a miniature consciousness can be supported by examining how making and reading a film works in conjunction with the self. Through film, Tikka introduces the topic of narrative as an epiphenomenon of socioemotional interaction into the discussion of consciousness in order to insist on enactment as a condition for qualitative knowledge. It is through narrative and imagination that we can gain the illusion that we are engaged in knowing without material interaction. The necessary switching between real and imagined states in narrative is a form of enactment that enables us to engage with, or more exactly resonate with another mind. What then if the biological system is 'corrupted' as for example in the presence of a film to produce a false body state? Tikka, like all the previous contributors, rejects the realist position in favour of the idea of emotional situatedness that raises historical questions about survival dreams relative to technology, suggesting finally that the mind has adapted to the shortfall of evolution by inventing forms that simulate dangers relevant to the period.

Regarding the self as 'an active agency within a dynamically changing experienced world' as Susan Stuart puts it in the penultimate essay is a concept shared with varying degrees of commitment by many of the contributors. How in a 'closed' system in which the world is its own best model can there ever be an 'other'? The active construction of a necessary, but contradictory condition, informs Susan Stuart's essay on some philosophical aspects of the concept of self-consciousness. Drawing on Kant, she develops the idea of mind as a distributed dynamic that is neither in nor out of the body because there is no self as a differential entity, it is however a necessary concept whose negation and reinstatement is a crucial aspect of our cognitive processes. Our own sense of body, provided it is not impaired, appears to provide us with constant information about our position in the world, and yet we can also become technologically extended with robots horses of cups. Yet as Stuart points out, the sense of realness derives exclusively from our own sensory experiences, and perhaps the best we can affirm is that our consciousness is distributed as material. Where this view presents its most interesting challenge is in the emergence of technologies such as virtual reality that hitherto were the product of speculation. Such a philosophical conundrum leads Stuart to wonder if, in a technological environment such as that depicted in *The Matrix*, indeed the self will turn out to be nothing more than a prosthesis.

Finally Robert Pepperell tackles the question of the mind as screen by asking 'where is it?' Does the screen of consciousness on which the world appears have specific form and place or is it beyond the fabric of the brain and out there at the very limits of the cosmos? His approach is not to weigh the arguments according to a personal bias but, consistent with one of the underlying themes of this collection, to acknowledge — even welcome — the incompatibility between the positions as a productivity. His contribution revisits some of the key ideas around visual perception and the cinema to show how both internalist and externalist approaches are sustainable up to certain limits, yet even so each camp claims intellectual victory. In some ways this category of explanatory competition mimics the cognitive processes seen in optical illusions and the cinema as subjective experience and objective reality provide contradictory data. Whether the screen is in our minds or out there is of less consequence to Pepperell than the larger problems posed by a double reality. In particular he is concerned with what might be achieved by dispensing with the screen and rephrasing the question relative to the mind. In a re-reading of Descartes, he asserts that far from distinguishing between mind and body he regarded their union as axiomatic. This is a key mover for Pepperell who goes onto suggest that the dialethic state in which the mind or the screen could be both in here and out there is consistent with a mainstream philosophical argument, which initially could not accommodate its own implications. By condoning contradiction the concept of distributed consciousness can be understood in the realm of indeterminacy, a concept that opens the way for transdisciplinary methodologies which might be seen to have value in tackling the more intransigent problems of Consciousness Studies.

In the preparation of this book we included all the essays that we commissioned and imposed few editorial constraints. We certainly outlined a thesis and structure and were quite clear about who we would approach based on previous work that we had read and seen. But in retrospect the idea that drove this collection of essays seems to have been realized with remarkable coherence and it perhaps should have been less of a surprise to us that it has come together quite so well. The fact that it has is evidence of a dynamic debate thriving on the edges of the mainstream of Consciousness Studies, reflected in the contributions here, each in their own way dealing with issues and questions that some of us have been thinking about for many years in many different contexts, things such as the nature of film, cinema, world, mind, and so on. Those of us fascinated by these diverse yet related issues had always felt we were working in a disciplinary no-man's-land. Now suddenly it seems they have a coherent intellectual home in Consciousness Studies, albeit one that is self-consciously eclectic. Irritating as this must be to specialists, its value lies in the fact that the entrenched divisiveness referred to earlier is being re-placed in academia by a generous curiosity about diversity and even incompatibility. Of course, it has to be said that with the benefit of hindsight it is possible to weave a theoretical narrative through any number of loosely related essays and indeed that may be all that this introduction shows. But however dubious that might sound to us as academics, it is strangely reiterative of a single theme that we have found in all the contributions: that the world, with all its complexities, inconsistencies and vagaries, is its own best model of what's real.

Locating the Artist within Views of Consciousness: Perception, Reception, and Art History

Amy Ione

Recent technological innovations have allowed both artists and scientists to rethink historical theories of vision, sensory experience, and the relationship between image and text. Examining how contemporary research has redefined tenets of Art History that relate to Consciousness Studies, this essay probes the role of transdisciplinary analysis in defining the 'place' of art in consciousness theories.

Looking back at the 1990s (the decade of the Brain) we can identify a number of events indicating that the status of Consciousness Studies was on the upswing. Among them was the launch of several journals that encouraged researchers to combine brain research with Consciousness Studies. One of these, the *Journal of Consciousness Studies*, placed the phase "controversies in science and the humanities" on the cover of every issue.[1]

As an early subscriber, I can recall looking at the words with some instinctive reservations about the way science and the humanities seemed to relegate art to a peripheral position. Although I recognized the idiom is commonly used, it simply failed to hit the right note in my mind. Over a decade later, I find my earlier ambivalence towards this way of dividing perspectives remains, although I now have a broader understanding of the history behind it. In a general sense, the science/humanities distinction is embedded within our thinking, as is the historical inclusion of art within the humanities.

As I argue below, this has limited engagement with the qualities of art that are difficult to fit into the humanities and, by extension hampers efforts to locate the artist within views of consciousness. Excluded qualities include (among other things) the way one artist might contrive an optically titillating piece that has no narrative story to tell while another might invent new materials when no known substances do what the artist aspires to accomplish.[2]

The Framework

As is well known, the enthusiasm for the complex conundrum of consciousness has offered a means to revisit all ways of knowing and, as I have argued in detail elsewhere (Ione 2000, 2002, 2005), the science/humanities pairing has a history that relegated art to a secondary position. For example, we can date the elevation of language over visual art back to Plato's disdain for representation.[3] It is also well known that with the early Renaissance, artists further complicated our ability to 'see' art on its own terms by highlighting rhetoric and theory in a desire to elevate their professional position. By downplaying *praxis* and experimentation, the artists succeeded. The effect of their success, however, remains with us today in a way that is particularly evident when we place art within the narrow 'two cultures' matrix that pits science against the humanities.

Why the 'two cultures' idea is problematic clarifies when we review some of the history behind it. The phrase is easily dated to a title C.P. Snow used for his 1959 Rede Lecture and the books he later published of these lectures (Snow 1959, 1964). Here he adopted the pairing to highlight his view that literary intellectuals and natural scientists distrusted one another. The talks allowed Snow to voice his apprehension about the impact of the model on British education as well as the future of the world.

Snow's overall intention was to ask how curricula in Britain could better serve both branches of knowledge in a global society. Nonetheless, since introduced, the idiom has taken on a life far from his concerns. More often than not, those who use it fail to acknowledge that Snow's aim was to highlight a widening gap he saw forming between rich and poor countries as well as a gap between the technologically trained and untrained. More important in terms of consciousness, his contrast of the literary intellectual and the natural scientist is rooted in events we can place within nineteenth century intellectual history[4] that often serve as the unacknowledged framework for consciousness models (Ione 2002, 2005).

One trajectory that typifies the mindset that was taking hold in the nineteenth century clarifies when we look at the way the word 'scientist' gained credence. It was adopted after the Cambridge Professor William Whewell (1794–1866)[5] suggested; "We need a name to describe a cultivator of science in general. I should incline to call him a *scientist*. Thus we might say, that as an artist is a musician, painter, or poet, a scientist is a mathematician, physicist, or naturalist"[6]

(Whewell 1967: cxii). In other words, despite the general assumption that the word 'scientist' has a classical origin, we can categorically place it in the early nineteenth century, when many felt there was an increasing need to replace the term 'natural philosopher' with one that would acknowledge the emerging distinction between the lofty goals of philosophy and the experimental method of the natural sciences.[7]

Few ask why Whewell contrasted the 'scientist' with the 'artist' and not the 'humanist'. Rather the typical response is that 'scientists' have a long history, one that goes back further than the nineteenth century. Yet, when we look closely, what we find is that the term 'scientist' was indeed new, although the adjective 'scientific' can be traced to Aristotle. In English, the term appears to date to about 1600. At this point it was synonymous with knowledge and referred to demonstrable knowledge (as compared with intuitive knowledge), which was aligned with natural philosophy. We can additionally relate the English term to the 1620 publication of Francis Bacon's *Novum Organum*, which ushered in a shifting of the philosophical point of view from deductive logic. This accompanied Bacon's belief in inductive logic and the urge to move toward the experimental method, which made it possible to discover and understand new facts about the world. Bacon's view is best summed up in *Novum Organum*, aphorism 1.95, which reads:

> Those who have written about the sciences are either empiricists or dogmatists. Empiricists are like ants, who only collect things and make use of them. Rationalists are like spiders, who weave webs out of their own bodies. But the bee has a middle policy: it extracts material from the flowers of the gardens and meadows and digests and transforms it by its own powers. The genuine task of philosophy is much the same: it does not depend only or mainly on the powers of the mind; nor does it deposit the raw materials supplied by natural history and mechanical observations in the memory just as they are, but as they have been worked over and transformed by the understanding. Therefore there is much to be hoped for from a closer marriage (which has not yet taken place) between these faculties, namely the experiential and the rational (1965).

Reviewing the nineteenth century dynamics that led to the entry of the word 'scientist' into our lexicon exposes how varied opinions were initially. Thomas Huxley, for example, wrote (in 1894) that he thought it was about as pleasing as the word 'electrocution' (Huxley 1894). It must have sounded to him the way that 'scientologist' sounds to scientists in our times. Today, despite the well-documented early resistance to this term, few reject it. To the contrary, the community (including the scientific community) has become quite comfortable with the esteem associated with the title. What we see is that Whewell's proposition had a tremendous impact first in Europe, later the United States and now globally. As a result, those who previously saw more value in the larger purview of the natural philosophers (which included morals, ethics and a list of concerns not amenable to empirical analysis) eventually took a back seat. This reversal is apparent in the easy way the word 'scientist' rolls off the tongue today and in the accolades now given to proposals offered by 'scientific men', a trend strikingly evident in Consciousness Studies.

The idea of the 'scientist' as an analogy to the 'artist' is a bit more confusing, to say the least. It also offers some ground for separating the artist and the humanist.[8] The dynamic that wedged art into the humanistic mould was adopted as the Middle Ages turned toward the Renaissance. Then the interpretation of nature was generally regarded as but one element in the all-embracing enterprise of natural philosophy. Only by the seventeenth century, in the course of what historians were to later dub 'the scientific revolution', did achievements in the study of the natural world come to be widely regarded as setting new standards for what could count as genuine knowledge. Thereafter the methods employed by the 'natural philosophers' (as they were still termed) enjoyed a special cultural authority. One outcome evident during the eighteenth century was the aspiration to be 'the Newton of the moral sciences', a goal that testifies to the prestige of 'the experimental method' generally associated with Newtonian science, despite the hollowness of the goal to apply it to the essentially non-empirical domain of ethics.

There are two sides to this. If we look back before the Middle Ages we find that classical Greek art, like Greek science and philosophy, produced a wide range of options in regard to the value of art, comparable to the many opinions about art in the postmodern world. On the other hand, one significant difference between the Greeks and our postmodern worldview is that they had no separate term for fine art. This concept developed as the character of the culture changed. *Techné*, which was often associated with art, meant, more precisely, the orderly application of knowledge to produce a specific, predetermined product[9] (Pollitt 1972). This definitional distinction takes on new meaning when we consider how much exceptional art the Greeks produced and "old quarrel between philosophy and poetry" Plato talks of in *The Republic* (1989).

With the renewed interest in Greek knowledge that we associate with the Renaissance we find that Plato's ideas had a powerful effect on the intellectual history of art, but not our understanding of what is unique to art. Or, as E.H. Gombrich, the late doyen of Art History concisely stated in his book, *The Preference for the Primitive*:

> The well-known dictum by the philosopher Alfred N. Whitehead, that the whole history of Western philosophy is but a series of footnotes to the writings of Plato, applies with special force to the philosophy of the arts... (2001: 11).

Plato's ambivalence is best summed up when we recall that he sided with philosophy, ultimately banning the artists from his republic. [10] Thus it is not surprising that the concept of 'fine art' we associate with the resurging interest in Greek thought we see with the Renaissance had a strong philosophical foundation, easily equated with the Platonic influence on intellectual life at that time. In addition, this view further congealed as artists began to seek the professionalism that could only be achieved through elevating artistic cognition to a higher level, one associated with humanistic thinking and the liberal arts. Convincing all that artists used their mind, and thus were not mere craftspeople, necessitated reframing artistic practice in a way that de-emphasized craft, technology, and experimentation (Ione 2005). Nonetheless, while this raised the artist's social place, the awkward positioning mitigated understanding of art on its own terms.

Recently, with the emergence of Visual Culture Studies and the increased awareness of the confluence of art, science, and technology in innovative projects, earlier biases are being exposed. For example, Francis Ames-Lewis writes that she was mistaken (at the beginning of her career) to argue that early Renaissance painters and sculptors were essentially artisans with few ideas. She now recognizes that they engaged with intellectual activities as well.

Early on in my academic career I tended to encourage in my students the view that early Renaissance painters and sculptors were essentially artisans in outlook. Painters were appreciated, I suggested and experienced in the craft practices commended by Cennino Cennini in his *Craftsman's Handbook*. They had little time or inclination to engage with ideas that circulated in the world beyond the confines of their workshops... I argued (I think now mistakenly), painters and sculptors continued throughout the fifteenth century to aspire to be no more than high quality craftsmen... During the course of the fifteenth century artists also engaged increasingly in intellectual activities... As a result, they encouraged a wider recognition among their public of the validity of claims that painting and sculpture should be seen as liberal arts (Ames-Lewis 2000: ix).

One of the chief aims of the artist was to reconceptualise the biblical and other historical stories in ways that brought them to life for their contemporaries. This was incremental, but required extensive knowledge of the background, and is full of innovative representations through the fourteenth through sixteenth centuries. Moreover, as Pamela H. Smith ably details, craft was never put aside once art gained entry into the 'liberal arts'. As she explains:

> A distinction has often been drawn between the theoretical knowledge of scholars or scientists, which draws knowledge into a system and practical craft knowledge, which is usually seen to be composed of a collection of recipes or rules that are followed more or less mindlessly. Although there is a useful distinction to be made between theory and practice, investigation into the workshop practices of artisans belies such a view of craft knowledge. Instead, the expertise of craftspeople still astounds museum conservators as well as the art historians who have recently begun a more intensive examination of workshop practices (Smith 2004: 6-7).

The conjunction of the intuitive and experimental mind as scientific practices began to gain a footing is frequently noted. Less well known is that during the late sixteenth and seventeenth centuries, when experimental methodology was becoming an attractive option, many natural philosophers (scientists) sought out artists. Those turning to experimental analysis were attracted to the artist's intimate, hands-on knowledge of natural materials and the ways they had learned to manipulate them over time (Smith 2004). The active process of experimentation used in developing their artwork is (and was) subsumed in abstract, humanities-based theories.

The impact of adopting the artist as humanist model crystallized with the scientific advances and theoretical fashions of the scientific revolution. By the beginning of the nineteenth century, with the advent of romanticism, the mould took on a new form. Romanticism emerged as a reaction to and a fusion of the two definitions of classicism that had evolved. Historically classicism had come to mean "of or pertaining to Greek and Roman culture" (Pollitt 1972: 2). In a qualitative sense, classicism was the term used to express recognition of a standard of perfection within a particular genre. The Romantic sensibility fused these perceptions in a *stylistic* way. The result was that the technical classicism in art began to be defined as if it were only technique, while the art preferred by the Romantics included an emotional quality. This separation of the emotional and the technical reversed the Platonic concern. While Plato had favoured a *logical rather than an emotional approach*, the Romantics saw a conflict between emotion and reason, and valued the emotional.[11]

With the qualitative difference fused into the historical one several elements stand out. One easily identified is that the contributions of artists to scientific and technological developments were rarely highlighted although it is known that their innovative techniques yielded analytic and projective geometry and art furthered map-making, biology, and physics, as exemplified by the multi-fold interests and explorations of Leonardo da Vinci (Kline 1953).

Locating the Artist

Another manifestation of the outcomes of equating art with the humanities is the tendency to equate art with emotion, transcendence, and 'other' ways of knowing. As I have noted elsewhere, this identification invariably confuses the issues further. Yet, on the other hand, recent scientific studies have allowed us to come to terms with some of these confusions, particularly evident when we look at some of the naïve aspects of the romantic and transcendental perspectives. This is particularly apparent when we look at the complex life of the late nineteenth century solitary visionary — Vincent van Gogh.

The circumstances of this artist's life have fostered much debate. An artist sustained by a spiritual vision, we know from his letters that he exulted in finding a sacred space while painting. We also know that this was not enough to sustain his life. Van Gogh was not *only* a spiritual painter who could express his subjective reality with a great passion that now deeply touches many, he was also a human who developed his craft through the tragedy and isolation of a life ultimately defined through art. While his art spoke of a spiritual depth and a depth of compassion, his life spoke of how even his art could not actually hold his spirit transcendent all the time. When he was not painting, van Gogh was keenly aware that all that he loved and believed in was offered to others in paintings no one wanted.[12]

This circularity cannot be overstated, nor can the ease with which his spirituality can be misrepresented when equated with some higher level of consciousness. Van Gogh was a human who desperately wanted to communicate with others. In painting, he found that even in the cataclysm of his life the canvases retained their quietude (Van Gogh 1963), as he wrote to his brother Theo. Still, although he emptied his living passion and his intense beliefs into the more than 800 oil canvases he produced, this dialogue with his canvases was all he had outside of the friendship with his brother. Few, including most painters of his time, could read or feel what his work said. While today many of us deeply experience his canvases, most of us, even his greatest admirers, would not want to emulate his life. Antonin Artaud summed up the futility of this painter's consciousness when he termed him an "artist suicided by society" (Argüelles 1975). In his penultimate letter to Theo, found on his body after his suicide on July 27th, 1890, Vincent in effect confirms this, writing:

> Well, the truth is, we can only make our pictures speak... and I repeat it once more with all earnestness that can be imparted by an effort of a mind diligently fixed on trying to do as well as one can... Well, my own work, I am risking my life for it and... I think, acting with true humanity, but what's the use? (Van Gogh 1963: 339-340)

When we look at the specifics of his story, the romance must be balanced with the possibility that there might be physiological rationales to explain his actions and the events of his life. While there is no consensus, medical suggestions range from epilepsy, schizophrenia, neurosyphilis, bipolar disorder, and Meniere's disease to, substance abuse (smoking, drinking, absinthe poisoning), delirium tremens, lead poisoning and acute intermittent porphyria (Rose 2004). This effort to engage a larger picture reminds us that although science is unlikely to penetrate the mysteries of art and consciousness, it does allow us to bracket out possibilities, separate transcendence from physical attributes, and endeavour to honestly attempt to locate the artist and his or her consciousness when we develop our theories.

Adapting a quite different vantage point we find that science has aided in 'normalizing' aspects of artistic experience. For example, although synaesthesia was long seen as aberrant, studies have now identified genetic 'normals' have this experience. In other words, synaesthesia is generally defined as a condition in which a sensory stimulation evokes a perception in more than one modality. This means that one might associate a colour with a musical note or a taste with a shape (Cytowic 1983; Harrison 2001; Dann 1998; Baron-Cohen & Harrison 1997). Although the responses are idiosyncratic, and vary across synaesthetes, all seem to agree that recent research has creatively shown there is a genetic base for this subjective experience.

The high ratio of artists with synaesthesia may, in part, be a consequence of the artistic urge to stimulate multiple senses through the artwork. This aspect of artistic processing is not only now seen as 'real', we are also able to acknowledge that the earlier conclusions that the sensation was only metaphorical were too quickly adopted. Moreover, in terms of art and consciousness, Synaesthesia Studies offer a unique vantage point from which to evaluate emergence, the developmental mind, and the developmental model that so resonates with what we have recently learned about art cognition. Briefly, just as we know that the brain of a specialist differs from that of a novice, there is evidence to show that the perception of newborns is synaesthetic, and that their synaesthesia may resemble that of synaesthetic adults (Maurer 1997). From a developmental perspective, the high incidence of synaesthesia in artists is an area worthy of greater consideration since so many artists are enthusiastic about enhancing cross-modal experience and heightened sensitivity. Indeed, laboratory experiments have not only distinguished novice processing from that of the specialist, for example (Solso 1999; Miall & Tchalenko 2001; Solso 2001). They have permitted us to relate optical and perceptual experiences (Solso 1994, 2003; Livingstone 2002; Zeki 1999). Thus, although we do not necessarily know how an artist intuitively translates the percept, we can develop a deeper sensitivity for the subtle aspect of what artists present to their audiences.

These examples are not intended to suggest that science alone broadens our perspective. Artists, too, allow us to dissolve some of the old myths about art. Their knowledge of history and practice, moreover, aids in ferreting out fashions, separating bias from theory, and grounding the view that art is about the sublime. In terms of art and consciousness, a dialogue between the painter Richard Diebenkorn and curator Maurice Tuchman comes to mind. The curator had invited Diebenkorn to participate in the *The Spiritual in Art: Abstract Painting 1890-1985* exhibition and the artist refused the invitation. Diebenkorn explained that he rejected the show's aim to highlight the spiritual, mystical and abstract. As he correctly recognized, Tuchman was inclined to demonstrate the genesis of modern art through spiritual movements, and hoped to convey the desire of spiritual artists to express spiritual, utopian or metaphysical ideas. Tuchman was also presenting the view that these desires were not expressed in traditional pictorial terms. Choosing to reject the rhetorical matrix of art history, he adopted a spiritual one instead. This rejection of the art historical canon in favour of a spiritual matrix is frequently applied to art by consciousness theorists due to the division of spirit and science that became so pronounced in the nineteenth century (Ione 2002).

Diebenkorn responded that it is easy to confuse intentions in art and that, in his view, the show was being put together in a way that did just this. He wrote:

> The overall impression I get from your *alternative* interpretation is that you give it all to the mystics and spiritualists in regard to the genesis and development of abstract and non-objective painting. For me, in large part, the prospectus shapes up as a kind of refutation of the traditional viewpoint rather than a much needed illumination of the total picture... abstract painting *was a formal invention*... What seems to get lost in your prospectus is that the formalist line from Cézanne through Cubism arrived at a point on the threshold of total abstraction wherein it was implicit, and for the most astute artists a clear option... From my view, in about 1910, advanced artists were presented, so to speak, with a vehicle, which in the case of mystics and spiritualists was made to order for their expressive needs (Tuchman 1987: 17).

Conclusion

An illumination of the larger picture does not negate the premise that questions about art and consciousness are perhaps irresolvable. Rather I would claim, it reveals that when we engage with perception, reception and art history we can locate the artist's context, examine art practices and discover that the complex beauty of art's mystery becomes more mysterious as it reveals its nature to us. This seems to suggest that the whole is larger than the discrete parts. One thinks of Plato, who had a creative mind and was in awe of artistic inspiration in the sense that he saw it as divinely inspired, yet had reservations about art, especially in relationship to the value he placed on a moral purpose. Although his ambivalence toward art is largely ignored, the spiritual dimension associated with his ideas has clearly informed views of consciousness and are often mapped onto art. One thinks of Leonardo and Michelangelo secretly drawing in the morgue to better *see* the human body while aspiring to wear the humanistic label. Their remarkable achievements as practitioners also stimulate our minds to ask: what art is? One thinks of van Gogh, who suffered for his art, not surviving to know how deeply it later spoke to others. None of these complex stories solve the amorphous realms of art and consciousness. Rather, what we can discover deepens our respect for what is unknowable, as it urges us to separate the wheat from the chaff.

Bibliography

Ames-Lewi, Francis. 2000. *The Intellectual Life of the Early Renaissance Artist*. New Haven and London: Yale University Press.

Argüelles, Jose. A. 1975. *The Transformative Vision*. Berkeley: Shambhala Publications Inc.

Bacon, Francis. 1965 (1620). 'Novum Organum' in Burtt, E. A. (ed.) *The English Philosopher: From Bacon to Mill*. New York: The Modern Library.

Bambrough, Renford. 1963. *The Philosophy of Aristotle*. New York: Mentor Books.

Baron-Cohen, S., & Harrison, John. 1997. *Synaesthesia: Classic and Contemporary Readings*. Cambridge, MA: Blackwell Publishers.

Briggs, John. 1990. *Fire in the Crucible: The Self-Creation of Creativity and Genius*. Los Angeles: Jeremy P. Tarcher Inc.

Collini, Stefan. 1993. *Introduction to C.P. Snow's Two Cultures*. Cambridge: Cambridge University Press.

Cytowic, R. E. 1983. *The Man Who Tasted Shapes*. New York: Putnam.

Dann, Kevin T. 1998. *Bright Colors Falsely Seen: Synaesthesia and the Search for Transcendental Knowledge*. New Haven: Yale University Press.

Gogh, Vincent van. 1963. The Letters of Vincent Van Gogh. ed. Roskill, M. New York: Atheneum.

Goguen, Joseph A. & Myin, Erik. 2000. *Art and the Brain II: Investigations into the Science of Art*. Vol 7 (8-9).

Goguen, Joseph A., & Myin, Erik. 2004. *Art and the Brain: Controversies in Science & the Humanities (Part III)*. Vol 11 (3-4).

Goguen, Joseph A. 1999. 'Art and the Brain' in *Journal of Consciousness Studies* (6).

Gombrich, Ernst H. 2001. *The Preference for the Primitive: Episodes in the History of Western Taste and Art*. Phaidon: London and New York.

Harrison, John. 2001. *Synaesthesia: The Strangest Thing*. Oxford: Oxford University Press.

Havelock, Eric C. 1982. *Preface to Plato*. Cambridge, Massachusetts and London, England: The Belknap Press.

Huxley, Thomas H. 1894. Letter, *Science-Gossip*, 1.

Ione, Amy. 2000. 'Science: Method, Myth, Metaphor?' in *Alexandria* 5: 353-391.

— 2002. *Nature Exposed to Our Method of Questioning*. Berkeley: Diatrope Press.

— 2005. *Visualization and Innovation: Trajectories, Strategies, and Myths*. Amsterdam and New York: Rodopi.

Ione, Amy & Tyler, C. W. 2004. 'Synesthesia: Is F-Sharp Colored Violet?' in *Journal of the History of the Neurosciences*, 13.

Janson, H. W. 1970. *History of Art*. Englewood Cliffs: Prentice Hall.

Kline, Morris. 1953. *Mathematics in Western Culture*. New York: Oxford University Press.

Livingstone, Margaret. 2002. *Vision and Art: The Biology of Seeing*. New York: Harry N. Abrams.

Maurer, Daphne. 1997. 'Neonatal synaesthesia: implications for the processing of speech and faces' in Baron-Cohen, S. & Harrison, J. (eds.) *Synaesthesia: Classic and Contemporary Readings*. Cambridge, MA: Blackwell Publishers.

Miall, R. C., and John Tchalenko. 2001. 'A Painter's Eye Movements: A Study of Eye and Hand Movement During Portrait Drawing' in *Leonardo* 34 (1).

Murdoch, Iris. 1977. *The Fire and the Sun: Why Plato Banned the Artists*. Oxford: Oxford University Press.

Plato. 1989 (Book X, 607b). *The Collected Dialogues of Plato*. Hamilton, E. & Cairns, H. (eds.): Bollingen, Princeton University Press.

Pollitt, J.J. 1972. *Art and Experience in Classical Greece*. Cambridge: Cambridge University Press.

Rilke, Rainer Maria. 1952 (2nd ed.). *Letters on Cézanne*. (tr. Agee, J.) New York: Fromm International Publishing Corporation.

Rose, F. Clifford. 2004. *Neurology of the Arts: Painting, Music, Literature*. London: Imperial College Press.

Ross, Sydney. 1991. *Nineteenth-Century Attitudes: Men of Science*. Dordrecht, Boston, London: Kluwer Academic Publishers: 1-40

Smith, Pamela H. 2004. *The Body of the Artisan: Art and Experience in the Scientific Revolution*. Chicago: The University of Chicago Press.

Bibby, Cyril. 1959. *T.H. Huxley: Scientist, Humanist, and Educator*. London: CA Watts & Co.

Snow, C. P. 1959. *Two Cultures*. Cambridge: Cambridge University Press.

Snow, C. P. 1964. *Two Cultures and the Scientific Revolution*. Cambridge: Cambridge University Press.

Solso, Robert L. 1994. *Cognition and the Visual Arts*. Cambridge, MA and London: A Bradford Book.

— 2001. 'Brain Activities in a Skilled Versus a Novice Artist: An fMRI Study' in *Leonardo* 34 (1).

— 2003. *The Psychology of Art and the Evolution of the Conscious Brain*. Cambridge: MIT Press.

— 1999. 'Brain Activities in an Expert Versus a Novice Artist: An fMRI Study' in *Journal of Consciousness Studies* 7(8-9): Special Issue on Art and the Brain, Part II (ed.) Joseph A. and Myin Gougen, Erik. Exeter, UK: Imprint Academic.

Tuchman, Maurice. 1987. *The Spiritual in Art: Abstract Painting 1890–1985*. New York: Abbeville Press Inc.

Whewell, William. 1967 (1840). *The Philosophy of the Inductive Sciences*. London: Frank Cass & Co. Ltd.

— 1859. *History of the Inductive Sciences, from the Earliest to the Present Times*. Vol. 1-2; New York: D. Appleton and Company.

Yeo, Richard R. 2003. *Defining Science: William Whewell, Natural Knowledge and Public Debate in Early Victorian Britain*. Cambridge: Cambridge University Press.

Zeki, Semir. 1999. *Inner Visions: An Exploration of Art and the Brain*. Oxford: Oxford University Press.

Notes

[1] Other early journals include *Cognition and Consciousness*, launched in 1992, and *PSYCHE*, in 1993. Both of these were sponsored by the Association for the Scientific Study of Consciousness and, since their inception, have offered scientifically rigorous forums that are also open to novel theoretical contributions. While they accept both empirical research and speculative articles, their interdisciplinary emphasis is primarily intended to bring together the disciplines of cognitive science, philosophy, psychology, physics, neuroscience, artificial intelligence, linguistics, and anthropology.

[2] Indeed, even the *Journal of Consciousness Studies* recognized in time that art needed to be examined on its own terms. Since the publication's inception, it has published three issued devoted almost exclusively to consciousness and art (Goguen 1999; Goguen & Myin 2000, 2004), all of which have proved quite instrumental in clarifying issues unique to art and consciousness.

[3] "Then the mimetic art is far removed from truth, and this, it seems is the reason why it can produce everything, because it touches or lays hold of only a small part of the object and that a phantom, as, for example, a painter, we say, will paint us a cobbler, a carpenter, and other craftsmen, though he himself has no expertness in any of these arts, but nevertheless if he were a good painter, by exhibiting at a distance his picture of a carpenter he would deceive children and foolish men, and make them believe it to be a real carpenter... When anyone reports to us of someone, that he has met a man who knows all the crafts and everything else that men severally know, and that there

is nothing that he does not know more exactly than anybody else, our tacit rejoinder must be that he is a simple fellow, who apparently has met some magician or sleigh-of-hand man and imitator and has been deceived by him into the belief that he is all-wise, because of his own inability to put to the proof and distinguish knowledge, ignorance, and imitation." (Hamilton & Cairns, 1989: 598)

[4] Stefan Collini's recent introduction to the Canto edition of Snow's book offers an excellent summary of this relationship (Collini 1993; Snow 1959, 1964).

[5] William Whewell spent most of his career at Trinity College, Cambridge, where he studied, tutored and served as Professor of Mineralogy (1828–32), Professor of Moral Philosophy (1838–55) and College Master (1841–66). He was also Vice Chancellor of the university (1842).

[6] A concise summary of this episode is detailed by Sydney Ross, in his short essay "*Scientist*: The Story of a Word" (1991). Included in Ross' survey are many quotes from primary sources associated with the debates. Richard Yeo's *Defining Science: William Whewell, Natural Knowledge and Public Debate in Early Victorian Britain* (2003) is another useful reference.

[7] This turn is documented in the *Oxford English Dictionary*, where the nineteenth century compilers recognized that no example of science in the narrow sense of just physical or natural science as we use it today was evident before the 1860s (Collini 1993).

[8] The changing nature of art is examined in my *Innovation and Visualization* (Ione 2005)

[9] In Greek, the word *téchne* covers art, craft and skill.

[10] In all fairness it should be mentioned that Aristotle was more sympathetic to the arts in some ways. For Aristotle, poetry and myth were more important than history because "the one describes what has happened, the other what might. Hence poetry is something more philosophic and serious than history; for poetry speaks of what is universal, history of what is particular." (*Poetics* 1461 b, 3. *In* Bambrough 1963)

[11] "In the world of Goethe and Byron it was recognized that the measured, restrained, balanced, and orderly nature of Greek and Roman poetry contrasted with the more openly enraptured effusive art of the Romantic era. 'Classical' came to imply a style that was highly formal and ordered as opposed to one which was intensely 'emotional" (Pollitt 1972: 2).

[12] Van Gogh received no recognition during his lifetime and only sold one painting while he was alive.

Tomorrow's World That We Shall Build Today[1]

Angela Ndalianis

This essay analyses the impact that science fiction (SF) has had on envisioning real cities. In 1939 the New York World's Fair imagined the utopian techno-city of the future, yet by the late c20th, such imaginings had become realities. Drawing on examples like Odaiba in Japan and Futuroscope in Poitiers, France, this essay explores the ways in which these emerging spaces have embraced the idea of the filmic SF city, while also drawing on the theme park's similar rationale — as filtered through the world fair. Aside from realising architectural tropes from SF, Odaiba and Futuroscope also realise the idea of expanding human consciousness by integrating robotic consciousness into the social fabric.

Astro Boy, Godzilla and the Attack on Tokyo Bay

Tetsuwan Atom first graced the science fiction screen of manga comics in 1951. This super-boy robot, who came to be known in the western world as Astro Boy, was the creation of Osamu Tezuka who later gave the Astro Boy movement in the form of a science fiction animated television show — also called *Astro Boy*. Astro Boy's fictional birthday — April 7, 2003 — finally arrived when reality caught up with fiction and, to make this reality even more 'real', the urbanscape of the future envisioned by Tezuka (the super-transport systems, the gleaming architecture, and a world where human and robot live in harmony) also appeared to have arrived. Having influenced an entire generation of Japanese roboticists, it comes as no surprise that Astro Boy has become an iconic figure who embodies the future now. Furthermore, Astro Boy's birthday celebrations began on April 6, 2003 "with the launch of a new Tetsuwan Atom Japanese animated series on the Fuji TV network"[2] (Nakada 2003). Beyond the robot star that it promotes, the Fuji TV network recalls additional science fiction iconography as it rises majestically like a network matrix in all of its metallic glory, centered by a mega-ton globe that appears to defy gravity — the structure is one of the many impressive symbols that reflect the futuristic imperatives that drive urban development on the island of Odaiba, a man-made island that is situated just outside Tokyo in Tokyo Bay.

I've seen the future, and it is Odaiba. Odaiba is one of the many islands first constructed in the early c17th when Shogun Tokugawa Ieyasu ordered the drainage of swamp land and the creation of these *daiba* (cannon emplacements) as strategic locations where soldiers could defend Edo, the new capital of Japan, from invaders. These military posts also became integral to fending off western colonizers and traders, perhaps most famously in 1853, which was the year U.S. Commodore Matthew Perry arrived in Tokyo Bay, demanding that the Japanese open up trade with the West. Perry was sent on his way, but another invader — also a product of the West — was to make an attack on Tokyo Bay a century later. His name was Godzilla, and his creation was the result of the devastating realities of science and technology. Godzilla — in addition to Mothra, Ghydra, Biollante and many other mutant and robotic friends — became a symbolic manifes-tation, within a science fiction context, of the destructive possibilities of science as embodied in this instance by the U.S. government's atomic attack on Japan. Godzilla's arrival from the depths of Tokyo Bay in 1954 was to seal a contemporary relationship between Odaiba and science fiction.

Fifty years after Godzilla's inception, he would again be brought to life in Tokyo Bay — this time finding a home on the island of Odaiba within the walls of the National Museum of Emerging Science and Innovation. In 2003, the museum opened an exhibition that developed on the themes of science fiction's close rapport with scientific reality. Through a display of the *Godzilla* film series — its mutant monsters, robots, destructive military weapons — the show explored the ways in which science fiction has always been closely enmeshed in the social fabric. The mutant creatures, robots and advanced weapons all had their roots in scientific and technological realities that had or which would become concrete beyond the fictional spaces of the *Godzilla* films. The National Museum of Emerging Science and Innovation expounds a philosophy that is integral to Odaiba in general. As its title suggests — and in collaboration with the Science and Technology departments of the local university — exhibitions like that showcasing the International Space Station and advances in space travel, or the frequent exhibitions that display current developments in robotics through the performance of 'real' robots like Honda's Asimo and Sony's QRIO, aim to educate the public. The lesson? That science fiction no longer exists beyond our reach, far away into the future: it is with us now.

The central logic behind emerging cities such as Odaiba is the principle of the 'learning city' — a city that promotes scientific and technological innovation by integrating it into its economic operational plan and by training and teaching its citizens the importance that innovations in the fields of information and communication technology have for competition in the global market. Combining retail developments with industry and technology, to quote Kurt Larsen, learning cities act "as drivers for the knowledge-based societies of the 21st century" (1999). Yet, while appearing to be focused on the present, because they borrow so many tropes from science fiction (whether consciously or unconsciously) these learning cities are imbued with an undeniable 'future' quality.

The one haunting memory that remains of my first trip to Odaiba in 2003 is the extent to which it felt like I'd entered a series of science fiction films from the post-1950s period. I was both overjoyed by the sensation, but also overcome by an uneasy feeling. The mise-en-scene was indisputable: the spotless, meticulously manicured urbanscape with the metallic and monochromatic building surfaces of structures like Tokyo Big Shot and the Telecom complex; the expedient people movers littered throughout Aqua City and Decks Tokyo Beach (the two destination shopping malls that include a 'reconstruction' of 1950's Hong Kong); the super-velocity driverless monorail that travels from mainland Tokyo to Odaiba; the mega-architectural structures that stand as monuments to corporations like Fuji TV, Telecom, Panasonic and telecommunication companies like NTT, which has its offices in the skyscraper called 'Tokyo Teleport' — all seem to be straight out of films like *2001: a Space Odyssey* (1968), *Logan's Run* (1976), and *THX1138* (1971) or television shows like *Star Trek*. The technologically-controlled, computer reliant infrastructure of the entire city (that includes the visible presence of robots), computer games in the Joypolis game city, cutting edge entertainment complexes such as Mediage, Toyota's Mega Web, the Panasonic Center and the Sony Complex, as well as the hi-tech surveillance system that monitors every move that citizens make, recall *The Forbin Project* (1970), *Westworld* (1973) and *TRON* (1982). In shopping complexes like Venus Fort, a women's shopping complex (and a small scale version of Caesar's Palace in Las Vegas) that caters to and celebrates the 'perfect' woman consumer, I couldn't quite shake off the feeling that I had entered a bizarre revision of *The Stepford Wives* (2004) — and as I wandered around, mesmerized by the spectacular homage to female beauty, I was also overcome by the fear that I would be caught out as the not-too-perfect woman and be submitted to central control for re-programming. And, as if we've reached a time like that predicted in *Blade Runner* (1982) when human kind has finally initiated the extinction of numerous animal species, we can visit Dog Town (*Inutama*) and Cat's Park (*Nekotama*), dog and cat 'theme parks' where we can pat and play with these 'real' animals —and even rent a dog for a couple of hours to take him walking. All of this science fiction mise-en-scene, and the narratives we create within it, speak of a utopian existence — an environment where human and machine come together in perfect unison for the betterment of human kind. The dystopian implications of these spaces are hidden from view, but every utopia has its dark dystopian double, doesn't it? Or maybe I've seen too many science fiction films.

In his book *The Aesthetics of Ambivalence*, Brooks Landon extends our understanding of science fiction. He argues that our society has become science fictional as a result of emerging technologies that include advances in bio-genetics, military warfare technology and, in particular, special effects technologies that make possible the illusions of science fiction film narratives. Writing in 1992, Landon's comments about science fiction are still applicable today. In *Minority Report* (2002), for example, the narrative links the future with our present through technological familiarity. Writing for *The New York Times*, Michel Marriott explains that; "Bonnie Curtis, one of the producers of *Minority Report*, said Mr.Spielberg largely depended on a group of futurists and his own imagination for much of the technological applications in the movie."[3] Spielberg turned to major industry corporations to design the film's 'future' technologies: NOKIA designed the film's phones, and LEXUS designed the cars — both the red sports car driven by Tom Cruise's character, John Anderton, and the private Pod that rides on the Mag-Lev (magnetic levitation) system. Likewise, many other technologies envisioned in the film have predecessors in our real space: augmented reality and surveillance technologies like the retinal identification system are already in operation, as are the security identification systems — the Spyders, which had an earlier life in our history as insect robots like the Mars pathfinder. The technology that made possible the direct address to Anderton's stolen identity (when he enters the GAP in the mall scene) is already in place: Stephan Finch and his company, Thinking Pictures, have been designing movie posters in theatre lobbies that, using patrons' 'smart cards', will eventually address individual movie goers according to their personal tastes.

At times, as in the case of *Minority Report,* the illusionistic and spectacular contents contained within the screen narrativise changes in society (in the plot's concerns with the implications of genetic engineering, computer technology, and the simulated experiences offered by augmented reality technology). But in many instances, contemporary science fiction films also employ special effects technologies that reveal the remarkable transformations occurring in our own culture from the perspective of scientific and technological advancements. Beyond the diegetic collapse of current technological progress and the projection of that technology into the future, in order to create their effects illusions, many blockbuster films rely on technologies that were once considered as belonging to the realm of science fiction. New soft and hardware is being developed to provide more 'realistic' effects in the fictional spaces that audiences consume as entertainment. Yet these effects are also altering the role played by the cinema within a broader cultural context. For example, the film industry (in conjunction with the computer games industry) has taken the lead in advances in artificial intelligence (AI) and artificial life (A-Life). One of the most astounding "science fictional modes of depicting", to use Landon's term, is to be found in film special effects used in the *Lord of the Rings* trilogy (2000-3). Introducing the science fiction concern of evolving artificial life forms familiar to films like *A.I.* (2001), *Thirteenth Floor* (1999) and *I, Robot* (2004) into their film worlds, in *Lord of the Rings* we actually witness the rudimentary beginnings of virtual, computer-generated beings that have the ability to evolve and think. 'Massive' (Multiple Agent Simulation System in Virtual Environment) is a software programme created by Steve Regelous of the *WETA* effects company in order to create realistic battle scenes.[4] The huge armies are, in reality, hordes of computer-generated soldiers that rely on AI models. 'Massive' endows each character with a digital brain and gives it the power to act independent of human interference. Each character can perceive, interpret and respond to what's happening around it: to make decisions and act. In fact, in early tests of the battle scenes, some of the A-Life soldiers decided not to fight but to run away.[5] The 'Massive' programme is now on sale, allowing users to create their own digital creatures within computer spaces.

Landon is concerned with the ways in which new imagining technologies are producing similar science fiction effects, but I want to also
extend Landon's fundamental premise and argue that the science
fictional has infiltrated our reality in more architecturally and socially
invasive ways. The themes, narratives and technologies that were
contained within the parameters of science fiction cinema are now
slipping into the public sphere in very real ways. I began with the
examples of Astro Boy, Godzilla and Odaiba because they encapsulate
the issues that concern me in this essay — the relationship between
our fictions of science that have found a voice in real terms in our
urban spaces — a relationship that was forged earlier in the last century by world expositions. Odaiba was itself originally planned as a
possible venue for a World Expo in the late 1980s but plans (after a
great deal of building authorized by two mayors Suzuki and Aoshima)
were, in the wake of the Bubble Economy, finally abandoned by
Mayor Aoshima in the early 1990s.

I Have Seen the Future... at the World's Fair

Kihlstedt has stated that:

> Mass utopias are mere figments of the imagination, and most are 'embodied
> only in literature. Even in the nineteenth century, when some small utopian
> communities were actually built, utopian endeavors remained primarily lit-
> erary. In the twentieth century, however, visionary images of the future
> were brought to life and offered to the public at world's fairs (1986: 97).

In the early 21st century this is even more the case, for the projected
utopias have also escaped the fairs and expositions and entered the
city space, but before returning to our own utopias I'd like to travel
back in time to these earlier visions of utopian communities.

Since the Chicago World's Fair of 1893, world expositions and
fairs returned continuously to the concern with creating idealized
cities. The Chicago Fair was especially significant in establishing
what would later become integral not only to the logic of expositions,
but to theme parks like Disneyland and EPCOT (Experimental Proto-
type Community of Tomorrow) and urban destinations like Odaiba
that would follow in their wake — in all instances, a ready-made ideal
city was created, one that was technologically-driven and reliant on
commercial imperatives and popular culture[6]. As James Gilbert has
explained when discussing early Expo visitors; "the visible future they
encountered was a carefully engineered vision, a prophecy... of the

coming relationship between work, leisure, and culture" (1991: 37). But unlike the dystopian futures often delineated in science fiction, in the future visions of the expositions, the inclusion of technological and scientific innovation within the social environment could only result in the creation of utopian spaces.

Expositions like the Chicago Century of Progress Exposition of 1933-1934 and the New York World's Fair of 1939 took the first important steps not only in forging a relationship between science and society, but also integrating these concerns with the visions and consumer pleasures offered by science fiction and entertainment. Rydell explains that, in the wake of the Great Depression; "1930s scientists, confronted by a 'revolt against science', joined corporate backers of the fairs in trying to pin popular hopes for national recovery on the positive results expected from the fusion of science and business" (1993: 526). Specifically, combining speculation familiar to science fiction with the realities of the scientific and technological innovations of the time, these fairs specialized in presenting the public with utopias of the future.

It was the New York World's Fair of 1939 that became one of the most famous examples to showcase a new urban landscape — one that figured the utopian possibilities of technology and science. Appropriately, on the opening night, Albert Einstein switched on the lights that would bring life to the Fair's motto: 'Designing the World of Tomorrow'. The New York World's Fair proceeded to create a vision of a world in which; "science could become a way of life and utopia would be nigh" (Rydell 1993:111). Showcasing the latest technologies offered by corporations (and, in addition to displaying Rotolactor, an automatic cow-milking machine), numerous other technological inventions were presented to an eager public — Voder, a synthetic human-speech device by AT&T; television sets by RCA, GE and Westinghouse; and Elektro, a walking and talking robot by Westinghouse[7] — it was the representation of a 'City of the Future' that drew the crowds in by the millions.

The plans for this 'City of the Future', which were conceived by the industrial designer Norman Bel Geddes, set the foundations for cities that were riddled with massive freeway systems, cars and soaring skyscrapers. In Geddes' Futurama 'Highways and Horizons' exhibit sponsored by General Motors, viewers sat high above a miniature city of the future in 1960 while a motorized belt moved them along in a full circle. As they looked down on a 36,000 sq ft. model city of superhighways and skyscrapers designed by Geddes, through speakers built into the backs of their seats, a narrator asked the audience to imagine how the traffic and housing problems of the present United States would be solved through these technological and industrial wonders by the year 1960. Provided with souvenir pins that read 'I have seen the future', as Morshed explains, the Futurama exhibition reinforced two things: 'The first is the idea of the Future as spectacle, and the second is the process of seeing that spectacle' (Morshed 2004: 74).

In addition to inspiring Walt Disney's design of Disneyland in the 1950s, and in presenting a glimpse of the highways and skyscrapers of the metropolis that would later dominate our contemporary city spaces, the New York Fair's *World of Tomorrow* was a mediator that provided a bridge between science fiction and reality. It was the stepping-stone to later urban designs and its inspiration came directly from the realm of science fiction. Geddes drew inspiration from *Le Corbusier* (in particular his *Ville Contemporaine* of 1922 and *la Ville Radieuse* of 1930)[8] and other utopianist urban planners of the 1920s and 30s but, whereas *Le Corbusier's* inspiration for the transcendental themes that are evident in his ideal cities drew directly from religious traditions and iconography, Geddes turned to another form of religious experience — that provided by the prophetic wisdom of science fiction and popular culture. In this 'ride' into the future, the audience had entered a science fiction narrative.

The futuristic, technologically reliant cities that populated the Buck Rogers comic strips of the 1920s and film serials of the 30s had a great impact on this glimpse into the world of tomorrow, as did the science fiction novels of Edward Bellamy and H.G.Wells. In Bellamy's *Looking Backward* of 1888, Mr.West (the hero) wakes up to find himself in the year 2000 and a; "High-tech' world of soaring skyscrapers, streets covered with transparent material, and music piped into the home" (Kihlstedt 1986: 100). Similarly, in Wells' *When the Sleeper Wakes* of 1899 the hero falls into a trance and comes to 2100. The technological city he finds himself in relies on windowless houses, central lighting, air conditioning, and an urban environment that worships mechanization and the wonders of science and technology, very like the Futurama exhibit of the New York World's Fair (Kihlstedt 1986: 101). Again, like the participants in the Futurama ride, Bert Smallways, the central character in Wells' novel *The War in the Air* (1908) explores the futuristic city from the window of his aircraft, and in 1939, the artist Julian Krupa's vision of 'Cities of Tomorrow' was published in *Amazing Stories*, one of the first science fiction magazines. "The city of tomorrow, *Amazing Stories* prophesied, would consist of an idyllic, vertically stratified urbanscape in which 'dwellers and workers... may go weeks without setting foot on the ground, or the ground level" (Morshed 2004: 74). In addition, the moving chairs in the General Motors Futurama display (which would become integral to Disney and later theme park ride technology) were called 'Time Machines' in a deliberate allusion to Wells' novel of the same name. It was no surprise that, during the fair, H.G. Wells was asked to write the lead article about the fair and how it equated with his version of the future in the *New York Times*.[9]

When You Wish Upon a Star: Disney, Disneyland and Project X

Expositions like the New York World's Fair would have a dramatic impact on real-world spaces that would be built a decade later — most memorably in the form of Walt Disney's Disneyland, which finally opened its doors to a utopian landscape in Anaheim, California in July 1955. Clearly, in his conception of Disneyland, Walt Disney was inspired by the exposition structure: the pavilions and corporate sponsored exhibits were transformed into 'lands' — *Adventureland, Tomorrowland, Frontierland, Fantasyland* — and the corporate sponsor was now the Disney Corporation and its technologies were now on display in the form of cutting edge rides that were 'themed' according to Disney films, including *Dumbo* (1941), *Alice in Wonderland* (1951) and *Cinderella* (1950). In addition, many of the utopianist writings of the 1920s-30s also impacted on Disney, but what was most interesting was that while Disney embraced the desire to build the future now and to construct utopian environments that pushed the envelope when it came to scientific and technological innovation, he rejected many of the visions of how this future would be conceived.[10] Already in the 1950s, the freeways riddled with automobiles and super-scrapers that towered towards the heavens, which had been central tropes of science fiction writers, utopianists and expositions, had become a reality — and Disney was not impressed with this version of the future. Instead, in Disneyland, he set about creating his version of science fiction, one that later filtered into our conception of contemporary urban spaces. Marling has argued that Disneyland:

> ... presented a powerful critique of the manifest ills of Los Angeles in 1955... Disneyland included pedestrian spaces free from vehicular traffic. In the form of rides (or 'attractions', in park lingo), it spotlighted every imaginable kind of people-moving device that did not entail a driver pilot-

ing himself through increasingly congested streets — and chewing up the landscape in the process: trains, monorails, passenger pods, canal boats, riverboats, and double-decker buses (1997: 30).

Wanting to escape the increasing attack by the Los Angeles urbanscape on Disneyland in Anaheim in the 1950s, Disney proceeded to purchase thousands of acres of property in Florida, which would become the home of the new *Magic Kingdom* in the 1970s. Here, the realities of Norman Bel Geddes' imagined skyscrapers and automobile society would find it difficult to infiltrate Disney's vision of the future. Disney's allegiance with science fiction was clear when he hired the famous science fiction author Ray Bradbury to work at the Disney Imagineering Studio. Bradbury had met Disney when *Tomorrowland* was being conceptualized and Bradbury had expressed his interest in collaborating on the design of this land. But, while recognizing the value of such an alliance, Disney had insisted that such a partnership between two geniuses would be doomed to failure. Nevertheless, Bradbury's talents as creative consultant were later put to use not only in the design of the U.S. Pavilion at the 1964 New York World's Fair, but in the planning of *Spaceship Earth* — one of the central attractions at Disneyworld's EPCOT theme park — in 1982 (Bradbury 1999: 7).

EPCOT was loosely based on Walt Disney's plans to create a futuristic community — plans that never came to be according to Disney's vision because of his death. Called Project X,

> ... the original EPCOT was a bold New Town scheme intended to show that the problems of present-day American cities were not beyond solution. That it was possible, for example, to eliminate the automobile from the urban equation, or at least minimize its depredations by running service roads under and around city centers and providing cheap, efficient forms of mass transit (Marling: 1997: 31).

Disney's 'utopian dream of a real city' not only focused on building a community with "dependable public transportation", but this perfect city would also be "covered by an all-weather dome" and its factories and key industries (which would be "concealed in greenbelts that were readily accessible to workers housed in idyllic suburban subdivisions") would embody the latest innovations in science and technology (Marling 1997: 31). Disney's Project X was the original 'learning city' that would later influence cities like Odaiba.

Despite Disney's death, Project X was to finally be transformed into two realities — albeit in revised form. Firstly, in the form of the town 'Celebration' that occupies Disney property in Florida and which went through various stages of development in the 1990s and early 2000s: this community attempts to bring life to Walt Disney's dream by time travelling back to a utopian and idealized version of a non-existent past when small town America embodied the aspirations of the *American Dream*. While fascinating as a study of utopian ideals, its conception of a 'future now' is, in actuality, more about the 'past now'. Celebration, in fact, is more aligned with the horror genre than science fiction and, as such, lies beyond the scope of this essay — only to say that, it comes as no surprise that the kind of community it idealizes was indeed the stuff of horror in episodes of *The X-Files* and *Millennium*. More importantly, the second development that Disney's Project X took was in the form of the EPCOT Center, a Disney Corporation theme park that opened its doors in 1982, and which has, as its central theme, the future — specifically, a future supported by the possibilities of scientific and technological advancement in the hands of multinational corporations. As Marling has stated, EPCOT "became a kind of permanent World's Fair" complete with corporate sponsored pavilions (1997: 31).

Both 'lands' — *Future World* and *World Showcase* — owe a great deal to the conventions and philosophical concerns established in the Fairs. *The World Showcase*, which themes the world by including miniaturised versions of France, Morocco, Japan and Germany, updates the displays of different cultures that were found in the Midway section of the expos and fairs in the c20[th]. But it is *Future World* that displays the most dramatic inspiration of fairs and science fiction. Radiating around *Spaceship Earth*, the giant geosphere that dominates the theme park, are numerous themed attractions — *Innoventions, Journey into the Imagination, Universe of Energy* — all of which are sponsored by major corporations. It is *Spaceship Earth*, however, that displays the most dramatic connection to science fiction. The earlier *Futurama* ride of 1939 took visitors forward in time to experience the city of the future in 1960. On *Spaceship Earth* visitors enter a time machine that takes them back in time, to travel a 15-minute journey through the history of technology and communication. Displaying this history through a series of animatronic performers, and beginning with a Cro-Magnon shaman who recounts the story of a hunt while others record it on cave walls, viewers witness a series of communications milestones — the Phoenician and Greek alphabets, the printing press, the telegraph, radio, film, television — even outerspace where the power of satellite systems is on display. Finally, exiting the ride, participants find themselves in a pavilion sponsored by another com-

munications giant, AT&T, and invited to sample a range of technological goodies — from computer games to simulation rides — all
made possible by the company's electronic network.

Neon Glitz and Experience Architecture

Since Disneyland opened its doors in 1955, the theme park slowly
became an important feature not only of contemporary retail and
leisure culture, but also as venues, which like their World Exposition
predecessors, showcased the possibilities of new technologies. For
film studios such as Universal, Warner Brothers, Paramount and 20th
Century Fox, the theme park became both a marketing tool for its film
products (where popular films were 'themed' as rides or environments), and a spectacular symbol of the power and economic potential
of cutting edge technology delivered in an entertainment package, a
concern that obviously drives EPCOT. Since entering the new millennium, our urban spaces have continued to embrace the logic of the
theme park with an amazing zeal. One of the most fascinating revi-
sions of the theme park/Exposition foray into science fiction realities
is the 'theme park' *Futuroscope*, which is situated in Poitiers, France.
Initiated by the local politician, Rene Monory, who wanted to build a
park that was the "centrepiece of a new-tech industrial estate", Futuroscope, which opened in 1987, was built with the support of the local
Council of Poitiers and assisted by national government funding. Over
the last five years, it has become radically revised as a 'learning city'
more aligned with Odaiba.
    Situated 200 miles outside Paris, in the 1990s it offered Disneyland
Paris some serious competition while also boosting the local economy
in the role it serves as an entertainment destination. The theme park's
premise is to use entertainment attractions in order to educate and
acclimatize audiences to new imaging technologies. Scattered across
an idyllic landscape are a series of futuristic looking buildings that
appear to be part of a science fiction film set (one is shaped like a
giant crystal, another like an enormous set of glass organ pipes, and
another still looks like a 1950s retro spaceship), and within these
buildings, audiences can experience some of the most amazing audiovisual technologies that the entertainment industry has to offer. The
attractions (which are sponsored by hi-tech corporations) include: a
360-degree cinema; a 3-D Cinema experience; a Kinemax-IMAX
Theater; a Dynamic Motion Simulator using the Showscan system
devised by Douglas Trumbull (the effects guru who was responsible

for the effects of films like *2001: a Space Odyssey* and *Blade Runner*); a dual IMAX cinema with one vertical and one horizontal screen; a Multi-Screen Show with ten 35mm projectors projecting onto 10 screens of different sizes (including the hemispherical Omnimax screen); the 'Cineautomate', an interactive film; and an hourly night show that features a computer generated 'Water Symphony' (*à la* the Belaggio in Las Vegas) that comprises of dancing water fountains, laser lights, fireworks and music.

The park director Daniel Bulliard has stated that; "The park's theme of image is based on the observation that 'easy, daily access to reality or dream, the omnipresent image is the backdrop to our lives and changes how we see the world. It seduces, captivates and invades our professional being and devours our leisure time", and Isabelle Houllier, assistant to the director extends on this: "By offering a wide array of contemporary images, the park educates as well as entertains. 'People have a tendency to not understand technology they see every day... Here, they can learn and see technology through cinema, and have fun at the same time." Clearly, *Futuroscope* has adopted an identity as a 'learning city' in that it aims to promote innovation through its showcase of cutting edge technologies. But, in addition to what is contained within the walls of the theme park, unlike EPCOT or the expositions of the past, it extends the promotion of innovation beyond its walls into the social realm that contains and surrounds it. The park itself has become a hub around which an entire industry in multimedia, computer and communication technology has evolved.

Larsen explains that for *Futuroscope*;

> ... research and development with education and leisure activities, is the focus of its strategy. Thus far, it has attracted 70 firms and created 1,500 jobs in the park and 12,000 jobs indirectly in the whole region. It is also a major tourist site, drawing visitors from around the world" (Larsen 1999).

Importantly, since 2000, the area around the theme park has undergone a dramatic transformation: hotels, residential areas, big business sectors have flourished. Recalling *Star Trek*, 'Teleport' is the technology park near the theme park that companies like Telecom France and e-Qual (a company with specialization in IP-based network solutions and satellite communications) call home. Near Teleport, and part of the training and research area, is France's first combined experimental high school and university; "where students matriculate from high school directly into the same area of study in college. Engineering and technology degrees are emphasized"; and also included as part of the complex is the International Institute of Long-Term Forecasting (Larsen 1999). Like the New Bad Future films of the 1980s — *Robocop* (1987), *Total Recall* (1990), *Blade Runner* — corporations combine forces with the government to control the products of science and technology and, in turn, the shape of the society that develops around them.

So, science fiction books and films impact upon the New York Fair's 1939 vision of the tomorrow of 1960, which eventually becomes tomorrow by being incorporated into theme park and urban spaces that are then reincorporated as images of the future in science fiction films like *Blade Runner, A.I.* and *Minority Report*. In many respects, *Blade Runner* is a paradigmatic example of the complex interchange that occurs between society, as reality, and the realities of science fiction. The film inspired architects to redesign the urban landscape by using the film's focus on neons to unify buildings. In his thought-provoking book *The History of Forgetting*, Norman Klein writes how:

> In February 1990, at a public lecture series on art in Los Angeles, three out of five leading urban planners agreed that they hoped L.A. would someday look like the film *Blade Runner*... By 1990, Frank Gehry's architecture is praised in a mainstream review as 'post-apocalyptic', having a '*Blade Runner*' inventiveness... The film *Blade Runner* has indeed achieved something rare in the history of the cinema. It has become a paradigm for the future of cities (Klein 1997: 94-95).

The effects of *Blade Runner* were felt not only in the buildings of Frank Gehry but in the Jerde Partnership's designs for Universal City Walk in Los Angeles, which is the micro-city that is the thoroughfare to Universal's theme park complex. Relying on the bold and funky colours of neon lights to decorate the facades of the buildings of this urban entertainment destination, a melodic rhythm is created that unites the distinct complexes. While *Blade Runner*'s mise-en-scene is clearly an inspiration, Jerde's unified city space (which Klein argues succumbs to the logic of an 'electronic baroque')[11] strips away the dystopian vision that marks Ridley Scott's film. Here, in Universal City, citizens inhabit a science fiction utopia. Then, in 2001, Universal City Walk was science-fictionalized for the Spielberg directed film *A.I.* Rewriting the famous arched entrance that marks the separation between Universal Studios and the City Walk, the film's set designers 'technologized' the actual city icon by transforming the stone archway into one comprising fluorescent neon lights favoured by Jon Jerde via *Blade Runner* for the City Walk. In *A.I.,* the Universal arch becomes the illuminated icon of the futuristic and fictional metropolis 'Rouge City'. This time, reflecting the science fiction film tradition, this iconic image gives voice to a darker, more apocalyptic double — a fact that is marked by the highway entrance to 'Rouge City', which takes the form of a 'mouth of Hell' familiar to painted depictions of the underworld since the c15th.

Learning cities and urban destinations like University City and its CityWalk rely on what is known as 'experience architecture'. Beyard et al explain that:

> The field of experience architecture blends environmental design, media technology, and narrative to create compelling 'event-places'... [furthermore] These projects exemplify the social tradition of making places that are designed to remove us from everyday life (2001: 8).

Like the World Expositions, or theme parks like Disney's EPCOT, integral to this removal from everyday life is our placement within the future. However, Beyard et al. make a very significant distinction — one that clarifies the ways in which our contemporary environments differ from the earlier models. One of the central features of environments that rely on 'experience architecture' is that "the future is in retreat. Experience architecture has always thrived on innovation — and supported concepts that promote a social contract between environments and progress. World's fairs typically hosted offerings with futuristic themes, and expositions showcased industrial — and then technological — leaps forward", however, the fascination with the 'future now' has undergone a transformation. The gap has closed further still. "Simply put", says Beyard, "the future isn't cool anymore. What we have only imagined can now be experienced. Of the dreams we had postponed in search of technology, much — perhaps too much — is available today" (2001: 9).

From Elektro to Asimo: do Androids Dream of Electric Aibos?

As mentioned, the New York World's Fair of 1939 was dramatically important in framing (and predicting) our future in a science fiction light. In addition to displaying future cities and houses filled with technological gadgets, the fair emphasized the role robotics would play in making our lives free of mundane activities. In the *Hall of Electrical Living*, viewers could be entertained by Elektro, the amazing Westinghouse Moto-Man. Influenced especially by the hundreds of robots that had made appearances in science fiction films like

Metropolis (1927); and the *Buck Rogers* (1939) and *Flash Gordon* (1980) film serial tradition, Westinghouse's mechanical man (despite looking like an anthropomorphized washing machine) was to have a dramatic impact on public consciousness. Like the *Futurama City* of 1960, Elektro embodied the technological possibilities of the future.

Robots are closer to being norms in our everyday environment. To paraphrase Beyard, as a dream we had once postponed, robots are now available today. Honda's android Asimo (in an obvious homage to Asimov — father of the laws of robotics) has made many media appearances in the last couple of years — and his battery pack gets less bulky every time we see him. In the last year, he has been making public appearances in Odaiba. In early 2003, in Odaiba's Museum of Emerging Science (and next door to the Godzilla and technology exhibit), visitors could see Asimo walk, talk and perform his very own robot-version of the chicken dance.

In his book *Robots: the Quest for Living Machines* Geoff Simons has stated that:

> ... the robot dream has existed in the human mind from antiquity to the present day. Fantasy precedes coherent theory, which in turn precedes practical realization: there were many ancient dreams about humanoid artifacts before the earliest engineers and craftsmen began to shape their working models (1992).

Simons understands these "robot dreams" as reflecting the way human beings struggle "to cope with an incomprehensible universe" (1992: 32). From the ancient Greek legends of Pygmalion (who breathed life into a statue Galatea) to Dr. Victor Frankenstein (who animated the flesh of human corpses with electricity to create his monster), the myths and legends that deal with the creation of artificial life are as old as human history. As Simons suggests, creation myths are not only common in most cultures, they "often have an interest in robotics" (1992: 16). The early myths posed many important questions: where did the world come from? What is the genesis of human beings? What happens, however, when these legends move beyond fiction and enter reality?

We have come a long way since the days of Pygmalion, Frankenstein and Elektro. Current prototypes in robotics are already revealing the collaborations between multinational corporations, scientists, the government and military institutions — associations that have featured as narrative scenarios to be feared in science fiction since the 1950s. In the western world — and, in particular, the U.S. — robotics has primarily entered the private and public sphere in the form of entertainment products found in films and theme park attractions. Particularly significant is the escalation of so-called 'entertainment robots' that has occurred in the last decade — especially within Japan. During the mid-1990s, Tatsuzo Ishida, Sony Corporation's robotics engineer (who had, since the 1980s, overseen the production of entertainment technologies such as walkmen, handycams, and game consoles) proposed that Sony engineer a new species of humanoid entertainment robots along the lines of C-3PO, the famous screen robot of the blockbuster science fiction film *Star Wars* (1977). The Sony Corporation agreed, and with fellow roboticists Yoshihiro Kuroki and Shingo Tamura, Development Chief at Waseda University's famed robotics lab, they began designing entertainment robots. Toshoi Doi, Sony corporate Vice President and President of Sony Computer Science Laboratories, believes that "such 'entertainment robots' will create 'a new industry' for emotionally gratifying mechanical playthings".[12] Unlike the robots that operate within the service industry, or Hollywood's animatronics (which focus on repeated, pre-programmed movements), these entertainment robots lack a functional drive: they are meant to entertain and offer amusement to their owner and their behaviour develops in a random way. Behind this seemingly empty rationale, however, lies an extremely focused one. The freedom and lack of specific function makes possible the robot's ability to advance in intelligence through adaptive learning. The random interactions with its environment are conducive to learning.

The entertainment giant Sony — the company that introduced radios, televisions, walkmen and Playstation consoles to the general public has, since the mid 1990s, developed a lucrative market for its entertainment robots. In fact, Sony has become a leader in this field. In 1998 Sony announced Aibo the pet robot dog — a pet companion who plays ball, recognizes its owner, and performs a variety of tricks. As the most popular entertainment robot released in the market, Sony could barely meet demand for sales and on November 16, 2000 the second Aibo model went on sale in Japan (and online) for $3,200. Being one of the most advanced examples of artificial intelligence, currently, the latest model of Aibo (who, admittedly, I was besotted with when I first saw it in action) is available worldwide via some department stores and Sony's website. Aibo is also on sale and regularly performs at the amazing Sony Complex in Odaiba.

In 1999, Honda Motor Corporation unveiled a bipedal robot dubbed 'P-2'. Since 1999, P-2 has evolved through various prototypes. The current version is called Asimo, who is not only another one of the regular robot stars to make appearances at venues in Odaiba, but whose name is a clear homage to the famous scientist and science fiction writer Isaac Asimov who 'invented' the 'Three Laws of Robotics' in his 1942 science fiction story *Runaround*.[13] Asimov's robophilia and his specialization in robotics and artificial intelligence (in his novels) have had a significant impact on roboticists. In 2002 Honda added more complex artificial intelligence technology to Asimo's programming and it has become one of the most advanced robots ever produced. In addition to being able to access the internet for relevant information, Asimo can move with incredible agility, is capable of interpreting gestures, can recognize faces, voices and environment, and he responds to questions in real time by using a vocabulary of hundreds of words. Asimo is the world's first humanoid robot to exhibit such a broad range of intelligent capabilities, and with further improvements planned in his programming, he will become even more capable of adaptive learning[14].

In addition to being influenced by the science fiction writings of Asimov, it is a Japanese fictional robot that has had the most dramatic impact on Japanese robotics. Since introducing Tetsuwan Atomu/ Astro Boy in 1951, the popularity of Tezuka's creation was to retain an amazing presence in public consciousness — especially in Japan, but also on a global scale. The impact of Astro Boy was clear when, in 2003, Honda Motor Co. promoted its Asimo rental business (renting Asimo to make public appearances) to coincide with Astro Boy's 'birthday' on April 7. The sentiment is evident in the following words spoken by Minoru Asada, an Osaka University robotics researcher: "Astro Boy was like our religion" (Larimer 2000). And the connection between the science fiction character Astro Boy and real life science continues to become stronger. In 2000, Sony built a small humanoid robot that it called the SDR-3X (Sony Dream Robot), to be followed by the SDR-4X. In 2004, the SDR-X4 was superseded by QRIO who has more advanced artificial intelligence programming than both the SDR series and the Aibo dog-robots. QRIO — whose name stands for 'Quest for Curiosity' — can listen to and follow commands, walk, fall and pick himself up. He also sings and dances, revealing an agility lacking even in Asimo. Information on the Sony website explains that:

> QRIO knows your voice. It can determine who is speaking by analyzing the sounds it hears with its built-in microphones... It knows tens of thousands of words already, but can also learn new ones... It will ask what sort of things you like and remember them, getting to know you better all the

time... QRIO has its own emotions - and expresses them in a variety of ways, such as through its movements, actions, sounds or colors". (Online at: http://www.sony.net/SonyInfo/QRIO)

In the realm of robotics, QRIO is emblematic of the fact that the science fiction robot has become a reality. While its pre-engineering phase was inspired by robots like *Star Wars'* C3P0, it is, again, Astro Boy who has left his mark on this boy-like creature. QRIO is about the height of a small child (like Astro Boy), and it even starred in the new series of the *Astro Boy* cartoon (Fuji-TV). Appearing in episode 43, titled "A Robot that Admires Humans", QRIO starred as itself. It was the first time a robot actually starred in a film, and to add to QRIO's talents, it was also responsible for dubbing its own voice in the episode. Like the examples of urban architecture mentioned above, an invention of advanced scientific reality actually migrated into the realm of science fiction, thus sealing the slippery nature of the rapport that these two concepts — science fiction and science fact — have always had with one another. However, in more recent times, it is the 'real' scientific creations that enter the realm of science fiction, lending a sense of futuristic legitimacy to the fictional spaces. It is as if the present has surpassed science fiction in its depiction of 'future-ness'.

In 1950, the scientist Alan Turing proposed a very science fictional concept when he devised the Turing Test, which determined when or if a machine can be said to possess human intelligence. The Turing Test asked: "can machines think?" (1950) Further to this, does the fact that a machine can duplicate human thought mean that the machine possesses human-like consciousness? Until recently, it was believed that this was a question that would be addressed within the confines of science fiction, but the gap between reality and fiction is increasingly closing. In quite real, yet rudimentary ways these robots reflect the beginnings of the struggle between human and machine, a struggle that has always obsessed science fiction cinema. Science fiction films like *Metropolis, Frankenstein* (1931), *I, Robot* and *A.I.* all revolve around individuals who seek to reverse the laws of nature by creating life through technology and science. According to Moore's Law (which claims that integrated circuitry doubles its capacity every two years), by the year 2020 computers will achieve the "memory capacity and computing speed of the human brain" (Kurzweil 1999: 3, 26-32). Science *fictions* have become science *realities*. Society is experiencing a major turning point — it is following a journey along the path of Moore's Law.

While sharing the enthusiasm for 'future-now' urbanscapes, eastern and western cultural attitudes to robots differ markedly. In western culture, the anxiety regarding humans taking on the role of creator has been present since early pre-Christian myths, but it is with the rise of Christianity and Judaism that this anxiety reached a pinnacle. From the c16th, science and technology began to advance to a point where the creation of artificial beings that appeared to move of their own volition were becoming a reality. The Church's response was a negative one in that the role of creation was one that was associated with God as Creator. Human-as-creator of artificial life was considered blasphemous. This anxiety regarding artificial life has continued into contemporary culture. It is experienced most dramatically in science fiction cinema, which has always warned of the dangers of creating artificial beings: since the time of Shelley's *Frankenstein*, these products of 'man' inevitably turn on their makers. Perhaps this age-old anxiety about artificial life is one of the reasons that western culture has been more hesitant about accepting robot technology to the extent of the Japanese, and it certainly explains the persistent presence of religious subtexts in science fiction films like *Minority Report*; the *Matrix* trilogy (1999-2003); *I, Robot* and *A.I.*

The situation in Japan is very different. Writing in response to the start of the modern robot era in Japan, writers have drawn attention to the Buddhist and Shinto beliefs that have encouraged the Japanese to embrace robots (Simons 1992: 29). For example, in his book *The Buddha in the Robot,* Japanese philosopher and roboticist Masahiro Mori states that robots have a Buddha-nature within them. Relying on animist traditions, Shinto religion posits that many objects (living and artificial) possess a soul or spirit. As Simons explains, samurai swords can have their own souls, as can robots (1981: 29). In fact, it is quite common in robot industrial plants to hold religious ceremonies to welcome the new robot soul in the world on the day of its activation. The belief systems that are present in Shinto and Buddhism (which are absent in Christianity and Judaism) encourage an enthusiastic attitude to robot culture that has accepted the robot as potential equal of the human within the social sphere — a fact evident in science fiction anime from *Astro Boy* and *Gigantor* to *Laputa* and *Ghost in the Shell*.

We are living in exciting times. This era has witnessed the birth of the intelligent machine and has placed it within an environment that once was the stuff of science fiction. Soon enough we'll be responding to Turing's question "Can machines think?" with a resounding "Yes!"

Bibliography

Anderson, Colleen 1999. 'Japan's Friendly Robots' in *Technocopia*. On line at: http://www.technocopia.com

Beyard, Michael D. et al. 2001. *Developing Retail Entertainment Destinations*. Washington: Urban Land Institute.

Bradbury, Ray. 1999. 'Free Pass at Heaven's Gate' in The Jerde International Partnership (ed.). *You Are Here*. London: Phaidon.

Corn, Joseph J. (ed.) 1986. *Imagining Tomorrow: History Technology and the American Future*. Massachusetts: MIT Press.

Fordham, Joe. 2003. 'Middle-Earth Strikes Back' in *Cinefex* 92: 70-142.

Frampton, Kenneth. 2001. *Le Corbusier*. London: Thames & Hudson.

Gilbert, James Burkhart. 1991. *Perfect cities: Chicago's utopias of 1893*. Chicago: University of Chicago Press.

Kihlstedt, Folke T. 1986. 'Utopia Realized: The World's Fairs of the 1930s' in Joseph Corn, J. (ed.) *Imagining Tomorrow: History, Technology, and the American Future*. Cambridge, MA: MIT Press: 97-118.

Klein, Norman. 1997. *The History of Forgetting: Los Angeles and the Erasure of Memory*. London & New York: Verso: 94-5.

— 1999. 'The Electronic Baroque: Jerde Cities' in The Jerde International Partnership (ed.) *You Are Here*. London: Phaidon: 112-22.

Kurzweil, Ray. 1999. *The Age of Spiritual Machines*. London: Phoenix.

Kuznick, Peter J. 1994. 'Losing the World of Tomorrow: The Battle Over the Presentation of Science at the 1939 New York World's Fair' in *American Quarterly* 46(3): 341-373. On line at http://www.jstor.org (consulted 07. 05. 03)

Landon, Brooks. 1992. *The Aesthetics of Ambivalence: Rethinking Science Fiction Film in the Age of Electronic (Re)production*. Westport: Greenwood Press.

Larimer, Tim. 2000. 'Rage for the Machine' in *Time* (5 January 2000). Available at: http://www .time.com/time/asia/magazine/2000/0501/cover1.html

Larsen, Kurt. 1999. 'Learning Cities: the New Recipe in Regional Development' in *The Organization for Economic Cooperation and Development Observer*. On line at: http://www.findarticles.com

Lehane, Scott. 2001. 'The Lord of the Rings' in *Film and Video*. On line at: http://www. filmandvideomagazine.com

Marling, Karal Ann (ed.) 1997. *Designing Disney's Theme parks: the Architecture of Reassurance*. Paris & New York: Flammarion.

Marriott, Michel. 2002. 'Movie Posters that Talk Back' in *The New York Times* (12 December 2002). On line at: http://www.nytimes.com/2002/12/12/technology/circuits/12post .html?ex=1040748097&ei=1&en=27c86fc1540ed60e

Mori, Masahiro. 1981. *The Buddha in the robot*. Tokyo: Kosei.

Morshed, Adnan. 2004. 'The Aesthetics of Ascension in Norman Bel Geddes's Futurama' in *Journal Of The Society Of Architectural Historians*. 63(1): 74-99.

Nakada, Gail. 2003. Birthday 'bot: Japan's most famous superhero is back in a big way. *Japan Inc*. 4/1/2003. Available at: http://www.highbeam.com

Rydell, Robert. 1993. *World of Fairs: the Century-of-Progress Expositions*. Chicago: University of Chicago Press.

Simons, Geoff. 1992. *Robots: the Quest for Living Machines*. London: Cassell.

'Sony Breaks New Ground with Entertainment Robot'. On line at http:// www.sony. com.au/article.jsp?id=2917

Turing, Alan M. 1950. 'Computing Machinery and Intelligence' in *Mind*, 59 (236): 433-460.

Notes

[1] This is taken from the theme song of the New York World's Fair. The complete passage is:
"We're the rising tide coming from far and wide
Marching side by side on our way
For a brave new world,
Tomorrow's world that we shall build today" (Rydell 1993:132).

[2] Nakada 2003, n.p.

[3] Marriott 2002, n.p.

[4] See http://www.Massivesoftware.com

[5] See Lehane 2001 and Fordham 2003.

[6] See Gilbert. Gilbert explains that; "The Fair organizers, in this instance, attempted to demarcate a boundary between the two in identifying the ideal city with the neo-classical architecture that came to be known as the Expo's White City and the popular and commercial with the Midway zone, which offered all sorts of amusements and displays. Progressing into the c20[th], this attempted binary increasingly broke down" (1991: 15).

[7] Kuznick 1994: 341.

[8] For more on Le Corbusier, see Frampton 2001.

[9] For detailed accounts of the impact of science fiction literature, see Nancy Knight, "'The New Light': X-Rays and Medical Futurism" and Folke T. Kihlstedt, "Utopia Realized: The World's Fairs of the 1930s", in Corn, Joseph J. (ed.) 1986. *Imagining Tomorrow: History Technology and the American Future*. Massachusetts: MIT Press. (10-34 & 97-118)

[10] At the New York World's Fair, "Disney was represented by a specially commissioned Mickey Mouse cartoon in the Nabisco pavilion" (Marling 1997: 35).

[11] See Klein 1999.

[12] Anderson 1999.

[13]   i) A robot may not injure a human being or, through inaction, allow a human being to come to harm.

ii) A robot must obey the orders given to it by human beings, except where such orders would conflict with the First Law.

iii) A robot must protect its own existence as long as such protection does not conflict with the First or Second Law.

[14] See http://world.honda.com/ASIMO/history/

So Far, so Close: *Island of Lost Souls* as a Laboratory of Life.

Sybille Lammes

In this chapter 'Island of Lost Souls' (1932) will be analysed as a laboratory where notions of eugenic purity and pollution are played out. By analysing the isolated laboratory as a Latourian technoscientific network, this chapter will map the processes of eugenic purification and hybridisation that are taking place in the film. It will be argued that the depicted laboratory of Dr. Moreau functions as a locus for discussing the place techno-science and eugenics have in daily life. As all islands in films, it is a paradoxical locus in that it entails both distance and proximity.

Science fiction as a laboratory

Although techno-science could be said to be the most obvious determinant of science fiction film as a genre, it is rarely mentioned as a topic for analysis in Film Studies. Much attention has been paid to the social functions of science fiction film in shaping and contesting social issues, but rarely are such social questions considered as intertwined with techno-science. This disregard maybe due to the still widespread supposition that technology and science are no social categories, an assumption that has been disputed by many academics in the field of STS (Science and Technology Studies). It may also be due to the strong psychoanalytical thrust of Film Studies in the last decades of the 20th century. Whatever may be the reason behind this oversight, the fact of the matter remains that an important function of the genre thus remains largely uncharted, namely the role that science fiction films can play in making sense of the place of techno-science in everyday life.

In this chapter, I will put techno-science on the agenda as a category worth studying in relation to film. I will do so by crossing disciplines, that is by using insights that have been developed in the field of STS, mainly by the French philosopher and anthropologist of science Bruno Latour. I take his idea that techno-scientific laboratories should be approached as part of daily life to overcome asymmetries between these production centres and the 'world outside' by treating films as part of the techno-scientific domain. Thus films are not so much approached as a reflection of a social context, but rather as producers of techno-science. Extending his approach, I will consider science fiction films as cultural laboratories where one can discern how frictions or asymmetries are played out between closed-off production centres and places where no direct access to the workings of techno-science is granted.

Using the actor-network theory as my main method, I will analyse Erle C. Kenton's *Island of Lost Souls* as a techno-scientific network. Strong centres in this network are the places in the film where techno-science is produced. Domains where such direct power of production is lacking are considered as weak links. To be able to analyse the dynamic between these different areas, I will make use of Latour's concept of mediation. Mediation or translation is an important principle of the actor-network theory, since it allows for an analysis that does not deny that asymmetrical power relationships exist, but at the same time, offers a counterbalance by concentrating methodologically on ever-changeable translations, which shape techno-scientific networks. Techno-scientific networks should be conceived of as areas of tension, which shift and shape themselves through a constant process of mediation.

Latour states that asymmetrical relations such as those between faith and science, fiction and fact, text and context or even between different academic disciplines are paradoxes, because one can only think in such oppositions by simultaneously presuming that the two sides of such dichotomies have something in common. Opposition thus entails translation. When such translations are not acknowledged, mediations become monsters. But when one takes such translations as a starting point, a different picture emerges and categories come into being via such mediations. The actor-network theory aims precisely at this by taking these hybrids as the central principle of its method (Law & Hassard 1999; Latour 1987).

In line with this approach, techno-scientific practices in the film are being treated as webs in which categories are changeable and fluid and have no pre-given meaning. This approach also has consequences for the way in which the relation between techno-scientific processes and gender, class and ethnicity are approached. These three social identities will be considered in the locality of their production. Thus, ideological presuppositions about their meaning and demarcation are being avoided. By using a method that eschews assumptions about the meaning of categories, different pictures of techno-science emerge, where social categories become fluid, interactive and changeable.

So far, so close

The aforementioned Latourian asymmetry between powerful techno-scientific production centres and the large domains that don't have access to such centres, is often addressed in science fiction films: a scientist has retreated to a remote place to be able to conduct difficult and controversial research. The carried out experiments or developed applications form an imminent danger to the world at large. If the endeavours eventually 'leak' out, efforts are made to stop the scientist's research and to keep it to an isolated incident. Such dystopic films often end with an implosion of the isolated workplace before it can really affect the rest of the world. Situating techno-scientific laboratories in spacecrafts, on islands, mountains or remote planets, creates a multitude of possibilities to address and try questions about the accountability and limits of techno-science. A strong contrast is set up between such techno-scientific autocracies and the presumed civilized world where such experiments are taboo.[1]

Laboratory-islands thus offer ample opportunities to bring to the fore the closed-off character of western techno-scientific production centres. To phrase it in the spirit of Bruno Latour (1993), through the reality and image of these distant islands a techno-scientific paradox is addressed. This paradox concerns an asymmetrical relation between powerful and isolated laboratories where techno-science is produced and vast domains outside such production centres with very limited access to such insular practices.

The *Island of Lost Souls* concerns a 1930s adaptation of H.G. Wells' *fin de siecle* novella *The Island of Dr. Moreau*. In the *Island of Lost Souls* the bio-anthropologist[2], Dr. Moreau has retreated to a remote island to escape the law so as to be able to dedicate himself to his interest in evolution theories and to bring some of his hypotheses into practice. At the beginning of the film a ship arrives on the island, carrying a freight of animals and a shipwrecked young man called Parker. Together with the animals he is left on the island.

During his involuntary stay on the island it starts to dawn on Parker that Dr. Moreau and his assistant-surgeon, Montgomery are using the delivered animals for conducting experiments. They attempt to accelerate processes of evolution, by transforming animals in such a way that they shoot up the evolutionary ladder. So far they have succeeded in creating a versatile group of male humanoids and a female panther woman named, Lota. Parker also begins to realise that he is not only imprisoned on the island, but that they are planning to use him as research material.

Paradoxical spaces

According to Latour (1993) hybridisation and purification are 'modern' practices that are mutually dependent on each other, while excluding each other at the same time. Therefore they maintain a paradoxical relationship. The practice of cleansing generates dichotomies between, for example, humans and non-humans, nature and culture, and science and the outer world, while the practice of hybridisation or translation seeks for transitions between such positions and thus creates new mediated ways of being. On different levels such movements of mixing and isolation can be discerned in the film.

Such a paradoxical movement can be immediately distinguished at the beginning of the film. A boat moors on the island, which implies a journey, a translation. However, by leaving Parker (and the animals) on the island, a sharp line is drawn. By this purifying act a new process of translation is instigated since non-natives are left on the island. Parker is becoming a hybrid, not being able to forget about where he came from, at the same time gradually losing his distance from the place where he has arrived. As I will show throughout this analysis this paradox of distance and proximity mainly centres around the ethics of techno-science — how much distance is a scientist allowed from the 'outer' world.

From the moment Parker is left on the island, a process takes place in which Parker functions as a guest who constantly translates between the isolated workplace of Moreau and his own world. This translation mainly focuses on the understanding of techno-science. Eventually this process of translation makes place for an ultimate cleansing ritual in which the island is destroyed by fire. When the game of hybridisation and purification is over, the guest retreats from the island and takes distance. He essentially distances himself from Moreau's ideas about the hybridisation of different species and different races. However, the apparent hardening of categories that takes place at the end of the film entails yet another kind of mediation: the view on what is pure science that prevails at the end of the film involves a translation between the asymmetrical category, knowledge and belief in which is argued for Christian informed kind of science.

Traversing borders

The bio-anthropologist Moreau arrived on the island bringing very little with him. Educated in the western sciences he brought his knowledge of anthropology, biology and evolutionary theories with him. What he left behind is the possibility of being controlled in how he applies this knowledge. Without such control he is able to set-up his secret workplace, called 'the house of pain'. In this house the imported animals are subjected to painful and excruciating operations that are meant to bring them onto a higher evolutionary plane.

The house of pain is such a secret place that Parker is not allowed to come near it. Like a bluebeard, Moreau declares this space out of bounds for his guest. It will nevertheless not take long before Parker finds out more about what's happening in Moreau's laboratory of life. In the scene where Parker is introduced to the only female inhabitant of the island, Lota, awful screams emanate from the house of pain. Although Lota has received explicit instructions from Moreau never to mention the house of pain in Parker's presence, she cannot help but scream its name out loud. Before anyone can stop him, Parker runs towards the house of pain and enters the surgeon's theatre. In the middle of the room lies a hairy creature tied to an operation table. It beats its head from side to side and screams. Moreau and Montgomery are standing next to the table. When they notice Parker they start to yell at him: "Get out!" Parker turns away in shock. In modern science the soundness of scientific experiments is often emphasised and ensured by letting spectators watch actual experiments. By having 'modest witnesses' present during conducted experiments, the scientific status of laboratory practices gets ensured and strengthened.

Moreau clearly doesn't subscribe to this practice and wants nobody to testify or see what is taking place in his workplace. In this respect a parallel can be made between Moreau's laboratory and an alchemical workplace. According to the historians of science Shapin and Schaffer alchemical or hermetic practices can be characterised as closed and not open to witnesses (1985). Different from modern experimental practices, external witnesses are not considered an essential part of the process. In a similar vein, Moreau does not find it necessary to have

outsiders visit his lab and even actively tries to avoid any onlookers by
retreating to a remote island.

Even though this parallel is strengthened by the resemblance
between Moreau and the alchemist, Prospero in *The Tempest*, it would
be too simple to maintain that the activities that take place in the
house of pain are alchemical and therefore unscientific. First of all, it
may be Moreau's intention to have a hermetic workplace, but a witness does enter it in the end. Parker and the viewer thus become
'modest witnesses.' Secondly, the equipment in the theatre we eventually see does not substantiate the claim that Moreau is an alchemist at
work. There are no astrological maps, homunculi or stones of wisdom
to be found. Instead we see an operation table and a man in a surgeon's outfit.

Later in the film the scientific status of the lab is further stressed
when Parker is invited for a tour of Moreau's grounds. Moreau first
shows him his botanical garden. He explains that he has retreated to
this island to conduct evolutionary experiments, not being impeded by
the British law or curious journalists. He then shows Parker around his
house of pain, which is actually part of a much larger building. We see
a sterile white room equipped with several machines, an adjustable
anatomical table and a display case with surgical instruments. A
surgeon's table stands in the middle of the theatre. On it lays a creature covered by a white sheet. Moreau uncovers the head of the still
moaning being and inspects his jaw.

In this scene Moreau openly invites a witness to inspect his scientific practice. He shows his research subjects (plants and animals),
explains his theories and gives Parker the opportunity to see his laboratory with his own eyes. Although it remains questionable how much
of an external witness Parker is by now (after all he has lost contact
with the rest of the world), in this instance both he and the viewer can
inspect Moreau's practice.

Moreau presents his scientific practice as being organised and
rational. In this sense the film subscribes to a representation of techno-
science as factual and logical, according to Latour a face so often put
on by scientific production centres when presenting themselves to the
outer world (1987). But this factual and cold image of techno-science
is not judged positively in *Island of Lost Souls*. Moreau is represented
as a cold, unethical and amoral scientist. He hasn't retreated to an
island because he is afraid that his practice will be criticised on rational grounds, but is more afraid of disapproval on ethical grounds.

On top of the world

Moreau clearly feels superior to the male hybrids on the island. When the hybrids become too wild and aggressive, Moreau controls them by conducting an obedience ritual that involves a whip, a gong and a chanting session. After using his whip to calm them down, Moreau beats a gong. He then asks the hybrids; "What is the law?"; on which the leader of the group answers; "Not run on all fours, that is the law." Then the whole group replies; "We are not men." This routine is repeated three times in which only the lines of the leader vary. "Not to eat meat, that is the law"; and "Not to spill blood, that is the law." "We are not men", the other male hybrids reply every time in a similar vein. At the end of the ritual, the leader reaches his hand out to Moreau:

> His is the hand that made.
> His is the hand that heals.
> His is the hand of pain. [3]

As with so many scientists, Moreau tries to keep a distance between himself and the objects of his research. He treats the hybrids as raw material and wishes to have no personal ties with them.[4] But in his case the demarcation between himself and his research material is unstable and not a given. Moreau has to use a lot of measures to keep his material at a distance and under control.

The male hybrids are unreliable and difficult to manage, yet Moreau's attitude towards them is aggressive and tyrannical. He treats them as primitive beings who can only be managed by a whip and a sedating ritual in which he plays the high priest. He sees himself as an absolute higher being who cannot be compared with anything that sprouted from his hands. He looks down on his creations and does everything in his power to distance himself from them. Whilst trying to blur demarcation between animals and human beings, he sees himself as separate and higher than any other life-form.

The way in which Moreau treats his animals can be characterised as a mixture between a cold-blooded scientist and a colonialist. His white tropical uniform, his British accent and his priest-like demeanour during the submission ritual all point to the latter direction. He rules his hybrids like a slave-driver and even beats them when they don't obey. Hence the distance between the bio-anthropologist and his research material is typified as a western colonial desire to have power over everything that can be described as wild or belonging to nature[5].

Godly rivalry

The evolutionary ideas that Moreau advocates contain a contradictory drift. In his scientific practices he employs a clear difference between high and low beings, whilst at the same time trying to merge and change such demarcations. During the tour of his botanical garden he speaks of human beings as "the present climax of a long process of organic evolution." The animals he uses for his experiments are in his own words "lower animals", while the hybrids he has produced hold a slightly higher position. In this sense his views on evolution are linear and hierarchical. At the same time, Moreau conceives these positions as gradual and changeable since hybridity is a central part of his project. He speaks of evolution as a "process" and of the animals as "organisms" that only differ gradually from each other. His main goal is to create a being that surpasses the development of the Homo Sapiens. Hence, whereas he propagates a hierarchical categorization, he also seeks for mediations between these categories.

As a scientist, Moreau feels closer to God ("Do you know how it feels to be God?"; he asks Parker at one point). He puts himself on the highest rung of the imaginary evolutionary ladder. By characterising an evolution theorist as a challenger of Godly creation, the film can be placed in a discussion that took place in the 1920s and 30s about the problematic relationship between evolution theory and Christian principles. Evolution theories can collide with biblical views on the fundamental difference between human beings and other animals. They also don't combine well with the Christian beliefs about the Godly genesis, fate and superiority. Around the release of the film a heated debate took place in the United States concerning such issues. A large movement strongly opposed the implications of evolution theories that the world didn't come into being in seven days and that humans are animals as well[6].

This conflict came to a head in the famous Scopes Trial of 1925. In this court case the teacher, Scopes objected to his dismissal as a teacher on the grounds that he lectured on evolution theories. Although Scopes won the case, it caused many schools to remove evolution theories from their curriculum. In the 1930s the subject of evolution was only taught in 30 percent of the American schools (Caudill 1989: 1-26). *Island of Lost Souls* seems to subscribe to such fundamentalist opinions by characterising the scientist as blasphemous according to the film. Seeking such translations and hybridisation between categories is not good scientific practice.

A soulless nation

A few months after the release of the film in the Unites States a message appears in *Variety* under the title 'London Sans Souls':

> Island of Lost Souls (Par) has been rejected in toto by the British censors because it is considered too horrible. Considerable of a blow to Paramount, because the picture was made from an H.G. Wells story and features Charles Laughton, both British[7].

The journalist of *Variety* is surprised by the fact that a film that has so many British 'flavours' cannot be accepted by the British censors[8]. It can be argued though that the allusions that are made in the film about British culture are less innocent than the critic wants us to believe. To put it bluntly: British culture is presented in a very negative way in *Island of Lost Souls*. By connecting the scientific practice on the island to British culture, 'bad science' is placed within a non-American culture. Consequently a process of mediation and differentiation can take place.

The Britishness of the scientist Moreau is emphasised in more than one way. First of all, Moreau is being characterised as a 'true gentleman', who is always polite and keeps offering cups of tea to his guest. While Parker speaks his mind straightforwardly, Moreau uses stereotypical British phrases that are polite and composed. As a critic of the *New York Herald Tribune* described Moreau; "He can answer the hero's indignant 'You rat you don't deserve to live' with a querulous 'I beg your pardon (...)"[9]. Furthermore, Moreau's Britishness is stressed in the scene where Parker gets a tour of the island. He tells Parker that both him and Montgomery are wanted by the British Crown for conducting unethical and illegal experiments. Although this explanation points to the fact that such experiments are also illegal in Europe, it nevertheless emphasises the non-American and British origins of 'bad science.'

The British character of unethical scientific behaviour is also amplified in another important way. By situating Moreau's laboratory on an island both an analogy is made with the British Isles and a clear reference is made to a sixteenth century play that can be considered as part of British cultural legacy: *The Tempest*. In Shakespeare's play a group of aristocrats becomes stranded on a remote island that is only inhabited by the alchemist Prospero, the adolescent Miranda and an ape-like creature called Caliban. Moreau is a 1930s version of Prospero, Lota is comparable to the naive Miranda and the hybrids are Caliban in plural. Parker has run aground on the island, just as the aristocrats in *The Tempest*.

Like the shipwrecked aristocrats, Parker comes to have more to do with the situation on the island than he had expected. Reminiscent of the Italian aristocrats that land on the island to find their relatives, Parker ends up as a guest of a far-related Anglo-Saxon family member he never thought to meet.

Cultural historian David Lowenthal notes in his book *The Past is a Foreign Country* that white North-American culture has to deal with a friction between the wish to be free from its past and the feeling of lacking a clear past (1985). Founded as a nation by its separation from its (British) colonial forefathers, it still teeters between disregarding its British past and creating nostalgic celebration of its history. In an attempt to close itself off from its British roots, American culture is described as timeless and ahistorical. Whereas the old world is conceived as the degenerated, false, tyrannical and contaminated forefather; American culture is hailed as possessing eternal youth. Paradoxically this contempt for the past is being complemented by a nostalgic need for a past in which British culture plays an important part.

In *Island of Lost Souls* this cultural friction is primarily played out at the level of science. On the one hand, 'bad science' is firmly situated in the old world and in a place far removed from American culture. This image is reinforced by associating Moreau's practice with alchemy and by contrasting the older Moreau with the young American hero. Moreau's scientific drive is thus strongly tied in with a British imperial mentality that is far removed from the new world. By creating a strong resemblance between Moreau's island and that of Prospero, both a temporal and spatial fracture is created between the United States and the United Kingdom.

However, on the other hand the antagonist and protagonist share quite literally the same language and the film leans heavily on a fascination for British culture and the old world. It needs this comparison to give shape to what American scientific culture means. In this sense one can speak of a proximity between both cultures, and Parker's presence on the island should be conceived as a practice of mediation through which Parker can formulate an American definition of 'good science'. In other words, the film shows that the process of cultural distancing and closeness of which Lowenthal speaks can also be given shape at the level of science and its ethical dimensions.

Male hybrids

In the submission ritual described earlier one can clearly see how diverse and dissimilar the hybrids look. Some of them are small and skinny, others large and heavy. Their skin colour differs and some have curly hair while others straight. What they share is their unclean and untidy appearance. They look unwashed, unshaven and frequently walk around bare-chested. The trousers they wear look grubby and worn, and their naked torsos are often covered with matted hair.

By contrast the westerners on the island, including Moreau, couldn't differ more in appearance. They all look clean and groomed, and have a rather uniform appearance in their pristine white tropical outfits. Also, in this respect it is clear that Moreau and his visitor have more in common than might seem at first glance.

As a heterogeneous group, the hybrids form an intangible threat that is difficult to control. This becomes clear in the ritual that Moreau conducts, but also at other moments in the film. Especially when the creatures see women (Lota and Parker's fiancée at the end of the film) they show their intimidating nature by sneakily following them around. In more than one respect the male hybrids incorporate a volatile mixture of merging and contradictory characteristics. As misshaped translations between nature and culture, as a result of the compromise of asymmetrical categories, they form an imminent danger. This heterogeneous group can be described as a mixture of everything that white Anglo-Saxons would like to keep out of their own idea of order.

When Parker is shown around the house of pain he passes a tread-mill that is kept in motion by a group of small and deformed looking male hybrids. Moreau points to the creatures; "Those are some of my less successful experiments. They supply the power to create others." Moreau's explanation indicates that efficiency is crucial in his work-place, but it also shows that he uses his experimental outcomes as a workforce. A workforce with very few rights, indeed. These mishaps are treated as an underclass. The same goes for the hybrids that live in the forest — they have no houses to live in, have to search for food in the forest and are clad in rags. They live an almost inhuman existence. They are needy creatures that live on the brink between a human and bestial existence.

The hybrids on the island belong to a lower class, while the humans present there clearly belong to a higher class. While the hybrids are roaming outside, Moreau and his guests sleep in decent rooms, have dinner parties and are always dressed meticulously in white. And they would like to keep it that way. Nevertheless, the hierarchy they wish for is by no means stable and the male hybrids are grumbling outside. They are often tempestuous and have difficulties obeying Moreau. The unequal and unsteady relations between the hybrids and the Anglo-Saxon humans point to a conflict in which the poor hybrids try to undermine the privileged position of the human islanders.

By characterising the hybrids simultaneously as less evolved and as lower in class, and the 'real' humans on the island as biologically more developed and affluent, a direct link is forged between the degree of power and wealth, and evolutionary development. In line with a social Darwinian opinion that thrived in conservative eugenic circles, the film approves of the assumption that poverty is not so much a social but rather a biological phenomenon (Hawkins 1997).

Although Moreau has used many different species for his experiments, it is striking that most hybrids look like a mixture of primate and human. Like anthropoids they often walk with bent backs. Furthermore, they are hairy, they make monkey-like gestures and hurl themselves through the jungle, swinging from lianas and branches. Their human side is prevalent in their ability to speak and to walk on their hind legs[10]. It is not surprising that the *New York Herald Tribune* refers to them as "Neanderthal extras" and that the review in *Variety* suggests that they are a kind of "gorilla along human lines"[11]. As a missing link they occupy a no-man's-land that lies between humans and primates.

Sometimes the creatures are also epitomized as the colonial 'other.' This association is for example strongly emphasised in the aforementioned ritual of obedience in which Moreau treats them as a slave trader. This suggests that the imported creatures are primitive converts that have to abide by the rules of their missionary. Also Parker presumes immediately that the hybrids are 'natives' of the island. He even tells Moreau that his "natives behave like beasts." The last comment comes close to the opinion that the colonial other and animals are interchangeable categories that are at a similar stage of evolutionary development.

It should be stressed again that the creatures can by no means be described as a stable and homogeneous category. On the contrary, as hybrids they incorporate dissimilar features that enable the white category of human beings to define and defend their homogeneity. As the "other they are a collection of everything that is needed to delineate what this white category entails" (Bhabha 1994: 66-84).

It is via this intangible group that the male humans on the island are also able to state and defend their definition of masculinity. This process can be clearly discerned in the film when Parker's fiancée arrives on the island to rescue him. The hybrids are very interested in this young blonde woman and keep following her around. When she goes to sleep in a bedroom adjacent but separate from Parker's room, their imminent threat becomes more real. She has just gone to sleep when one of them breaks into her well-secured room. Parker has to come to her rescue. After this incident, Montgomery and Moreau are seen having a heated argument in which it becomes apparent that Moreau hoped a rape would take place to advance his experiments.

The bestial hybrids are depicted as sexually obsessed and as barely able to control their sexual needs. Their 'lower' male disposition is not suppressed by moral principles and without Moreau's whip they would form a criminal danger. They are depicted as quasi-subjects that are too close to nature to control their wild lusts.[12] Yet it is striking that Parker is not totally opposite to the hybrids in this regard. Like them he cannot always control his sexual needs. At one point in the film during an encounter with Lota, his passion gets the better of him. Their encounter is a set-up of Moreau who imagines that a sexual encounter between them could result in an interesting outcome.

At the moment of their encounter Parker is reading a book; "(…) from Dr. Moreau's library about the electric wireless (…)." As he explains to Lota, he plans to build a radio to make contact with the mainland in order to leave the island. Lota doesn't want Parker to, and throws the book in the water. Parker now tells Lota that he is already engaged to another woman. What follows is a kiss that is clearly initiated by Parker. After this act of uncontrolled passion, Parker regains himself and walks off. When Lota desperately flings her arms around him, Parker notices that she has hair growing on her fingers.

In H. G. Wells' book *The Island of Doctor Moreau* Parker is introduced as a former student of biology at University College London. Wells openly refers here to his own background since he attended the famous lectures of the British evolutionary, T. H. Huxley at the same university (Green 1985). One of the points emphasised in the work of this influential social Darwinist is that evolutionary theories involve an ethical dilemma since they work from the assumption that humans are animals that are inclined to use (sexual) violence if their survival and continuation is at stake. It was, according to Huxley, essential that humans used their unique moral abilities to counter such natural tendencies (Hawkins 1997). Parker's reaction to Lota's infatuation follows a similar pattern to Huxley's argumentation. He admits briefly to his attraction to Lota, admitting to his 'natural' side. He manages however to regain himself. He suppresses his sexual longings and decides to stick to his own kind. He tames the beast in himself and thus purifies the category human from any inhuman aspects.

Tainted blood

Both the experiments that Moreau wants to conduct with the white guests on the island and his experiments with the hybrids can be described as an attempt at amalgamating two asymmetrical categories, namely the human and the animal. This is clearly associated with class and ethnicity.

Amalgamation doesn't lead to a positive outcome in the film. The results are only shortly lived: Moreau's operations are not yet that successful and after the surgical procedure the hybrids start to change back to their 'original' animal state. Another operation is necessary to stop this process of decline.

Lota and the male hybrids are physically and mentally unstable. It costs them great effort to maintain themselves and they often fall 'back' into uncontrolled and animal-like behaviour. In addition they are not that intelligent and haven't developed speech to its full extent. The male hybrids are even more unstable than Lota since they are also depicted as potential who cannot control their lusts. Furthermore, they are shown as scared and restless creatures. Especially the sounds emanating from the operating theatre make them agitated. Moreau needs to conduct a ritual to calm them down and to prevent a riot.

These weak characteristics of the male hybrids neatly fit descriptions used in conservative eugenic circles to portray so-called "hereditary defective lower groups." To name a few of the terms used to describe such groups: they are "criminals", "sexual offenders", "shiftless" and have a "weak physique". Mentally they can be described as having "amoral tendencies"; a "high grade of feeblemindedness" and as suffering from "imbecility" (Rafter 1988: 81-163).

In the 1920s and 30s eugenic issues were still being widely discussed in the United States. Conservative puritan voices maintained that Anglo-Saxon groups were biologically superior to other Northern-

Americans and had to protect their germ-pool from contamination. They saw in the economic depression proof that human degeneration had reached a crisis point. Hard measures were called for and sometimes even put into practice, such as the sterilisation of the "feeble minded" (Kevles 1985).

In the mean time such opinions were countered by other eugenic arguments that argued that hybridisation could also lead to a better race and that all ethnicities were the result of hybridisation (Kevles 1985; Young 1995: 28, 64-65). It is striking that at the time of the release of the film most pro-amalgamation arguments could be heard from scientists who, like Moreau, had a British background. British evolutionary biologists such as J. Huxley (the grandson of T.H. Huxley), L. Hogben, J.B.S. Haldane published material in which views about the correlation between amalgamation and degeneration were opposed. Their books and articles were also widely read in the United States (Barkan 1992). Correspondingly, it is a British scientist in *Island of Lost Souls* who appeals for amalgamation and believes in its positive effects.

The results of his experiments nevertheless prove him wrong. As hybrids they may have climbed higher up the evolutionary ladder, but it is precisely because of this that they form a threat to the well-being of the higher races on the island. Not surprisingly, it is literally at the moment that they taste real human blood that they start to revolt, steal the surgical instruments out of the display cabinets and put Moreau on his own operation table. As the review in *The New York World Telegram* summarizes it; "the half-humanized brutes revolt and give him a dose of his own medicine"[13]. By appropriating human instruments and possessions, the hybrids become a concrete threat to the Anglo-Saxon's position of purity.

In line with the conservative eugenic ideal to which the film subscribes, this threat is eventually antagonized. Not progression but degeneration remains the dominant feature of the hybrids. Without their leader they loose all control and become aggressive psychotic monsters. They burn the island down, thus both destroying Moreau's project and themselves. The weaker races and fallible science fall prey to their own degeneration.

Cleansing Rituals

Dr. Moreau and his assistant have travelled to a remote island to mediate between 'wild nature' and 'western culture.' Moreau's aspirations are to master the wild sphere to such an extent that both presumed categories loose their stability. Simultaneously, Moreau uses clear hierarchies that seem to contradict his practice of amalgamation. Hence the laboratory of Moreau serves as a paradoxical locus for practices of hybridisation and purification.

The same goes for the relation between the island and the mainland. By representing Moreau's practice as secluded, the film points to the tendency of scientific workplaces to isolate themselves. By the arrival of Parker this seal is broken. As an overseas controller he has an ethical function to mediate between Moreau's workplace and 'the outer world', thus preventing scientific practices from becoming a moral danger that cannot be controlled.

Parker would have wished to have never set foot on the island. But he has more to do with what he finds there than is at first apparent. As an American his final mission consists of purifying and re-establishing distinctions between categories such as human/animal and culture/nature. Problematic aspects of evolution theories that don't fit his American conservative eugenic ideal are thus sanitized. As also becomes clear in his rendezvous with Lota, he tries to translate between categories while at the same attempting to establish clear demarcations. Parker attempts to keep things at bay that are actually so dangerously close by.

In the film a dynamic play takes place between what Mary Douglas has called purity and contamination (1992). As the ritual comes to a close, Parker leaves the island, deciding to separate from the monsters, 'bad' science, his own wild temperament and his British past. The ritual of purification is completed and the monstrous mediations that are the outcome of evolutionary thinking are firmly placed outside American culture. By seemingly situating such outcomes far away, American science can be kept pure. "Don't look back", are Parker's words when they debark. Behind him, the island is destroyed in a sea of flames.

To conclude

Dr. Moreau's scientific practice is portrayed as a threat to social order. The experiments he conducts are described as impure and dangerous, and he is criticised for his attempts to flee moral responsibility by literally turning his back on the mainland. In this film, the scientific production centre is accused of having too much power and of avoiding outside control. Visitors from the mainland figure as a purifying force, while Moreau's island figures as a locus of contagion.

However, one cannot simply make such a distinction either. The evolutionary experiments that are conducted by Moreau, on the one hand, are aimed at amalgamation and the hybridisation of humans and animals. On the other hand, Moreau's experiments are based on the presumption that hierarchies between high and low, human and animal, or Godly and primitive can be easily made. As an evolutionary theorist, Moreau explores the development and order of species, a paradoxical enterprise that implicates translation and purification.

I have shown that the insular location of Moreau's practice is in itself a paradox. By situating his island in the remote Pacific Ocean, a multitude of possibilities are created to discuss scientific issues that may otherwise come uncomfortably close. The island is characterised as different, un-American and remote from civilization, thus offering a safe locus for discussing asymmetries that are at the heart of American techno-scientific culture. Accordingly, the American visitor to the island, Parker, who seems to have been stranded accidentally in this tropical hell, has more to do with Moreau than he can suspect. It is his mission to decontaminate the scientific practice. Parker mediates between two atmospheres and hence questions about the boundaries of evolutionary science are discussed and a judgement is made about what science and technology should mean.

Bibliography

Bergonzi, B. 1969. *The Early H.G. Wells: A Study of the Scientific Romances*. Manchester: Manchester University Press.

Bhabha H. K. 1994. *The Location of Culture*. London: Routledge.

Boednel, W. 'Island of Lost Souls' in *Review of Island of Lost Souls: New York World Telegram* (13 January 1933).

Caudill, E. 1989. *The Roots of Bias: An Empiricist Press and Coverage of the Scopes Trial*. Columbia, SC: Association for Education in Journalism and Mass Communication.

Doherty, Th. 1999. *Pre-code Hollywood: Sex, Immorality, and Insurrection in American Cinema, 1930-1934, Film and culture*. New York: Columbia University Press. P. 312

Douglas, M. 1992 (2nd edn.). *Purity and Danger: An Analysis of the Concepts of Pollution and Taboo*. London: Routledge.

Geertz, C. 2000 (3rd edn.). *Local Knowledge: Further Essays in Interpretive Anthropology*. New York: Basic Books.

Green, K. May 1985. 'Xavier Herbert, H.G. Wells and J.S. Huxley: Unexpected British Connections' in *Australian Literary Studies* 12 (1): 47-64.

Harding, S. G. 1986. *The Science Question in Feminism*. Ithaca: Cornell University Press.

Hardy, P. 1995 (2nd edn.). *Science Fiction: The Aurum Film Encyclopaedia*. London: Aurum Press.

Hawkins, M. 1997. *Social Darwinism in European and American Thought, 1860-1945: Nature as Model and Nature as Threat*. Cambridge: Cambridge University Press.

Kevles, D. J. 1985. *In the Name of Eugenics: Genetics and the Uses of Human Heredity*. New York: Knopf.

Latour, B. 1987. *Science in Action: How to Follow Scientists and Engineers through Society*. Cambridge, MA: Harvard University Press.

— 1993. *We Have Never Been Modern*. London: Harvester Wheatsheaf.

Law, John & John Hassard. 1999. *'Actor Network Theory and After'* in The Sociological Review. Oxford: Blackwell Publishers.

London Sans 'Souls'. *Variety* March 14, 1933.

Lowenthal, D. 1985. *The Past is a Foreign Country*. Cambridge: Cambridge University Press.

Merchant, C. 1980. *The Death of Nature: Women, Ecology, and the Scientific Revolution*. San Francisco: Harper & Row.

Rafter, N. 1988. *WhiteTrash: The Eugenic Family Studies, 1877-1919*. Boston: Northeastern University Press.

Said, E.W. 1978. *Orientalism*. 1st ed. New York: Pantheon Books.

Shakespeare, W. 1670. *The Tempest. Or, The Enchanted Island. A Comedy. As it is now Acted at His Highness the Duke of York's Theatre*. London: Printed by J. M. for Henry Herringman at the Blew Anchor in the Lower-Walk of the New-Exchange.

Shapin, S., and S. Schaffer. 1985. *Leviathan and the Air-pump: Hobbes, Boyle, and the Experimental Life: Including a Translation of Thomas Hobbes, Dialogues Physicus de Natura Aeris by Simon Schaffer*. Princeton, N.J.: Princeton University Press.

Shohat, E. 1991. 'Gender and Culture of Empire: Toward a Feminist Ethnography of the Cinema' in *Quarterly Review of Film Studies* 13 (1-3): 45-84.

Spencer, F. 1993. 'Pithekos to Pithecanthropus: An Abbreviated Review of Changing Scientific Views on the Relationship of the Anthropoid Apes to Homo Sapiens.' in Corbey, R. and Theunissen, B. Evaluative Proceedings of the Symposium: *Ape, Man, Apeman: Changing Views since 1600*. Leiden, the Netherlands: Department of Prehistory, Leiden University.

Richard Watts Jr. 1933. 'Island of Lost Souls'; Review of *Island of Lost Souls*, in *New York Herald Tribune* (13 January 1933).

Wells, H.G. 1995 (1896). *H.G. Wells: The Science Fiction*. London: Phoenix Giant.

Variety. January 17, 1933. Review of Island of Lost Souls.

Young, R. 1995. *Colonial Desire: Hybridity in Theory, Culture, and Race.* London, New York: Routledge.

Notes

[1] To name but a few examples: *Mysterious Island* (1929), *Abbott and Costello Meet Frankenstein* (1948), *Doctor NO* (1962), *Alien: Resurrection* (1997) and *Forbidden Planet* (1958).

[2] This is how Moreau describes himself in the film.

[3] A variation on the text in Wells' novella. H.G. Wells, *The Island of Doctor Moreau*, part one of *H.G. Wells: The Science Fiction*. 1995 (1896) London: Phoenix Giant: 121-23.

[4] Clifford Geertz calls this scientific attitude "experience-distant." Geertz Clifford. 1983. *Local Knowledge: Futher Essays in Interpretive Anthropology*. New York: Basic Books.

[5] Merchant, Carolyn. 1980. *The Death of Nature: Women, Ecology, and the Scientific Revolution*. San Francisco: Harper & Row; and Harding, Sandra, G. 1986. *The Science Question in Feminism.* Ithaca: Cornell University Press.

[6] About such confliction relations, see: *Colonial Desire*: 64-65.

[7] — "London Sans 'Souls'," *Variety*, March 14 1933.

[8] Exhibition of the film was prohibited for more than 30 years in the UK. See: Hardy, Phil. 1995. *Science Fiction: The Aurum Film Encyclopaedia* London: Aurum Press: 88.
As a result of the Production Code Administration only a shorter version of the film was allowed to be shown in the US after 1935, leaving out the scenes in which Moreau tries to mate humans and hybrids.
Doherty, Thomas Patrick. 1999. *Pre-code Hollywood: Sex, Immorality, and Insurrection in American Cinema, 1930-1934*, Film and Culture (New York: Columbia University Press: 312.

[9] Richard Watts Jr. 1933. 'Island of Lost Souls'; Review of *Island of Lost Souls*, in *New York Herald Tribune* (13 January 1933).

[10] In early depictions of anthropoids they are often shown as using a stick to support themselves, hence stressing their difference to humans.
See: Spencer, Frank. 1993. 'Pithekos to Pithecanthropus: An Abbreviated Review of Changing Scientific Views on the Relationship of the Anthropoid Apes To Homo Sapiens' in Corbey, R. and Bert, Theunissen (ed.) *Ape, Man, Apeman: Changing Views since 1600*. Leiden, the Netherlands: Department of Prehistory, Leiden University.

[11] Richard Watts Jr. 1933. 'Island of Lost Souls'; Review of *Island of Lost Souls*, in *New York Herald Tribune* (13 January 1933).

[12] In research on ethnicity and film such behaviour is often equated with the negative position of the non-white male as the rapist.

Shohat, Ella. 1991. 'Gender and Culture of Empire: Towards a Feminist Ethnography of the Cinema' in *Quarterly Review of Film Studies* 13 (1-3): 45-84.

[13] William Boednel, *New York World Telegram*, January 13, 1933.

Shaping Consciousness: New Media, Spirituality, and Identity

Michael Punt

This chapter will trace the rise and occlusion of the spirit realm from dominant discussions in 19ᵗʰ century science. It will argue that the rise of positivism was a temporary move designed to strategically consolidate scientific method at a moment when it was in danger of being overwhelmed by uncertainties. It will show how in the popular domain, especially in technologies of pleasure such as the cinema and the amusement park, the science technology and entertainment interface can be regarded as the site of healthy resistance to positivism. The author claims that in this sense the study of nineteenth century technology provides a conduit into popular consciousness.

Between *The Terminator* (1984) and *Terminator 2: Judgment Day* (1991) Arnold Schwarzenegger undergoes quite a radical transformation. From being the pitiless 'Terminator' sent back from 2029 to kill Sarah Connor, he reappears ten years later as a T880-Model 101 determined to protect her child from a murderous shape-shifting T1000. Such an about-face requires radical reinvention, and Schwarzenegger is reborn, fully grown, in a car park in downtown Los Angeles at the beginning of *Terminator 2: Judgment Day*. The new Arnie appears naked in the cold wet artificial light of the badlands, and in an extended vision of homoerotic excess is transformed from the alien to the angelic. The danger and pleasure of this confrontation for the viewer faced with so much body on the screen is defused in the following scene in an act of outrageous brutality thinly disguised as a strategy to acquire clothes to cover his nakedness. The trick of this dramatic opening is that we perceive Arnold as having become new through a reflection on our own internalised process in which we acknowledge the adjustment of our erotic orientation from one state to another, in order to understand what we are seeing. Schwarzenegger and his stylisation of becoming seem to speak to a vast number of

people in a popular art form such that they will invest him with political power over their destiny. The Terminator franchise may be politi-
cally incorrect schlock but it merely rehearses the same preoccupations that drive the finer arts. Arnie's namesake, Schönberg, (1874-
1951) for example was also fascinated by the moment when one thing
turns into another. What separates these two countrymen is the better
part of a human lifetime (three score years and ten) in which the
Modernist project in the arts was hijacked and redirected away from a
preoccupation with the custody of the spiritual dimensions of human
consciousness and towards a materialist assertion that the only thing
that mattered in the world was defining the essence of the perceptible
real. Modernism, or more precisely late Modernism did for the arts
what the bracketing of telepathy did for science; it restricted its epistemological realm to the banal.

Telepathy

In Britain and the USA in the 19th century, telepathy was not a mar-
ginal pursuit of the gullible, but stood as a general term for a range of
preoccupations in psychical research that viewed reality as a contin-
uum in which the material and immaterial were undifferentiated.
These ranged from such things as slate writing, fortune-telling, palm-
istry and clairvoyance, to personal mediumship and communication
with other people without material of connection. Telepathy was a
necessary component of scientific research if its realm of enquiry was
not to become trapped in a tautology in which the epistemology becomes nothing more than an exquisite demonstration of method. In the
19th century, telepathy's great achievement was to provide a rationale
that situated scientific objectivity inside the human observer. It stood
in opposition to Cartesian method, which had come to dominate
classical science, and insisted on the separation of the subject and the
object, so much so that, the greater the distance between the observer
and the observed, paradoxically, the more authority was bestowed on
the truth claim. In contrast however, telepathy regarded the human
mind as a transformative force so that, only through intimate entan-
glement, could it change the world about it. Experiments in telepathy
confirmed reality as a chaotic field of heterogeneous forces comprising rays, microwaves, electromagnetic emissions, and of course the
force of mind which some gifted, or impaired, individuals could,
under special conditions, perceive as a sensation. This meant that
telepathic communion was not a process of simple connection but was

fully interactive so that when some element in the spectrum of forces found a conduit, a moment of temporary tranquility was established in the chaos which made it intelligible to a wider community of observers. Consistent with this view of reality as a field of forces, the form of the conduit that temporarily imparted comprehensible order was not restricted to the mind of an individual human medium. Many experiments were developed in scientific laboratories to show for example how the processes that enabled human telepathic interaction were observable in a copper wire, or in the sympathetic communication between gas flames. Whatever form the medium took however, the pattern of forces in the world would be transformed by tapping into them, and any attempt by scientists to reduce this reciprocity (in experimental method) would be futile, producing, at best, skilful illusions and intellectual sleights of hand in which the observer's prior determination was concealed. As a consequence, to the spiritualist, the separation between mind and body was regarded as a dubious act of self subjugation to an unachievable ideal of objectivity; while in contrast any evidence of telepathy showed the world as a product of mind that became clearer the more fully it immersed the observer.

The implications of this worldview extended beyond the practical and entertaining; it confronted some of the basic tenets of realist ideology. For example, the scientific populariser, S. R. Bottone, described a process of photographing with electricity in which the passage of inductive electricity through light sensitive film produced an image without the need for any discharge of light (flash) (Bottone 1898). This proposed an ontology of photography which contradicted the dominant realist interpretation which flowed from Renaissance picture-making. As Bottone reveals, photography did not provide evidence of light writing itself but instead confirmed reality as the ever-present interaction of forces. Photography without the constraint of realism was metaphysics, magic, and science as a single continuous topic of practical research, little wonder that it was hijacked into the banalities of the quotidian. Even more problematic for the scientist steeped in Cartesian values was evidence from the discharges in a Crooke's Vacuum Tube that produced light with a different colour that seemed to have the power to attract small solid objects that were outside the glass. These tubes could be understood as miniature air-tight laboratories, which when complete with the necessary vacuum, produced the conditions of another world within a world, and the metaphysical implications of this were startling and not missed. Both Lenard and Röntgen also noticed that electrical discharges in very high vacua produced an invisible light that reversed the normal orders of opacity and transparency. They observed that altering the shape of the tubes and the metallic constitution of the anodes produced a variety of images in which the opacity of a material was no longer a prerequisite of visual cognition. Although much of this seemed perfectly verifiable within the laws of science in that what was visualised could be confirmed by dissection etc., fluorescent screens complicated the issue as these allowed rays to pass through them and an object behind them while at the same time leaving an outline on the screen — this was not only counter-intuitive but also counter-hegemonic. Each new turn in radiography seemed to move the condition of reality more away from the material and toward the phenomenal in every sense, it was a marvel that caught the public imagination and outshone the cinematograph as a fairground attraction. The tragic deaths of showmen and an overbearing rationalism reappropriated Crookes' and Röntgen's discoveries and the only surviving remnant which celebrates the mystery of it all is in the popular name, the X-ray.

Equally challenging to the prevailing scientific ideas about reality was the insistence by Marie Sklodowska (and her husband Pierre Curie) that atoms might decay and their transformation into light could be visible as radiated energy. Their selfless toiling over ten thousand kilograms of uranium is well known, as is their final reward: one tenth of a gram of a shining element, Radium, that refused to obey all the laws of classical nineteenth century science. Ra 226 (226 times heavier than Hydrogen) appeared to owe its existence to a transmutation of matter over a period of at least 5,000 million years. The suggestion that radioactive elements could transform, that heat could emanate from an apparently limitless source together with the confirmation of radioactive decay not only challenged classical physics but also had an impact in geology and this threw new challenges to Christian fundamentalism and the primacy of human significance in the order of things. Arguably, these two great discoveries of the 1890s, ones that transformed lives and human perception of its own importance, both pointed to interactive and phenomenal dimensions of the world about us. More particularly the coalition of Radium and the Röntgen X-ray tube opened a new field of enquiry into electromagnetic waves, that showed that, contrary to Leibniz' exclusive assertion, nature not only flowed, but it also jumped. This coexistence of contradictory conditions in a single coherent universe defied rationalism and opened the way for broader interpretations of the spiritual as a constituent element of reality.

The instrumental confirmation of other dimensions to reality challenged bourgeois reliance on the epistemology of vision and, along with the fascination with X-rays as a popular entertainment in fairgrounds, so too exhibitions of various technologies spoke of another dimension. The popular engagement with science and technology as an elevating and distracting spectacle in world's fairs, amusement parks, museums and public lectures extended to a fascination with interaction at a distance, and like serious scientific expositions, telepathic, spiritualist and mesmeric practices were often almost indistinguishable from amusing entertainment.[1] The historic fusion of all fields of scientific practice and entertainment, exemplified in these spectacles meant that the distinction between the paranormal and materialist science was not as clear as it later became either at the public or professional level. In this context, telepathy was not just a diversion for the bereaved, the easily ridiculed or the weak-minded and foolish; but a radical act of discovery, an intervention in a single-minded containment of knowledge that reduced the subject to an object. As such it was the natural accomplice to the highest achievements of those scientists experimenting with magnetism, electricity, Crooke's tubes and uranium. Nonetheless, it soon became apparent to influential members of the British Association for the Advancement of Science that any taint of superstition was counter-productive to the ambitions of some professionals who felt that a firm distinction should be made to distance themselves from practical technologists.[2] In order to secure the highest social status, the emerging profession of scientific naturalism was as relentless in its exposure of spiritualistic heresies as it was in its pursuit of new scientific knowledge. As a consequence, by the 1880s the Society for Psychical Research had collated strange mesmeric effects, spiritualist mediumship, apparitions and ghostly manifestations, Crooke's 'psychic forces' and Cox's psychism; and reconceived them through its principal organising term: telepathy. The term telepathy became the single conduit of distinction in the heterogeneous terrain of psychic manifestations. It also became the dominant manifestation of psychic phenomena to attract the scientific anti-spiritualists and its place in the contemporary practice and the history of science was temporarily lost.

Telepathy's expulsion from the canon was radical, abrupt and, in hindsight a somewhat shameful moment in the history of British science[3]. In 1876 Henry Slade was prosecuted under the vagrancy act and sentenced to three months hard labour. The verdict was overturned at appeal and while awaiting retrial he left Britain for the continent certain that he would not get a fair hearing. Slade was born in 1835 in Niagara County, New York and, according to his biographies, showed extraordinary powers as a teenager. By adulthood he became a famous slate writing medium who was alleged to have amassed, and squandered, a fortune made through his work. His fame encouraged him to tour Europe, and in England in 1876 he was subjected to a series of rigorous tests by August Cox, founder of the Psychological Society, and then by Dr. Carter Blake, a former Secretary of the Anthropological Society of Great Britain, neither of whom could find any evidence of deception. However, when Professor E. Ray Lankester subsequently tested him, there was apparently some evidence that Slade had prepared the slates in advance. After a brief and acrimonious exchange in the correspondence pages of *The Times*, Slade was charged with "unlawfully using certain subtle craft, means and devices to deceive and impose on certain of Her Majesty's subjects — to wit, E. Ray Lankester, T. J. Oldhams, Henry Sedwick, R. H. Hutton, Edmund Gurney and W. B. Carpenter"[4]. Evidence was given by the conjuror John Maskelyne who demonstrated how the trick might have been done. Although the evidence seems slight and inconclusive, Slade was found guilty by the magistrate, Mr. Flowers, on the basis that "he had used 'subtle craft' to try to deceive Lankester" and, he concluded, "I must decide according to the well known course of nature", and if Slade was seen to write on the slate as was alleged, then "it is impossible for me to doubt, whatever happened on the other occasion, Slade did on that occasion write those words on that slate in order to cheat Professor Lankester and Dr. Donkin"[5].

The significance of this trial in the history of ideas is that it was brought about by the reading of a paper at the British Association for the Advancement of Science by William Barrett, Professor of Physics at Dublin with the title 'On Some Phenomena Associated with Abnormal Conditions of the Mind' (Luckhurst 2002: 44). Its topic concerned mesmeric phenomena and 'community of sensation' between subject and investigators. The discussion that followed included the topic of spiritualism. The reaction to this was divisive with an essentialist complaint, principally from Edwin Lankester, that it was unscientific. It was this event, Luckhurst claims, which spurred Lankester to set a trap for a medium. He chose Henry Slade, not merely for his fame, but also because he featured in a challenge set out by William Stainton Moses, a respected medium who although he consistently refused to be tested himself had no hesitation in offering Slade up for scrutiny. The legal trial that followed was reminiscent of the old witch-hunts since it was orchestrated to excise spiritualist presence from rational science. Luckhurst sees this as a hollow victory: the retreat of rationalists to the courts may have curbed the exploration of the 'unnatural', but by "stepping into a non-scientific terrain Lankester invested the standards of evidence in legal discourse with greater authority than those of scientific naturalism" (2002: 47). It soon became apparent to influential members of the British Association for the Advancement of Science that a firm distinction should be made between science and spirit. But by bracketing the paranormal outside science, a new institution, the Society for Psychical Research, was enabled and legitimated. From the moment that psychical research had its own society, in Britain at least, science became an exclusively rationalist, empiricist exercise. Such an epistemological rupture appears to be a retrenchment and a return to the foundational mythology of Enlightenment science in the face of a serious challenge to materialism. However, as I will argue, this was not entirely as it seems — a moment of dismal ejection of imagination and colour from the rationalist project – but a timely suspension of the momentum of scientific knowledge in danger of being carried away from what Spinoza (1632-1677) described as the realm of impersonal rationality, disclosing the world to us under the 'aspect of eternity'[6].

Although the Henry Slade trial seems to be a characteristically nineteenth century squabble between a newly emerged spiritualist movement and scientific rationalism, its origins lay much further back in the history of science. Margaret and Kate Fox from Hydesville, USA, were exponents of typtology (table rapping) and they are often cited as founders of the spiritualist movement, in fact it preceded them but since they seemed to have caught the public imagination, they were used to launch the Spiritualism Movement in 1848. It rapidly gathered a substantial following that spread across the USA and into Europe. One explanation for the extraordinary popularity of spiritualism that has been offered was that a burgeoning materialist culture which linked the mechanical with the rational, provoked a certain popular resistance, but although this cannot be discounted, the roots lay much deeper, at the very core of science itself.

At its very beginnings, modern science was confronted by it own contradictory position relative to the experience of supernatural events. Justice Flower's invocation of the "well known course of nature" merely reiterated the interpretation of legal proof that lay at the very heart of seventeenth century science. As an experimental methodology it insisted that, for a fact to be classed as such, it had to be authenticated by reliable witnesses. But as Barbara Shapiro points out in a micro-history of the origins of scientific fact, witchcraft posed profound and almost insurmountable difficulties when testimony was reported by seemingly credible witnesses (1999: 179). It was a difficulty exacerbated by the particularity of crimes involving the supernatural in that the reliability of even the most eminent witness had to be discounted. Shapiro cites the declaration by Reginald Scott in 1594 that a; "jury would be wrong to convict if a man were seen in London the same day as a murder he was alleged to have committed in Berwick, even if he confessed and others deposed the same thing" (1999: 180). The significance of this assertion is that it imposed limits on witness credibility, drawn not from character or reliability but posited on what was considered possible in the natural world as it was rationally understood. In the Slade case, the witnesses were considered reliable, but the judgement seems to have had some difficulty with this and relegated their evidence to a secondary supporting confirmation. Instead, the key consideration in the judgement was the unnaturalness of the possibility of supernatural slate writing (in a scientific rational world). By appearing to support a scientific worldview it had the reverse effect, turning the epistemological clock back to the late sixteenth century and undoing the work of the pioneers of modern science such as Robert Boyle and the lesser known Joseph Glanvill.

In the 17th century Joseph Glanvill set out to collect and catalogue reliable evidence of the spirit world in order to support his own claims that if the proof was sufficient, matters of fact could not be denied just because they defied explanation. He collaborated with leading theological philosophers at the time, notably Samuel Clarke, Thomas Spratt and Robert Boyle who were anxious to prove the existence of the non-material in order to support the truth of Christianity. Shapiro reminds us of the particular case of Valentine Greatrakes, a famous, and apparently effective, 'stroker' who cured the sick in the seventeenth century and (like Slade) was also obliged to face charges of fraud. As she reports, Greatrakes assembled reliable witnesses from the scientific world including Robert Boyle to be present at his experiments in stroking. Boyle's work-diary entries of 6th April 1666 record him first witnessing, and then experimenting with Greatrakes' glove by stroking an afflicted patient.

> This day being present when Mr G. stroakd a Tincker that Dr Fairecloth & I had before examind, & who had been lame & gone upon Crutches between 7 & 8 year, having been thrice entertaind in St. Bartholomews hospital without at last receiving any amendment, I was informed by the patient, that he

he had been once stroackd before on Tuesday last with most sudden & wonderfull releife, & that yet his paines though incomparably lesse then before being not quite removd he came to be stroakd again, which I having desired that he might be, Mr. G. began to stroke his shoulder, where the patient complained of a pain, which by his stroacking being as the Tincker sayd presently removd unto his Elbow & thence toward his [d] hand, I tooke Mr G.'s Glove, [d] which was thick & sought, & turning the inside outward stroakd therewith the affected Arme, & (as I ghesse) within a minute of an hower drove the paine as the Tincker told me into his wrest where he sayd it much afflicted him, then stroaking that part also with the Glove, he told me felt a sharp paine in the middle joynts of his fingers, [d] & stroaking those parts also he sayd he felt it exceding uneasy under his Nailes, which being likewise stroakd he sayd his paine was quite gone from his shoulder, arme, & hand [7]

This incident shows us how at the beginning of the scientific project such 'supernatural' events were deemed worthy of scientific study and became a class of fact to be considered and incorporated in the universe that had to be explained. This was consistent with the founding belief of the Enlightenment that human knowledge was (as yet) incomplete, consequently catalogues of marvels were invested with sufficient importance as to suggest that the Royal Society collect the relative evidence. At the same time in order to resist a rising atheism associated with this new regime of knowing the world, the legitimate church was presented with the witnessed evidence of a supernatural. As science began to be the dominant epistemology it had to respond with increasing rationality (as Justice Flowers did two centuries later). As a consequence, by the early 1700s the inability to accommodate the unnatural (in scientific terms) meant that despite extensive witness testimony to supernatural events there was a decline in witchcraft trials since the courts (constrained by science) could only acknowledge the 'natural' as confirmed by reliable witnesses as their basis for concluding the facts of a case. Despite the internal contradictions, for the better part of three centuries, it seems that while there was certainly contention, there did not appear to be any incompatibility between the scientific and the supernatural, whether that immaterial existence was Christian or otherwise — at least as far as the Royal Society was concerned. In contrast, during the early nineteenth century in the Royal Institution, which comprised scientists who were more active, metaphysics was out of bounds. Founded by Benjamin Thomson, the Institution was originally envisioned as a centre for the dissemination of practical knowledge to the artisan classes. Nonetheless research into field theory by key figures in the Institution, such as Davy and Faraday, was driven by fundamentally metaphysical speculation and, despite their public image as empiricists, their personal intellectual investment appeared to be in transfiguring knowledge.

Perhaps given the judicial difficulties that the spiritual posed, it is not surprising that although Davy was an extremely practical scientist, for the majority of his career he harboured fundamental doubts about the exclusivity of materialist worldviews. Quite early in his life he seems to have been swayed toward Roger Joseph Boscovich's view, published in 1763, that Newtonian physics could not operate at the atomic level. Boscovich pointed out that if the atom was an irreducible object of infinite hardness, then there could be no compression and expansion as atoms collided (as there is in billiard balls for example). To remedy this deficit he suggested that atoms were structureless points that were surrounded by forces. His commitment to a non-Newtonian immaterial universe is evident in *Consolations in Travel* or, *The last Days of a Philosopher*, his final book, in which he became quite explicit with his metaphysical vision, he gave to it a third person voice in a character called 'The Unknown' (Williams 1965: 79). Boscovich's and Davy's metaphysics also had resonance with Faraday, and subsequently Maxwell Clarke who became convinced by philosophical discussion, experimental evidence and theoretical reasoning that the prevailing philosophy of matter was partial and that energy was not localised in matter but in the space around it. Not only did this begin to unify apparently discontinuous forces such as magnetism and electricity, but, for Faraday this early version of Field Theory provided a satisfactory continuity between his scientific research and his Sandemanian (Glasite) belief in spirit without denomination. As far as the public and most of their peers were concerned, Humphry Davy and Michael Faraday approached scientific and supernatural enquiries (including theology) as though they were exclusively concerned with the interrogation of forces as symptomatic of another (material) condition and (along with Thompson) excluded the supernatural de facto since they each felt that, whatever its validity, it promoted superstition which countered the overriding educational aspirations of the Institute.

In this context of a perceived epistemological regression from intuited, transfiguring knowledge to disconnected trivia running counter to the second creation narratives of a technologically driven Modernism, the bitter struggles surrounding spiritism during the same period take on a new dimension. The objections to spiritism were founded on the basis that it confronted the Institution's essentially practical aims of "diffusing the knowledge, and facilitating the general introduction, of useful mechanical inventions and improvements; and for teaching, by courses of philosophical lectures and experiments, the application of science to the common purposes of life"[8]. It was less of an affront to the members of the Royal Society who had their roots in natural philosophy and saw themselves as a more established and more learned coalition of scientists. What characteristically differentiated the two societies of scientists was their understanding of force relative to distinct frameworks of knowledge. Whereas the Royal Society saw scientific knowledge as transfiguring, the Institution with its populist agenda was more concerned with what might be understood as relatively intelligent knowledge. The various strategies of public engagement that were developed in the 19th century by the Royal Institution, and its lecture programmes in particular, promoted a more passive acceptance of the scientific project as a collection of discrete data to be learned with a view to self-advancement. This was a sort of directed trivia that necessarily precluded metaphysical speculation about the supernatural, and more significantly shifted the scientific emphasis away from the consideration of forces. In so doing, the Royal Institute inevitably undermined its own ambitions and paved the way for the passive enjoyment of science at the expense of active engagement in the epistemological project. As a consequence, the distinction between the paranormal séance and experimental science was not always clear to either professionals or the general public.

Revisiting the story of science and emphasising a history of continuity between the metaphysical and empirical, opens a new perspective on the intellectual polemic that was thought to have shaped the last century. This divide was perceived to be so extreme that in 1959 C. P. Snow referred to it most famously as 'Two Cultures', and the concept still appears to have some currency[9]. Viewed through the filter of a framework of knowledge however, the relationship between science and the humanities can be seen not so much as an epistemological bifurcation but more as a qualitative differentiation brought about as science forsook its earlier ambitions for transfiguration and limited them to "intelligent knowledge furnished by the ordinary sciences, which take care to organise their facts in terms of adequate ideas of the properties of things." It now seems from the writings of both Davy and Faraday that this was a deliberate and heroic intellectual sacrifice that was evidently necessary in order to manage the exponential growth in knowledge *per se* brought about by the burgeoning globalisation of experience. Although publicly antagonistic to transfiguration, there was neither disavowal of the spirit nor its extermination; instead certain constituencies, most notably artists, writers, poets, performers, public entertainers, etc. became custodians of a kind of knowledge that was understood as an essential component of the scientific project but which was expediently bracketed.

Snow's intervention is symptomatic of another powerful influence that insisted on the bracketing of the spiritual. As a consequence of the disavowal of the immaterial, by the 1880s the Society for Psychical Research had collated strange mesmeric effects, spiritualist medium-ship, apparations and ghostly manifestations, Crooke's 'psychic forces' and Cox's psychism, and reconceived them through its princi-pal organising term: telepathy. According to Luckhurst, telepathy became the single conduit of distinction in the heterogeneous terrain of psychic manifestations. It also became the dominant manifestation of psychic phenomena to attract the scientific anti-spiritualists as well as the more populist antagonists of superstition such as conjurors, and its place in the history of science was temporarily lost. But some scientists such as Crookes, *Röntgen* (and later Currie) seemed to provide instrumental confirmation of other dimensions of reality that challenged bourgeois reliance on the epistemology of vision and, along with the fascination with X-rays as a popular entertainment in fairgrounds, so too exhibitions of other technologies from cinema to heavier than air flight also spoke to another dimension. Quite per-versely it seems the popular engagement with science and technology as an elevating and distracting spectacle in World's fairs, museums and public lectures extended to, even insisted upon, a fascination with interaction at a distance, and like serious scientific expositions, tele-pathic, spiritualist and mesmeric practices in this context were often almost indistinguishable from amusing entertainment.

A bourgeois history of popular culture in the nineteenth century has tampered with our understanding of what was at stake in the mass engagement with science, how it took place and what it meant. De-spite the teleological claims of Modern(ist) historians, the cinema-tograph and the Kinetoscope, the X-ray's great fairground rivals, were not enlisted in a documentary project to represent life as we appar-ently perceived it, on the contrary many of the early pioneers, includ-ing Edison himself had a well-known fascination with the afterlife. The quite special possibilities the moving picture technology promised for transcending the physical world were (famously) noted at the idea stage of the Kinetoscope, and as the first reports of the Cinématogra-phe point out, despite its relatively degraded image quality, this kind of moving picture technology offered an opportunity to be in both this world and the next. More than post-mortem photography, moving picture technology seemed to provide a portal to an other-worldly experience beyond time measured by the decay of the body. Less morbidly, interaction between people, places and times regarded as separate according to the laws of science, became a dominant theme for the so-called 'living' picture shows. Phantom rides, actualities, and trick films reiterated many of the visual effects already achieved in magic lantern shows, as they also satisfied a long-standing popular fascination for practices that involved remote interaction in a context that showed a marked ambivalence to the hegemonic claims of science. Coupled with a discourse of bourgeois realism, however the cinema not only promised another realm but it did so in the dominant paradigm, which refusèd any possibility of it existing. As a critical intervention the cinema offered a double blow to an authority, which had progressively excluded them from its formation.

Although the cinematograph appears to have exploited the fruits of the systematic analysis of motion by Marey, Londe, Demény, Jansen et al., the public were uncertain about the nature of movement as divisible, and these machines appeared to present inclusive evidence about what movement is; the more the technicians worked on the problem the more the results seemed to argue both ways, not least by showing the sleight of hand that some procedures of scientific analysis could perpetrate on human senses. Henri Bergson became the respected voice of opposition to positivism and the idea of a finite divisible reality. He not only wielded significant populist support for his view of time as the only reality but also gave weight to the concept of intuition; arguing that the self-conscious positioning of the subject within the object was the only way to break the habitual materialisation of time as space. This philosophical intervention chimed with the public enthusiasm for the paranormal and transdimensional even though it was often obvious that hoaxes were being pulled: at either end of the intellectual spectrum there was a felt need to redress the argument between determinism and voluntarism in favour of experience. If, as scientists increasingly suggested, there was a determining logic to the universe that made our human direction (if not our individual destiny) inevitable, then in direct proportion, the strongest alternative to those suggestions came from inside science itself which had appeared to take a wrong turning in its dealings with telepathy by writing an important constituent of its make up out of the story.

While spiritualist pursuits remained popular, it was of course in the arts that the intellectual engagement with the immaterial was culti-

vated and refined in music, letters and visual art. For the last two
decades of the nineteenth century and the first couple of the twentieth,
a quite unguarded view of the comprehensible world as the consequence of an ongoing collision between partially present realities
informed art and popular culture. For Schönberg, this worldview
reaches a philosophical impasse in his great work *Moses and Aaron*,
(a work that occupied the last quarter of his life) in which rational
comprehensibility collapses under the contradiction that the concept of
an absolute truth poses. Schönberg saw the logical impossibility of
expressing the inexpressible in much the same way that four centuries
earlier Spinoza saw the impossibility of more than one substance, and
Deleuze (1925-1995) later understood as the inter-changeability of
immanence and transcendence. It was a similar sentiment that drove
Marcel Proust (1871-1922) to distinguish between the author and the
work in the novel's process of becoming. Epitomised by a description
of himself as Marcel became progressively aware of reality as a hidden entity that can only be fleetingly grasped by memory, the narra-
torís introspection produces a description of that awareness as a process that is independent of reality. In the visual arts in Europe the
Impressionists, following Cézanne (1839-1906), Manet (1832-1883)
and Degas (1834-1917) foreshadowed Proust and Schönberg by
insisting on visual impression as a unique effect of the moment. Light,
colour and movement, which have no absolute values save those
which social consensus imparts on them, became the topic of a medium in an art form which, until that time, had the main weight of its
intellectual investment in the depiction of matter as solid and the
spiritual as nothing more than a Platonic form of the quotidian. This
cultivation of the territory abandoned by science was gathered up into
a version of Modernism as an avant-garde movement informed by a
rejection of inherited values and worldviews. It launched a period of
intellectually driven creativity based on an extreme relativism that lost
its secessionist impulse and finally foundered in the absolutist ambitions of formalism. Devoid of any contact with political and social
realms, art lost its way as the custodian of spirit and swapped it for
faux science based on materialist chronologies, rationalism, Whig
histories and a baton race of influence in which white men always
seemed to lead the way (but never seemed to get anywhere).

It was during this period when science and art could be differentiated by their engagement with questions of the spiritual realm that the
art historian Aby Warburg (1866-1929) recognised that art could be
understood not as an epistemology of objects, but as the evidential

trace of a historically persistent human obsession with movement[10]. Warburg saw art as one of many activities, which ritually re-enacted the transient moment of 'becoming'. Art, according to him, was crucial because in painting and sculpture, for example, bringing into being an intention was revealed in the subordination of matter to human consciousness. For Warburg, the origins of the obsession with movement lay in the Dyonisian worldview that reveled in excess and boundless possibility. Although his ideas were influential, he fell into a certain obscurity, his work is known primarily through his students (Wind, Saxle and Panofsky especially) and certain forms of practice. However, for many contemporary artists, designers and art educators concerned with the interface between science and technology, understanding his work has become increasingly important in recent years. The more so as science begins to embrace again those speculative and metaphysical issues that it temporarily abandoned in the late nineteenth century.

Warburg's doctoral thesis on Botticelli's *Primavera and Birth of Venus* revealed them as works in which the programmed interaction of classical and modern forms were juxtaposed in such a way that in their surrender to a contemporary context there was a release of spirit. This exposed the function of art as the ritualistic liberation of the contained, and reiterated the Dionysian impulse that had been driven underground by stoic rationalism in the classical period. By following what might be called an ethicalist vision, Warburg showed the limitation of bounded disciplines in art history and the insufficiency of canonical terms such as 'The Renaissance' to fully account for the acts of human consciousness during its prescribed period. His approach to art was informed by the emerging confidence in Cultural Anthropology and (although it seldom appeared in his work directly) the cinema. The effect of these two key influences can be seen in the organisation of his library in Hamburg the KBW (*Kultur-wissenschaftliche Bibliothek Warburg*). It finally comprised some 60,000 volumes and was organised in an interdisciplinary structure. Under his hand, it was constantly re-organised as new thoughts and new kinds of relationships between ideas occurred to him.

In addition to the books, the library also contained over 20,000 images. Toward the end of his life he used this collection to produce a series of black painted boards on which he attached images of artefacts from quite different times and cultures to reveal a continuity of ideas that operated in contradiction to their temporal and geographic provenance. These boards, of which we have an incomplete record, were subsequently called the Mnemosyne Atlas. They stood purposefully against the shelves in his library and in this arrangement proposed a relationship between memory and culture that refused to reduce the human ritual of art to artefacts in the service of master narratives of influence and attribution. His constant rearrangement of images in the Mnemosynes and the library catalogues resembled the epistemological method of the eighteenth century wunderkammer. And just as these cabinets of curiosities were used to speculate on natural philosophy through the considered relationship between objects, which had very different origins in space and time, so the Mnemosynes used the space between the images (the dark matter of unrecoverable history) to uncover the centrality of ritualistic rehearsal of movement between states of being that drove art and which was quite independent of shifts in style, taste and cultural preference. To the classicist, this flexibility may seem like the reification of uncertainty, but the rearrangement of categories and speculation on new affiliations, irrespective of the orthodox laws of connection, shifted the scale of human consciousness from the universal to the particle. It turned the stacks of ossified scholarship eternally bound in a fixed catalogue into a particle world held together by causal and non-causal connections. It heralded the work on relativity in science and astronomy that has shaped the twentieth century, and chimed with an emerging avantgarde of which Schönberg, Proust, and Cezanne et al. are merely convenient milestones in the story of the inter-relationship between science and art at the turn of the twentieth century.

What these artists and Warburg share, apart from a commitment to reality as a contingency of human consciousness, is a sceptical view of time as an external absolute. Although much of their work is inaccessible to a broad audience, such relativism also found expression in popular culture as technologies initially used to support positivist worldviews were subverted to become instruments of frivolous pleasure. One of the most dramatic examples of this was the spectacle of the moving photographic image, which purported to reinforce the values of bourgeois realism as it simultaneously undermined them in an illusion of cultural consensus. The cinematograph, only one of the popular forms for showing moving pictures, was first exhibited on 28th December 1895. Within eighteen months there had been over 800,000 presentations of it at venues around the world. To account for its astonishing attraction has been one of the obsessions of some film scholars, most of who suggest it was the lure of a mysterious technology that stunned the audiences with its realism. Quite the reverse is true. There was no mystery for early audiences who fully understood the technology that was presented to them. They knew that the flow of life had been arrested temporarily, metonymically represented, and then reconstituted in a projection process that gave the illusion of perception. Like the Mnemosyne Atlas the cinema relied on the agility of the human mind to apprehend worlds, and to give sensible meaning to events even if they contradict the flow of dominant reality.

With the rise of the aesthetic of formal mastery and the displace-ment of the known audience with a constructed one (in the second part of the following centuries) art forsook its function as the keeper of all matters to do with spirit. At the same time some historians, to their shame, even allowed this version of the past to atrophy. In the place of art however a popular form of the Mnemosyne Atlas was rehearsed millions of times nightly in which the tension between human percep-tion and culturally determined reality nurtured the spiritual realm. As adventure and romance unfolds on the screen, the interrupted flow of light from the cinema projector affirms that 'in becoming' the world has a reality beyond our immediate perception. And in that space the constant theme of mainstream narrative film has been the significance of the moment: the coincidence, the accident, the deadline and the transformation has been rehearsed in ninety minute plays, which characteristically end when the extraordinary reverts to the banal. The reborn T 800-Model101, alias the Governor of California, may seem to be a strange reincarnation of the spirit of Schönberg, Proust and Cézanne, but just as his body has always defied sexual definition, so his films have shown little respect for the rational flow of time and space. Instead, at his most sublime, Schwarzenegger reminds us that the terms that we use to describe our experience are invariably insuffi-cient, and in the thrall of a technology of interruption and rupture we sometimes feel what we cannot usually see. This double life of the cinema, in which the fantastic and the real are visualised with equal conviction, is the direct legacy of the restraint of foolishness of scien-tists who expelled the possibility of the immaterial in favour of a rational universe. Without this expulsion, then the burgeoning realism of cinema in support of a bourgeois worldview would be merely a reiteration of the banal, but as it is, it becomes the site of conflict as the experience of a conscious being fully engages with a description of the human that disavows the very aspect which Warburg's research identified as a constant reflection on its own becoming.

Weidenfeld

Bibliography

Barbour, J. 1999. The *End of Time*. London:Weidenfeld and Nicholson.

Batz, F. 1965. *The Mind in the Middle Ages*. New York: Alfred A. Knopf.

Bessy, M. 1961. *A Pictorial History of the Supernatural*. London: Spring Books.

Bottone, Selimo Romeo. 1898. Radiography and the 'X' Rays in practice and theory, etc. Whittaker & Co.: London & New York.

Castle, T. 1995. *The Female Thermometer: Eighteenth Century Culture and the Invention of the Uncanny*. Oxford: .OUP

Coats, P. 1911. *Photographing the Invisible*. New York: Arno.

Curley, Edwin. 1994 eds. *A Spinoza Reader: The Ethics and Other Works*. Princeton: Princeton University Press.

Davy, H. 1889. *Consolations in Travel, or the Last Days of a Philosopher* London: Cassells.

Geley, G. 1927. *Clairvoyance and Materialisation: A Record of Experiments*. (Trans). Stanley De Bralth. London: Fisher and Unwin

Gettings, F. 1978. *Ghosts in Photographs: The Extraordinary Story of Spirit Photography*. New York: Harmony

Glendining, A. 1894. *The Veil Lifted: Modern Developments of Spirit Photography*. London: Whitaker and Co

Green, C. 1976. *The Decline and Fall of Science*. London: Hamish Hamilton.

Houghton, G. 1882. *Chronicles of the Photographs of Spiritual beings and Phenomena Invisible to the Material Eye*. London: E.W. Allen.

Inglis, B. 1992. *Natural and Supernatural: The History of the Supernatural*. UK: Prism.

— 1985. *The Paranormal: An Encyclopaedia of the Paranormal*. London:Paladin.

Jay, R. 1987. *Learned Pigs, and Fireproof Women*. London:Robert Hale.

Krauss. R.H. 1996. *Beyond Light and Shadow: The Role of Photography in Certain Paranormal Phenomena : An Historical Survey*. Tucson: Nazraeli Press.

————. 1978. The Importance of an Investigation into Spirit Photography, *October* 5:29-47.

Luckhurst, R. 2002. *The Invention of Telepathy.* Oxford: OUP.

Michaud, Phillippe-Alain. 2004. trans., Sophie Hawkes. *Aby Warburg and the Image in Motion.* New York: Zone Books.

Morus, I. 1992. 'Marketing the Machine: The Construction of Electrotherapeutics as Viable Medicine in Early Victorian England' in *Medical History* (36): 34-52

—— 1993. 'Currents from the underworld, Electricity and Technology of Display in Early Victorian England' in *ISIS* (84): 50-69.

Nasaw, D. 1993. *Going Out: The Rise and Fall of Public Amusements.* New York: Basic Books.

Noble, D. F. 1997. *The Religion of Technology.* New York: Alfred A, Knopf.

Pearsall, R. 1972. *The Table Rappers.* Michael Joseph: London

Remise, J., Remise, P., van de Walle, R. 1971. *Magie Lumineuse.* Paris: Balland.

Richet, C. 1906. *Phenomenes Dits de Materialisation.* Paris: Annales des Sciences Psychiques.

Schrenk-Notzing. 1920. *Phenomena and materialism: A Contribution to the Investigation of Mediumistic Teleplastics.* Trans. E.E. Fournier d'Albe. London: LKP,Trench,Trubner.

Shapiro, B. 1999. *A Culture of Fact.* New York: Cornell University Press.

Snow, C. P. 1993. *The Two Cultures* (with an introduction by Stefan Collini) Cambridge: Cambridge University Press.

Stafford, B. M. 2001. *Devices of Wonder: From World in a Box to Images on a Screen.* Los Angeles: Getty Publications.

Stafford, B. M. 1999. *Visual Analogy: Consciousness as the Art of Connecting.* Cambridge:MIT Press.

Stafford, B. 1994. *Artful Science.* Cambridge, MA: MIT Press.

Williams, L. 1965. *Michael Faraday and the Electric Dynamo.* London: Chapman & Hall.

Notes

[1] For a rich account of these entertaiments in the USA see, Nasaw, D. 1993. *Going Out: The Rise and Fall of Public Amusements.* New York: Basic Books.

[2] See my own work on this in *Early Cinema and the Technological Imaginary* and Morus, I. 1992. 'Marketing the Machine: The Construction of Electrotherapeutics as Viable Medicine in Early Victorian England' in *Medical History* (36): 34-52

— 1993. 'Currents from the underworld, Electricity and Technology of Display in Early Victorian England' In *ISIS* (84): 50-69.

[3] For a detailed exposition of this argument see Luckhurst pt. 1.

[4] Cited in Inglis, B. 1992. *Natural and Supernatural: A History of the Paranormal*. U.K.: Prism: 279.

[5] Ibid.

[6] For an introduction to Spinoza see: Curley, Edwin. 1994 (eds.). *A Spinoza Reader: The Ethics and Other Works*. Princeton: Princeton University Press.

[7] Boyle's work-diary entries of 6th April 1666. On line at: http://www.bbk.ac.uk/boyle/workdiaries/TOC.html.

[8] See http://www.rigb.org/rimain/index.jsp for a reiteration of their aims today.

[9] See the recent publication for a full text and subsequent afterthoughts. Snow, C. P. 1993. *The Two Cultures* (with an introduction by Stefan Collini) Cambridge: Cambridge University Press.

[10] For an overview of Warburg see: Michaud, Phillippe-Alain (trans. Sophie Hawkes) 2004. *Aby Warburg and the Image in Motion*. New York: Zone Books.

Clairvoyance, Cinema, and Consciousness[1]

Martha Blassnigg

The following chapter will present some outcomes of research into the topic of clairvoyance in a European context and the depiction of the spiritual in film in order to suggest that a cultural analysis of the phenomenon of clairvoyance can offer insights into the interrelation between the subject areas of cinema and consciousness. This research on clairvoyance began in 1997 as part of an interdisciplinary study arising out of the disciplines of Cultural Anthropology and Film Theory at the University of Amsterdam — it focussed on the phenomenon of the clairvoyant perception of angels and compared this with the treatment of the spiritual in film and the perception in cinema as multi-sensorial experiences. What follows will summarize these insights and situate them within a broader theoretical context in order to outline an initial discourse around the phenomenon of clairvoyance in an interdisciplinary discussion. In order to do so, this study will center on some aspects of the theoretical frameworks of Henri Bergson, Edgar Morin and Gilles Deleuze, all of whom share a philosophical basis that they have extended into the domains of cinema and the human mind; topics which have today found identity in distinct research disciplines.

In the discipline of Film Studies the discussion of film form as for example in popular cinema has been dominated by discourses around realism, while a more popular agenda of spiritual implications of the technology evident from the very beginning of its existence has remained hidden and underrated. When, what we now understand as cinema technology was being introduced to the public in the 1890s, the novelty occupied not only technicians, entrepreneurs and artists, but to some extent some contemporary scientists and thinkers concerned with the way the mind works. Amongst them was Henri Bergson who drew the cinema experience of his time into a discussion of cinema and consciousness when he stated that; "the mechanism of our ordinary knowledge is of a cinematographical kind" (Bergson 1964: 323) and demonstrates the necessary tendency of splitting the whole of matter into single sets of movements in space[2]. Cinema as technology, but equally important, the cinema experience and its implications for popular culture, as well as its relationship with science are crucial to a profound understanding of the alliances between the early cinema period and spiritualist practices of the time, particularly in the tradition of spirit photography. The extraordinary dimension to early cinema is best accounted for by understanding it as an expression of technology and the occult that was an undercurrent in the nineteenth century; in this respect it can be regarded as similar to esoteric tendencies in digital new media environments in recent years. To support this argument Michael Punt has shown in his work on cinema and film history how in its early years the cinema became pivotal in a dialogue between popular culture and science: not least because it embraced the paranormal and alternative approaches to science in its technological imaginary, after this had been abandoned by the established scientific community who wished to preserve the values of enlightenment science. Punt emphasizes how the scientific engine of cinema was not received as a device to enhance the impression and experience of 'reality', but that it was turned into a device of entertainment and the imaginary in popular culture that undermined the methods and paradigms of the professional scientific community (Punt 2000, 2005). Such a revision of attitudes to realism and a reconsideration of the history of the origins of cinema open up a discussion of the spiritual dimension in the cinema perception within film theory.

While Bergson treats the subject of cinema marginally, the novelty of his ideas has persisted in a variety of contemporary scientific fields. Gilles Deleuze in particular has taken up and resituated Bergson's thinking and applied it in his two books in which he develops a radical theory of cinema (first published in the 1980's). Bergson's importance, also with relevance to this research, lies in his establishment of a metaphysical correlation to modern science, combining scientific hypothesis and metaphysical thesis. This approach allows for a rigorous treatment of the subject of the 'spiritual', in this chapter defined as 'life force', 'breath of life', 'anime'[3], or as Bergson has called it 'elan vital'. In an interview in *Cahiers du cinéma* in 1986[4] after the publication of *Cinema 2: The Time Image,* Deleuze describes his initial fascination with cinema as "its unexpected ability to show not only behaviour but spiritual life [la vie spirituelle] as well" (Flaxman 2000: 366). This ability of cinema to enhance the spectator's perception, to some extent more drastically than other art forms have ever achieved, has on some occasions been treated ontologically as the 'magical' quality of cinema. The magical quality in this context has usually meant either the technology or the psychological effect or even the precondition of the human perception. In most cases, however, the notion of magic retains an understanding of the cinematographic experience within the unsatisfactory restrictions of a framework of representation and the dichotomies of body and mind or subject and object relations, as have been applied for example in the study of early cinema[5]. Deleuze's radicalism, however, offers an alternative approach in this context by invigorating Bergson's thinking in his cinema theory.

An exception to the general approach to the magic in cinema appeared in the 1950's in *Le Cinema ou l'Homme Imaginaire* by Edgar Morin. Morin transposed the idea of magic as an external force to an interiorized and subjective condition of an affective flux. When he talks about cosmomorphism and anthropo-morphism through the underlying principals of projection and identification, he applies an animistic worldview (he would call it a 'magic' one) where all beings and things are interrelated with each other and orthodox dualism dissolves. According to Morin, these psychological mechanisms consist of two important moments: the state of subjectivity and the state of the actual substantiation where the alienated, fixed, fetish projection becomes a 'thing': this, to Morin, is when one truly believes in duplicates, spirits, god, sorcery, possession or metamorphosis. Morin describes these spiritual entities as projections of our mind, as illusions, as the materialised duplicates of our mind. But nevertheless they effect and influence us and are part of one and the same perception, expressing a condition of immanence rather than transcendence; and in the case of cinema, this process of projection and identification integrates the spectator in the flux of the film, and the film into the psychical flux of the spectator.

Although never cited by Deleuze, despite relevant discussions of some of Bergson's ideas, Morin anticipated one of the most debated notions of Deleuze's cinema theory, a possible analogy between the screen and the brain[6], which is particularly evident when Morin writes on the anthropology of cinema and the cinematography of anthropos, exemplifying the imaginary reality of cinema and the imaginary reality of human beings. To him, all perceived forms of reality pass through our brain in the form of images: while similarly for Deleuze, based on Bergson's philosophy, the image has become thought (Deleuze 1995: 66); and "the brain becomes just one image among others" (Deleuze 1995: 42). Contrary to the orthodox visual concept of the image, Bergson understands images as 'things-as-they-appear' in between the realist notion of a 'thing' or object and the idealist notion of a representation. The moment of perception takes place in the thing to be perceived while internally, memories imbricate with the process of perception and shift from virtual into actual qualities (Bergson 2002). It could be claimed that cinema operates similarly with the virtual abilities of the human spirit as well as with the sensorial apparatus of our body — according to Morin it is an affective-magic flux:

> Cinema makes us understand not only the theatre, poetry, music, but also the interior theatre of the spirit: dreams, imaginations, representation: that little cinema that exists in our minds [7]. (1956: 207)

In this context Morin has introduced the concept of 'homo demens'[8], producer of fantasies, myths, ideologies and magic, understanding 'anthropos' as a complex spiritual, rational and emotional being. The implications of these concepts as they apply in particular to sensory perception are key to the consideration of the relationship between cinema and the spiritual, and this brings together Morin and Deleuze especially when the latter speaks of a cinema of thought. In this respect it is important to acknowledge that Deleuze makes clear that his comparison between the screen and the brain is not understood as a purely cognitive faculty:

> The whole of cinema can be assessed in terms of the cerebral circuits it establishes, simply because it's a moving image. Cerebral doesn't mean intellectual: the brain's emotive, impassioned too... (Deleuze 1995: 60)

Deleuze's notion that "the brain is the screen" is well-known and subject to widespread discussion[9]. It is based on Bergson's fundamental understanding of the whole of matter as a multiplicity of virtual images: "I call matter the aggregate of images, and perception of matter these same images referred to the eventual action of one particular image, my body" (Bergson 2002: 22). Although this concept forms a key to this chapter by relating cinema to the human mind, what follows is intended to move the debate in a new (although strongly related) direction, and will focus on the very implications of the affective qualities and the specific condition of time in Deleuze's approach that constitute contingent aspects in a parallel treatment of the cinema experience with the clairvoyant perception of the spiritual.

While the 'spiritual' is in theory commonly associated with a transcendental status in our thinking, in practice its perception is widely recognized as an immanent experience in various cultural contexts. Clairvoyance is a general term that refers to alleged psychic abilities to perceive things or events by an extended range of the power of our sensory system. It is associated with precognition, remote viewing, telepathy or extrasensory perception (ESP), which also includes clairaudience and sensations of a wider multi-sensorial range. It is commonly referred to as a prediction of the future, analogously as looking through a telescope, reducing the time it takes for the light or information from these distant places to reach our perception on earth. On the basis of my research however, I would like to suggest that clairvoyant perception can be better understood as a form of sensing comparable to a device such as the kaleidoscope, which breaks the very conditions of time and space we inhabit into various layers beyond the actual time and space coordinates. This confirms the clairvoyants' claims that spiritual perception, even remote in time (from the past or the future) takes place in the here and now, extending beyond the common systems of perception, resulting for example in the perception of auras or apparitions such as angels or the reappearance of the dead. In the best case (depending on the psychological constitution of the clairvoyant) it is a conscious activity that can be controlled and performed at will, and may be comparable to the creative process of 'becoming', establishing rhizomatic assemblages with the world and especially with other planes of consciousness.

Between 1997 and 2000 my research investigated experiences involved in the perception of clairvoyants in particular centring on the subject of angelic presences. The results were presented in a thesis and a documentary film (Blassnigg 2000), based on interviews with a number of Vienna-based clairvoyants who shared their experiences; and with artists who expressed their beliefs towards angels in their artworks. Through this research it was possible to outline some crucial underlying principles that seem to constitute the processes and experiences of the clairvoyant perception. To summarize briefly, these aspects include the importance of all the senses, and a call for a re-evaluation of their categorisation, as well as the deconstruction and extension of our three-dimensional perception and the condition of empathy in the communication with ethereal realms. When angelic presences appear in visions, it seems that they are not only perceived via internal images and inner voices, but clairvoyants distinguish them by particular scents and felt presences such as a tingling on the skin or colour and temperature sensations. Angels are characterized by their ubiquitous presence superceding the dimensions of time and space;

this is similar to the clairvoyant's access to past, present and future knowledge through the guidance of angels serving as intermediaries or interfaces. Some of these aspects are exemplified by the Austrian writer, Lotte Ingrisch in the following account (which one would be forgiven for confusing with a description of the cinema):

> It was on the 24th of June, when an angel suddenly answered. I sat in front of my typewriter in a trance-state and asked: 'Are those who are on the other side in the essence of love?' And none of them answered, then suddenly an angel replied: 'Love is the state of angels'. The following night, when I asked: 'Are you all present?', the angel replied: 'As many as you allow. We don't come or leave. We enter you when you are willing.' And I asked: 'Aren't we spatially separated?' The angel said: 'Not spatially nor temporally. Your own condition creates the illusion of distance.' And I said: 'Am I only dreaming you?' It said: 'We dream each other. But dream is the higher reality, the next stage.' Later on it said: 'Human beings seem to be something special. Not in their apparent hierarchy, but in their ability to merge with almost everything under certain circumstances.' The angel said: 'Everything flows whenever you finally start to flow. And everything is solid as long as you don't dissolve yourself'[10] (1996).

What is interesting here is that the clairvoyant worldview comprehends everything in the universe as being related and interconnected. The communication with spiritual realms in many cases functions via affect and telepathic understanding. The first observation resonates with Spinoza's understanding of one substance identified with God; and the second referring to telepathy, chimes with his notion of the first level of cognition in *Ethics*. This communication intends towards increasing an understanding of existential questions around life, spiritual realms and the universe in general, and it suggests that higher levels of cognition aim towards knowledge transfer, engagement and empowerment.

The fact that clairvoyance appears as a phenomenon of extra-sensory perception segues with ideas by Henri Bergson, Edgar Morin and Gilles Deleuze that in this context appear to be most useful in the way they shift focus from vision to the implication of the body as a whole in the process of perception. This establishes a discourse that decentralises vision as primary concept and as a consequence also questions the common term 'seer', which foregrounds vision in the range of clairvoyant abilities. As mentioned before, in this respect Deleuze makes clear that the brain in a comparison with the screen is not to be understood as a purely cognitive faculty, and he foregrounds the importance of the involved emotive qualities. This draws on Bergson's theory of perception, in which the brain as well as the whole body are instruments of action. Through the process of perception-affection-action the distinction between exterior movements/objects and the subjective affection of interior states unfolds and folds in one another and allows for the paradox of both states to co-exist. This segues with Deleuze's concept of the 'affection-image' that bears relevance to an understanding of clairvoyants's sensations as 'affection'[11]. Bergson has defined the affect as the interval between incoming perception and outgoing action (Bergson 2002: 233-234), and Deleuze shows that the affect has become one of the dominant expressions of contemporary cinema, as for example in the use of the close-up. According to Deleuze, in the 'affection-image' we no longer perceive space, the perception of space transforms into the perception of the dimension of time and the spirit: "the affection-image, (...), is abstracted from the spatio-temporal co-ordinates which would relate it to a state of things..."[12]. Dimensions of another order have opened: a fourth and fifth dimension, those of time and of spirit[13].

The affect can also be understood as 'being touched', as a form of touch in a more transitive sense referring to tactility and emotions. Although Deleuze does not refer here explicitly to the whole spectrum of the other senses, he creates a framework whereby we can think of them in totality[14]. In recent years, the senses themselves have gained increasing prominence in theoretical discussions[15]: while these usually adopt the common interpretation of an Aristotelian distinction of five separate perceptual experiences (analogous with the five elements: earth, air, fire, water and the quintessence), in the case of clairvoyance, the sensory perception is experienced in a rather transitive way pointing to an inner view rather than to ocular vision, to an inner voice rather than auditory perception and to touch as a virtual sensation, in the sense of feeling or being touched without physical contact[16]. In the expanded context of the clairvoyant's perception and affection of spiritual experiences, the orthodox scheme of the five senses proves to be a limited concept, which calls for a re-evaluation and possibly new definition of our sensory apparatus. Jojada Verrips has discussed this inadequacy extensively in his article "Haptic Screens' and Our 'Corporeal Eye", 2002, and offers an alternative by advocating a necessary epistemological shift from an "anthropology of the senses" to an "anthropology of the touch"; as touch, according to Verrips, involves an interplay of all the senses. By emphasizing the importance of the body, he sets a materially biased argument in contrast to the tendency to regard the body as a redundancy in the frequently claimed immateriality of contemporary technology environments such as in virtual

reality — an argument that can be extended to the commonly interpreted transcendent perception of spiritual experiences[17].

Verrips' emphasis on the sense of touch is pertinent with the way
Bergson acknowledges the faculty of touch in his theory of perception
when he states that; "there is nothing more in the visual perception of
the order of things in space than suggestion of tactile perception"
(Bergson 2002: 214). This aspect has also been pointed out by Ronald
Bogue with reference to Bergson's understanding of the body's surface as a site of both perception and the responding affection (Bogue
2003: 205). Significantly, touch in a commonly understood physical
sense is mostly related to our skin, the physical interface between us
and the world, analogous with the cinema screen and its pores breathing light and sound. Film and its expressions though, like spiritual
apparitions, enter directly into the affection of our mind and can touch
and make us feel, taste or smell; "It is through the body (and no longer
through the intermediary of the body) that cinema forms its alliance
with the spirit, with thought" (Deleuze 1989: 189).

In a comparison between the screen and the brain, the notion of the
'body' could at a first glance be overlooked and may seem expressed
by absence rather than by presence in terms of both the perceiver and
the perceived, though according to the previous discussion and in
particular the thinking of Bergson, it should be seen as an integral part
in the perceptive-affective process and as an alliance with the mind. In
addition to the implication of the body in the process of perception, it
is in a shift to content, where a discussion of the body also plays a
crucial role: in particular the immaterial, ethereal quality of the bodies
in the clairvoyant's encounter with apparitions[18]. In cinema the actors
themselves appear already without material bodies, but because of the
cinematographic illusion we are meant to perceive them as human
beings like ourselves. Patricia Pisters reminds us in this same collection that our neuro-system creates sensations in response to imaginary
stimuli, which are indistinguishable from those triggered by real
events. This is the very threshold by which Deleuze's cinema theory
builds on Bergson by referring to perception, even to the whole of
matter, in terms of images. Bogue points out that "If things are light,
then what we commonly call visual images, whether directly perceptual or cinematic, are made of the same 'matter'"; the image in itself is
a virtual image of a 'thing in the world' (Bogue 2003: 34). In this
connection Deleuze cites Jean-Louis Schefer when he speaks about
'unknown bodies' still hidden from our view, disturbances of the
visual and suspensions in our perception:

... the object of cinema is not to reconstitute a presence of bodies, in perception and action, but to carry out a primordial genesis of bodies in terms of a white, or a black or a grey (or even in terms of colours), in terms of a 'beginning of visible which is not yet a figure, which is not yet an action' (Deleuze 1989: 201).

This chimes with the earlier writings of Morin who proclaimed cinema as consisting of shapes of light and ghost-like apparitions: "... cinema itself has become a world of spirits where phantoms manifest themselves like a great number of the archaic mythologies: an ethereal world filled with omnipresent spirits"(Morin 1956: 43). In a further complication, whenever cinema shows 'incorporated' apparitions like spirits, ghosts or angels, it has to make clear in an explicit way that they represent apparitions next to the characters in the movie[19]. In a reversed analogy, Dovjenko prophesised in 1931 a cinema without screen, where the spectator would watch the film as if he found himself in the middle of the action. In this vision, the cinema screen has dissolved in space and has become itself a world of spirits where phantoms manifest themselves in great numbers of archaic mythologies: an ethereal world filled with omnipresent spirits (Morin 1956: 49). Morin has pushed this thought further in his vision of the future cinema, the 'telecinema futur' where in a correlation with our duplicates we would be surrounded by our own phantoms and virtual imaginations — possibly an analogy and an external visualisation of our regular psychical processes, the ultimate haptic exemplification of our mental apparatus, a Bergsonean universe of virtual images? To make this happen, according to Morin, cinema needs our participation for the characters on the screen to take our souls and bodies to become alive, fitting them to their measures and passions; "It is us who in the dark cinema space are their very phantoms, their ectoplasmic spectators. Provisionally dead, we watch the living..." (Morin 1956: 49). Contrary to the surpassed understanding of a passive audience, for Deleuze (and as it also is sometimes exemplified in films treating subjects such as death, ghosts and other spiritual apparitions) it is not a question of presence or absence of the body, but "that of a belief which is capable of restoring the world and the body to us on the basis of what signifies their absence" (Deleuze 1989: 202). This is one of the moments when Deleuze extends the framework of film theory in his cinema books to a wider philosophical implication of the cinematographic experience to his philosophy of the immanence of life. According to him, cinema does not treat stories any longer, but 'becomings', a concept deriving from Bergson and Nietzsche's theory of forces that sees being as essential flux, without sustainable stability or continuity. In this sense the concept of 'becoming' and not 'being' is the only possible way to think the chaotic reality and therefore thinking is a thinking in events, a constant change, a constant creation, fragmented in its mechanisms, yet thought of as a whole — comparable to the filmstrip running through the projector frame by frame, while always already existing in its entirety, perceived by our mind-bodies in the screen:

> But the whole is of a different nature, it relates to time: it ranges over all sets of things, and it's precisely what stops them completely fulfilling their own tendency to become completely closed. Bergson's always saying that Time is the Open, is what changes — is constantly changing nature — each moment. It's the whole, which isn't any set of things but the ceaseless passage from one set to another, the transformation of one set of things into another (Deleuze 1995: 55).

To understand objects as discrete as well as interrelated in expressions of duration — that is the Whole, and perception as being placed in the perceived objects and not the perceiver, implicates that the distinction between internal and external, between subject and object is (at least temporarily) overcome, as the 'spiritual' or 'virtual' not merely communicates with the 'material' but enters into a communion and mutual exchange. This displacement of the subject during perception into 'things' and the affection in the body in Bergson supports Morin's claim that the spectator becomes part of the flux of the film, entering perspectives and experiences of multiple characters in the movie[20], and part of the film's implications and suggestions enter the domain of the psychic/mental experiences of the spectator.

This is reflected in Deleuze as he moves away from the idea of 'a truth' or 'the real', by transposing his discourse around the 'actual' (the perceived) and the 'virtual' (memory, past), as defined by Bergson in *Matter and Memory*[21]. A practice of clairvoyance cannot promote a claim for a general truth either as it brings forth internal, subjective perceptions that underlie a condition of relativity in the sense of a Radical Constructivism, which advocates that "knowledge is a self-organised cognitive process of the human 'brain'. It is not aimed at a 'true' image of the 'real' world but at a viable organisation of the world as it is experienced"[22]. In my own research on clairvoyance it has never been a question as to whether extra-sensory perception/affection is for 'real' or not, or if angels exist ontologically or not. Clairvoyants perceive of such experiences not as illusions but as 'actual' events[23]; in this sense I shift the focus from the spiritual as belief to the spiritual as experience. This can be accounted for by Bergson's theory on perception and the hereto related qualities of Deleuze's 'time-image', which obliterate the dichotomy between the real and the imaginary, when the actual image enters in relation with its own virtual image as such:

> For the 'time-image' to be born, the actual image must enter into relation with its own virtual image as such; for the outset pure description must divide in two, 'repeat itself, take itself up again, fork, contradict itself'. An image which is double-sided, mutual, both actual and virtual, must be constituted (Deleuze 1989: 273).

With the concept of the 'time-image', drawing on Bergson's concept of 'durée', Deleuze defines a dimension where virtual images are in constant flux and oscillation between past, present and future, sometimes transforming into crystal images, opening up to a dimension of the spirit. According to him it is "this pure force of time which puts truth into crisis" (Deleuze 1989: 130). Cinema exemplifies this at its best, as it synthesizes fragmented time in three main aspects: the recording process fragments movements into single images; projection technology realigns these images as apparent sequential movement through the trick of holding each image still for a fracture of time while interrupting the light-beam twice by the shutter. Consequently the practice of montage has borne a new, fluid time, in which present, past and future overlap and intermingle. The film performance expresses a past, technologically actualised in the present of the spectators perception; in other words, every image itself already implies the character of the past: as the present we perceive is always already past. The cinematographic, translucent images in which time oscillates, can be compared to time experiences of clairvoyants who sometimes become affected with events happening in different moments in the past, the present or the future. Time becomes a new quality and expresses change in a constant flux:

> This is what happens when the image becomes time-image. The world has become memory, brain, superimposition of ages or lobes, but the brain itself has become consciousness, continuation of ages, creation or growth of ever new lobes, recreation of matter as with styrene. The screen itself is the cerebral membrane where immediate and direct confrontations take place between the past and the future, the inside and the outside, at a distance impossible to determine, independent of any fixed point. The image no longer has space and movement as its primary characteristics but topology and time (Deleuze 1989: 125).

The constant flux and change of our lives in a Bergsonean understanding describes human life as a transforming process of 'becoming'. It is not so much a transformation from one state into another, as
it is a fundamental principal of life of a constantly changing and
transforming movement going on in one's self. Cinema itself is a
place where we, as spectators, enforce the state of 'becoming' and
create translucent time-crystals in our perception as described by
Deleuze. We not only revisit memories both from the film and our
personal associations through recollection-images, but our minds enter
a flux of continuous exchange and transformation of images, it is, in a
Deleuzean understanding, itself an image, never to be grasped because
of its fluid and gaseous condition. The crystalline images in this way
open up to a new dimension, which Deleuze also calls the fifth dimension, which is profoundly spiritual (1989: 178).

To return briefly to Morin and his claim that it is the magic quality
that gives a body to the past, to memories and souvenirs, we can see
that it is in a similar sense that he speaks of a magical time, and also
of a psychological time, which he defines as subjective and affective.
Like Deleuze he refers to Bergson's concept of time:

> ... where past, present and future oscillate as in a state of osmosis just as in
> the human brain, memories, the imaginary future and the experienced mo-
> ment merge. This Bergsonean duration, the perceivable indefinite, it is the
> cinema that defines it (Morin 1956: 69).

Bergson's term *durée* (duration) extends itself from past to future
without interruption, and without that survival of the past in the present there would only be instantaneity. Therefore Bergson's *durée* is
something continually present and moving, a perpetual present similar
to how Lotte Ingrisch has perceived of the subjectivity of the condition of time while investigating the state of angels[24]. Deleuze interprets this Bergsonean understanding of time as follows:

> ... the only subjectivity is time, non-chronological time grasped in its foun-
> dation, and it is we who are internal to time, not the other way around. (...)
> Time is not the interior in us, but just the opposite, the interiority in which
> we are, in which we move, live and change. (...) Subjectivity is never ours,
> it is time, that is, the soul or the spirit, the virtual. The actual is always ob-
> jective, but the virtual is subjective: it was initially the affect, that which we
> experience in time; then time itself, pure virtuality which divides itself in
> two as affector and affected, 'the affection of self by self' as definition of
> time (Deleuze 1989: 82-83).

The inclusion of the discussion of consciousness (as for example introduced by Bergson in *Matter and Memory*), and in particular Gilles Deleuze's insights into the time-image cinema, draw us inexorably into the clairvoyant experience: the actors become seers (or should we call them 'pro-active sensors'?) and take over the part of the gaze of the spectator and transform it into a 'conscious seeing' (or sensing). The spectators themselves become 'seers' too, when they open their minds and bodies, in short all their senses to the cinematographic experience, which then becomes an event rather than a representation.[25]

Most importantly, as Bogue has pointed out, consciousness in a Bergsonean understanding is not anymore the agency illuminating the dark, but is itself a constituent component of light. He quotes Deleuze; "In short, it is not consciousness that is light, it is the set of images, or light, that is consciousness, immanent within matter" (Bogue 2003: 35). Spiritual seers and mediums, according to this research, merely manifest amplified capacities that exist in all of us and as a consequence, by this amplification they can render us 'seers', too, through their mediation, they can make us feel, perceive and understand through an extension of our own consciousness. By embracing the spiritual in the discussion, we can understand cinema as an expression of a variety of events embedded within the scope of our consciousness — or instead in a Bergsonean universe — our consciousness embedded within the 'matter-flow' or 'image-movement', in "the universe as cinema in itself, a metacinema" (Bogue 2003: 35), where the dancing beam of light between the image held in the gate of the projector and the screen becomes the pivot of his philosophy and diverts our focus away from the screen. In such a shift of attention the agents, mediators and receptors involved become entangled and interrelated: the mind, the screen, the skin, the emulsion layer of celluloid, light and sound vibrations, screen characters and angels, they all become refracted in a sensorial kaleidoscope of our internal crystallized perception.

Bibliography

Ackerman, D. 1990. *A Natural History of the Senses*. New York: Random House Inc.

Barker, J. 1998. 'Fascinating Rhythms: The Visceral Pleasure of the Cinema' in *Come to Your Senses! Event and Engagement —*

Workshop Reader, ASCA conference 25-29 May 1998, Amsterdam: 05-08.

Barnouw, E. 1981. *The Magician and the Cinema*. Oxford: Oxford University Press.

Bedicheck, R. 1960. *The Sense of Smell*. London: Michael Joseph Ltd.

Bergson, H. 2002. *Matter and Memory*, trans. N.M Paul and W.S. Palmer (*Matière et Mémoire*, 1896). New York: Zone Books.

— 1992. *The Creative Mind*, trans. Mabelle L. Andison (*La Pensée et le Mouvant*. 1946). New York: The Citadel Press.

— 1980. *Introduction to Metaphysics*. Indianapolis: Bobbs-Merrill.

— 1964. *Creative Evolution*, trans. Arthur Mitchell (*L'Evolution Creative*, 1907). London: MacMillan & Co Ltd.

— 1920. *Mind Energy*, trans. H. Wildon Carr (*L'Energie Spirituelle*, 1919). London: McMillan and Company.

— 1919. *Time and Free Will*, trans. F.L. Pogson. London: George Alenand Unwin. (*Essai Sur les Données Immédiates de la Conscience*, 1889).

Blassnigg, M. 2000. *Seeing Angels and the Spiritual in Film: An Interdisciplinary Study of a Sensuous Experience*. Unpublished MA-Thesis at the University of Amsterdam, Film Theory (Dep. Media and Culture) and Cultural Anthropology (and Non-Western Sociology).

— 2000. *Shapes of Light*. Documentary Film. Digital Video, 35 min. Vienna.

Bogue, R. (2003). *Deleuze on Cinema*. New York and London: Routledge.

Classen, C. (ed.) 2005. *The Book of Touch*. Oxford: Berg Publishers.

— 1998. *The Colors of Angels. Cosmology, Gender and the Aesthetic Imagination*. New York: Routledge.

— 1993. *Worlds of Sense. Exploring the Senses in History and Across Cultures*. London and New York: Routledge.

Classen, C., Howes D., and Synnott A. 1994. *Aroma. The Cultural History of Smell*. London and New York: Routledge.

Deleuze, G. 1997. Immanence. A Life... . In *Theory, Culture & Society. Explorations in Critical Social Science*. SAGE Publications: 14(2).

— 1995. *Negotiations. 1972-1990*. New York: Columbia University Press.

— 1993. *The Deleuze Reader*, ed. Constantin V. Boundas. New York: Columbia University Press.

— 1993. *The Fold. Leibniz and the Baroque*. London: Athlone Press.

— 1991. *Bergsonism*, trans. Hugh Tomlinson and Barbara Habberjam. New York: Zone Books. (*Le Bergsonisme*, 1966).

— 1986. *Cinema 1. The Movement-Image*. London: The Athlone Press. (*Cinéma 1: L'Image-Movement*, 1983).

— 1989. *Cinema 2. The Time-Image*. London: The Athlone Press. (*Cinéma 2: L'Image-Temps*, 1985).

Flaxman , G. 2000. *The Brain is the Screen. Deleuze and the Philosophy of Cinema*. Minneapolis: University of Minnesota Press.

Gunning, T. 1995. 'Phantom Images and Modern Manifestations: Spirit Photography, Magic Theater, Trick Films and Photography's Uncanny' in Patrice, P. *Fugitive Images: From Photography to Video*. Bloomington: Indiana University Press: 42-71.

Howes, D. (ed.) 2004. *Empire of the Senses: The Sensual Culture Reader*. Oxford and New York: Berg Publishers.

— 2003. *Sensual Relations: Engaging the Senses in Culture and Social Theory*. Ann Arbor, MI: University of Michigan Press.

— (ed.) 1991. *The Varieties of Sensory Experience: A Sourcebook in the Anthropology of the Senses*. Toronto: University of Toronto Press.

Ingrisch, L. 1996. *Das Leben beginnt mit dem Tod*. Wien: Verlag Österreichische Staatsdruckerei.

Moore, R. 2000. *Savage Theory. Cinema as Modern Magic*. Durham and London: Duke University Press.

Morgan, M.L. 2002 (ed.) *Baruch Spinoza: The Complete Works*. (Trans.) Samuel Shireley. Indianapolis: Hackett.

Morin, E. 1956. *Le Cinema ou l'Homme Imaginaire. Essay d'Anthropologie*. Paris: Les Editions de Minuit.

— 2005. *The Cinema, or The Imaginary Man*. (Trans.) Lorraine Mortimer. Minneapolis: University of Minnesota Press.

Pisters, P. 2003. *The Matrix of Visual Culture. Working with Deleuze in Film Theory*. USA: Stanford University Press.

— (ed.) 2001. *Micropolitics of Media Culture*. Amsterdam University Press.

— 1998. *From Eye to Brain. Gilles Deleuze: Refiguring the Subject in Film Theory*. Wageningen: Ponsen & Looijen.

Van der Pol, G. 1998. 'Angelic Touch'. *Come to your senses! Event and Engagement*, 64. Workshop Reader, ASCA conference 25-29 May 1998, Amsterdam.

Punt, M. 2005. 'What the Film Archive Can Tell Us About Technology in the Post-digital Era' in: *Design Issues*. 21(2): 48-62.

— 2000. *Early Cinema and the Technological Imaginary*. Trowbridge, Wiltshire: Cromwell Press.

Scruton, R. 2002. *Spinoza. A Very Short Introduction*. Oxford: Oxford University Press.

Seremetakis, N. 1994. *The Senses Still. Perception and Memory as Material Culture in Modernity*. Boulder: Westview Press Inc.

Sobchak, V. 2004. *Carnal Thoughts. Embodiment and Moving Image Culture*. Berkeley: University of California Press.

Stowasser, J.M., Losek F. 1994. *Der kleine Stowasser, Lateinisch-Deutsches Schulwörterbuch*. Oldenbourg Schulbuchverlag.

Stoller, P. 1986. *The Taste of Ethnographic Things*. University of Pennsylvania Press.

Verrips, J. 2005. Ecstasis, 'Aesthesis' and Cultural Anaesthesia. Keynote at the "Tage der Kultur-und Socialanthropologie" at the University of Vienna, 24-25 June 2005. (Unpublished keynote address).

— 2002. 'Haptic Screens and Our Corporeal Eye' in: *Etnofoor. Anthropologisch tijdschrift. Screens*. Amsterdam: Krips Repro, Meppel: 21-46.

Notes

[1] In this chapter the terms mind, brain and consciousness are used in ways which would undoubtedly be contentious in other circumstances. Here they are used simply to draw attention to some of the key concepts in the discussion of this topic. Where possible I have tried to retain Gilles Deleuze's specific use of the terms in his film theory.

[2] Ronald Bogue gives a very clear introduction to Bergson's impact on Deleuze's cinema theory; he states in this context: "Sets are merely subdivisions of the whole, but subdivisions whose organization creates the cinematographic illusion of solid bodies in a homogeneous space and an abstract time." Bogue, 2003, p. 25-26.

[3] From the Latin term 'spiritus' meaning 'breath' — in Greek the term 'psyche' stood for the principle of animation or life (Stowasser & Losek 1994). Translation from German by the author.

[4] *Cahiers du Cinema:* Issue 380: 25-32. Quoted in Flaxman 2000.

[5] See for example Moore 2000, Gunning 1995, and Barnouw 1981.

[6] The functions of the brain still seem to raise questions within the discipline of neuro-science. In *Matter and Memory*, Bergson has demystified the brain as functioning as storage for information and instead ascribes to it the coordination of perceptions with motor mechanisms that put the body in action. For contemporary discussions on the issue of the brain versus the mind and consciousness, see for examples the 6th Swiss Biennial on Science, Technics + Aesthetics on Consciousness and Teleportation, January 2005, Neue Galerie Luzern:

http://www.neugalu.ch/e_bienn_2005.html or the 7th Biennial Conference Toward a Science of Consciousness 2006 in Tucson: http://consciousness.arizona.edu/Tucson2006.htm.

[7] Translation by the author.

[8] 'Demens' derives from Latin meaning mad, senseless, insane, foolish, crazy. 'Dementia' refers to foolishness, insanity, madness (Stowasser 1994). Translation from German by the author.

[9] See for example Pisters 2003, or Flaxman 2000.

[10] The Austrian writer Lotte Ingrisch perceived this excerpt of a longer scéance while typing on her typewriter in a half-trance (Ingrisch 1996). Translation by the author.

[11] Ronald Bogue points out that Bergson does use the terms of 'sensation' and 'affection' in *Matter and Memory* somewhat casually. For the purpose of this chapter, I do not consider the distinction between the two as essential and treat them as interconnected (Bogue 2003: 205).

[12] The affection image lies in-between the 'perception-image' and the 'action-image', and finds its existence between a perception that is troubling in certain respects and a hesitant action. This is the moment when movement becomes an expression of power or a quality, producing pure optical- and sound situations (Deleuze 1986: 79).

[13] Patricia Pisters elaborates the argument of the spiritual in Deleuze's film theory more profoundly in her current research, as for example in this same collection in the chapter, *The Spiritual Dimension of the Brain as Screen — Zigzagging from Cosmos to Earth (and Back)*.

[14] C. Nadia Seremetakis states: "Although Deleuze's cognitations on taxonomies of the cinematic image are intellectually breathtaking, they describe abstractly the unique sensuousness of the cinema" (Seremetakis 1994: 111).

[15] See for example Ackerman 1990; Bedichek 1960; Classen 1993, 1998, 2005, Classen et al. 1994; Howes, 1991, 2003, 2004; Seremetakis 1994; Sobchak 2004; Stoller 1986.)

[16] In recent years film scholars have been working on the involvement of the whole range of the senses in the perception of the cinematographic experience, an approach that treats cinema as event rather than as a pure representation. See for example Jennifer M. Barker and her work on the haptic and visceral effects of cinema (Barker 1998) or Gerwin van der Pol who describes the haptic sensation of touch in cinema as the intention to touch in a more subtle sense: "Touch is not to hold, not to be in constant contact with something or someone else. Touch is a very momentary phase in a sequence of two subjects wanting to touch, touching, and having touched" (Van der Pol 1998).

[17] In his most recent article Verrips brings 'Aisthesis' to attention, the concept of a perception through all our corporeal senses, which has lost its original meaning to an emphasis on vision. 'Aisthesis' can be traced back to a less conventional interpretation of Aristotle's concept of the five senses in his *De Anima* in which they ultimately constitute an undividable whole; in this respect Verrips refers amongst others to the related 18th century term of 'Aesthetica', originally the science of sensitive knowing, which appears to bear relevance to an understanding of the clairvoyant perception (Verrips 2005).

[18] The German word 'feinstofflich' (ethereal or literally 'fine-material') expresses still the material, just a finer quality of matter. In this sense, the ethereal can be understood not as merely immaterial and 'without matter', but as a finer degree of matter or frequency. In this

respect it is interesting, as Bogue has pointed out, that Bergson understands *durée* as 'vibrational whole', and 'image-movement' and 'matter-flow' are strictly the same thing (Bogue 2003: 32-33).

[19] Kenji Mizoguchi succeeds with *Ugetsu Monogatari* (Japan 1953) in such an exercise with mastery without using the usual tricks of superimposition or transparent bodies, wings for angels or horrifying scares for the dead, when at the end of the film Genjuro returns to his wife who has died and merely through cinematographic mastery of camera work, lighting and editing, a dimension of an after-life is being created amongst the living. In more recent film history, Wim Wenders has become a classic for angelic presences in film beyond their stereotypical winged depiction with his *Wings of Desire* (1987), and the movies *The Sixth Sense* (1999) and *The Others* (2001) for example both play with the indistinguishable appearance of the dead and the living.

[20] The 'movie' is an adequate term in this context, as it aims to 'move' the spectators in an affective way.

[21] Bogue summarizes; "The past is conserved not in the material brain but in itself, and all past moments coexist in a virtual dimension" (Bogue 2003: 15).

[22] Although the use of the terms 'brain', 'true' and 'real' is problematic, as partially recognized through the parenthesis in the quote, it gives a general sense of how this concept can be understood in this context.
https://tspace.library.utoronto.ca/citd/holtorf/3.8.html

[23] The verb 'perceive' in German, 'wahrnehmen' is illuminating in this respect, as it could directly be translated into 'taken as true'.

[24] See quote on page 110 and footnote 10.

[25] The idea of opening up the body (and mind) to the world correlates with Morin's concept of cosmomorphisme mentioned earlier whereby the body gets penetrated by the cosmos. Deleuze refers to a similar event when he mentions that Jean Rouch through his films and ethnographic work actually became 'the other'; "Sometimes it is a character himself crossing a limit, and becoming another, in an act of story-telling which connects him to a people past or to come..." (Deleuze 1989: 275). In a different context this also resonates with Paul Stoller who advocates an aesthetic approach to scientific research in *The Taste of Ethnographic Things*, which does not exclude the actions of subjective data gathering and objective data analysis from one another. He suggests that like artists, scientists should open their 'bodies' to the world in order not only to penetrate the universe, but to let their senses be penetrated by the world and transform from scientific 'spectators into seers' (Stoller 1986: 40).

The Spiritual Dimension of the Brain as Screen Zigzagging from Cosmos to Earth (and Back)

Patricia Pisters

By connecting neurobiological findings to cinema and to Gilles Deleuze's philosophical claim that 'the brain is the screen', this chapter will look at the spiritual dimension of the brain. Considering a movie like a programme that is run on a processor, which is the mind, it will be argued that movies can modify our subjectivities such that the brain and mind are one. By focussing on the non-material qualities of the so-called cinematic 'time-image', the ways in which a spiritual dimension can manifest itself within the image and the brain will be looked at. Spirituality is thereby not defined as something ungraspable and transcendent but it is related to the domain of a 'cold choice'. Analyses of the films, 'Tierra' (1996) and 'Signs' (2002) will make these points clear.

In *The Abecedaire of Gilles Deleuze* as the last letter of the alphabet, Claire Parnet proposes the word 'zigzag'[1]. Deleuze loves ending with this word. 'There is no word after zigzag', Deleuze says, 'Zed is a great letter that establishes a return to A'. Zed as movement of the fly, as movement of lightening, is perhaps the elementary movement that presides at the creation of the world. Deleuze even proposes to replace the Big Bang by 'le zigzag'. For the creation of a universe, for any universe, for everything there is, he argues that the most elementary question is: How can a connection between two singular points, between two different fields of forces be created? One can imagine a chaos of potentials, so how to bring these into relation?

According to Deleuze, everything consists of connection, and these connections are rarely made in a linear or predictable fashion. Each connection is however prepared by a 'sombre precursor'. The trajectory of the sombre precursor is barely noticed, but brings about a reaction between two points/forces. And then we have the lightening, 'le zigzag', that creates an insight ('l'éclair qui fait voir'). This lightening (seen as a metaphor, but also literally as strikes of lightening and geometric patterns) can be brought about by philosophy, art and science. And what's more, philosophy, art and science need each other for comprehension[2]. In this chapter I hope to establish a few zigzagging movements and connections between philosophical, artistic and scientific thoughts associated with Deleuze's famous expression that 'the brain is the screen'[3]. Wondering about the spiritual potential of the brain as screen, the 'flashes of insight' are sparked off by a few Deleuzian concepts, some observations in neurobiology and Julio Medem's film *Tierra* (1996). At eye level, through the brain and the movements of its thoughts, this will take us on a travel from the enormity of the cosmos to the micro organization of the earth.

Flash One: *Tierra* — From Cosmos to Earth

Lightening is literally the most important feature and sign in *Tierra*. It is also a sign of the various zigzagging connections that will be made during the film. At the beginning of the film, Angel (Carmelo Gómes) arrives at an island where he is supposed to fumigate woodlice from the soil. The landscape he drives through is struck by lightening: the trees, a few sheep and their herd are all electrocuted. During the title sequence, just before Angel's arrival, the camera has moved from a cosmic space to the island and into the soil:

> *Camera moves through a cosmic night. Angel's voice-over:*
> Death is nothing but if you were completely dead you wouldn't hear me. So you're here Angel, in the middle of the widest, most unknown ocean you can imagine. Existence is accompanied by an inevitable background noise called anguish, which we can only half bear. But don't despair, you live in the only known light in the universe.
> *Camera descends and moves through the clouds to the earth seen from above:*
> A tiny island which is at your eye-level, but riddled with holes of mystery.
> *Extreme close-ups from woodlice in the soil:*
> A mystery: the woodlice, less than an inch, with twelve legs, it is what gives the wines of this area their earthy flavour.
> *Back to the cosmos again:*
> Another mystery — me. I am the part of you that died and I speak from the cosmos. You have transcended in life like the woodlice in wine. But you're the one who's here for something.
> *Angel driving in his car saying:*
> Come on! I'm half man, half angel, half alive, half dead. I'm the voice that speaks from your mind, uncontrollably.

Right from the beginning of the film, earthly qualities are mixed with celestial powers: the connection between the woodlice and the Angel; Angel declaring himself half man, half angel; half alive, half dead. Within the film, a logical explanation is given for this: Angel has been a psychiatric patient with a very big imagination and a split personality. He is almost cured and — perhaps as a sort of therapy — he has been given the assignment to fumigate the woodlice from the soil of the island. Here he will meet two women, Angela (Emma Suárez) and Mari (Silke). He feels attracted to both of them (his Angel side loves Angela, his man side prefers Mari) and a beautiful strange love story unfolds in which reality and surreality perfectly blend.

So at the level of the film's story, we see through Angel's eyes and Angel's schizophrenic brain tells us what to see and understand. But at another level, a meta-theoretical reading of the film that goes beyond the idea of a disturbed mind is also possible. At the end of the film, Angel refers to the brain explicitly. At the breakfast table with Angela, Mari and Alberto (Mari's brother, played by Nancho Novo) he asks: "Did you know that our brain contains a universe of 10,000 million neurons and 1,000 billion circuits? It only occupies 1,500 cubic centimetres. And it hides a black ocean that's unknown. There is no light. But it generates disorder. Its laws obey chance, so it makes a lot of mistakes. And it's a machine that makes noise, although you don't hear mental noise. Like cosmic dust, which I've never seen, have you?" This and other remarks by Angel, which will be addressed later in this chapter, allow investigating further into the film's philosophical idea of 'the brain as screen' and its relations to the cosmic and spiritual forces of life.

Flash Two: Deleuze — The Brain is the Screen

In the eighties Deleuze argued that the (then) current ways of studying cinema through models of linguistics and psychoanalysis, are not the most productive ways of understanding what cinema does. Deleuze sees a profound parallel to the way in which philosophy brings movement to thought and cinema brings movement to image: 'I went straight from philosophy to cinema and from cinema to philosophy'[4]. If there is a model, he says, we should look at the biology of the brain:

> The brain is unity. The brain is the screen. I don't believe that linguistics and psychoanalysis offer a great deal to the cinema. On the contrary, the biology of the brain — molecular biology — does. Thought is molecular. Molecular speeds make up the slow beings that we are. (...) The circuits and

linkages of the brain don't pre-exist the stimuli, corpuscles, and particles that trace them. (…) Cinema, precisely because it puts the image in motion, or rather endows the image with self-motion, never stops tracing the circuits of the brain (Flaxman 2000).

What Deleuze prefers in the biology of the brain is that it doesn't have the drawback of the other two disciplines of applying ready-made concepts: "We can consider the brain as a relatively undifferentiated mass and ask what circuits, the movement-image or time-image trace out, or invent, because the circuits aren't there to begin with" (Deleuze 1995: 60). In the conclusion of *What is Philosophy?*; entitled 'From Chaos to the Brain', Deleuze and Guattari argue that the brain is central to not only philosophy, but also art and science. Together they are the three aspects under which a brain becomes subject, 'thought-brain' (Deleuze & Guattari 1994: 210). It is the brain that thinks in the 'I conceive' of philosophy, the 'I feel or perceive' of art and the 'I know or I function' of science. In all three domains the brain confronts chaos. Chaos should be seen at the level of both the vastness of the universe and the microscopic (and smaller) level of the atoms. It's all a matter-flow of images that Deleuze calls the plane of immanence. In *Cinema 1: The Movement-Image,* he says; "It is rather a gaseous state. Me, my body, are rather a set of molecules and atoms which are constantly renewed. Can I even speak of atoms? They are not distinct from worlds, from interatomic influences. It is a state too hot for one to be able to distinguish solid bodies in it. It is a world of universal variation, of universal undulation, universal rippling" (1986: 58). By creating thoughts; philosophy, art and science refer back to chaos rendered consistent, like a mental 'chaosmos'.

Chaos however, is not the biggest struggle that philosophy, art and science need to fight. A much worse enemy is opinion. The misfortune of people comes from opinion, Deleuze and Guattari argue. It is quite understandable why opinions are so attractive: they seem to protect us from chaos like an umbrella. As Deleuze and Guattari explain; "We constantly loose our ideas. That's why we want to hang on to fixed opinions so much" (1994: 204). Philosophy, art and science however, want us to tear open the umbrella and plunge into chaos, "to let in a bit of free and windy chaos and to frame in a sudden light a vision that appears through the rent" (1994: 203). And the brain is the junction (not the unity) of the three planes. So this is not to say that these disciplines are all the same, or that they have to reflect on each other. Deleuze argues that the encounter between different disciplines starts when one discipline realizes that it has to resolve, for itself and by its own means, a problem similar to the one confronted by the other (1986: 367). So let us then look at some of the problems that film philosophy and sciences of the brain have in common[5].

Flash Three: Transdisciplinary Encounters — Neurobiology[6]

In *The Reality of Illusion*, Joseph Anderson gives an ecological approach to cognitive film theory, looking at the biological organisation of the brain and the modulations and changes that take place into the brain in perception and cognition of perception. One of the central problems in film theory addresses the question of reality or illusory characteristics of the film image. Usually there are two opposite schools of thought. On the one hand film is seen as the ultimate realistic form of art (Bazin, Kracauer), on the other hand is film considered to be the perfect illusory or artificial form of art (Metz, Eisenstein). Anderson now looks for instance at the Necker cube to see whether this can shed a new light on the problem. The Necker cube is a visual illusion: When you stare at the wire frame model of a cube for a while, the cube seems to flip its orientation between two possible interpretations of the picture. He then relates this to film viewing, stating that:

> It is not a matter of being in a semihypnotic state in a darkened theatre. It is not a matter of suspending disbelief. It is not a matter of being 'positioned' as a spectator or 'sutured' into a text, and it has nothing to do with dreaming. It is instead our perceptual system alternating between two incompatible sets of information (a three dimensional world or a flat screen with shadows on it) (1997: 48).

Luckily our brain has more areas and the neo-cortex can then process this visual information and generate thought, focus attention at will, and learn. Information is processed simultaneously through several modules of the brain in order to react on visual input and it does so at a high reaction speed. The visual system sees, the cortex interprets. And there is always the possibility of illusion, in which "the system follows its own internal structures, but arrives at a percept that is in error if compared to physical reality" (Anderson 1997: 20). Film viewing is such an illusion, but nevertheless one that triggers the activation of information within the neo-cortex, which allows us not only to see, but also to understand, learn from and interpret visual information. The workings of perception of reality and illusory perception of reality (like cinema) are quite similar.

Another phenomenon from the biology of the brain that demonstrates the similarity between the perception of reality and the perception of film is the so-called 'mirror-neuron'. Mirror-neurons are fired when we actually do something, but the same neurons are also fired when we see (or hear) somebody doing something[7]. And for the brain there is no difference between seeing someone in reality or seeing someone on film. Something we see literally touches areas in the brain that imitate the perceived actions or feelings. This means that images should not be considered as re-presentations of an objective reality, but that images have an internal power that creates certain effects in the brain. As Antonio Damasio argues in his book *Looking for Spinoza,* neural patterns and corresponding mental projections of objects and events outside the brain are creations of the brain that are related to the reality that causes these creations, but not a passive reflection of this reality[8]. Mirror-neurons and the way in which the brain is affected by images can give insights into the implications of Deleuze's 'the brain is the screen' for film theory, which still very often takes representation (albeit not only as a reflection of reality) as a starting point for thinking about the image.

Flash Four: Medem — Deleuze — Time-Image

Moving now from a meta-theoretical level to a theoretical level, the phenomenon of mirror-neurons, also shows how this is compatible with Deleuze's own classifications of images in his cinema books. In *The Movement-Image,* Deleuze classifies image categories such as the action-image, the affection-image, the impulse-image, the relation-image: they cause action, affection, impulses or thoughts in the brain. They touch the brain directly and as such they also modify our subjectivities; they are, what Deleuze calls 'material aspects' of our subjectivity in which the brain and the mind are one. In the time-image Deleuze also distinguishes non-material aspects of subjectivity:

> We have seen that subjectivity already emerged in the movement-image; it appears as soon as there is a gap between a perceived and an executed movement, an action and a reaction, a stimulation and a response, a perception-image and an action-image. And if affection itself is also a dimension of this first subjectivity, it is because it belongs to the gap, it constitutes its 'insides', it in a sense occupies it, but without fulfilling it. Now, on the contrary, the recollection-image comes to fill the gap and really does fulfil it (...) Subjectivity then, takes on a new sense, which is no longer motor or material, but temporal and spiritual (1989: 47).

Elsewhere I have given more precise analyses of how on the level of filmic texts these different image-types can function as aspects of subjectivity[9]. Here it is important to notice that in Medem's work subjectivity is mainly formed in a temporal and spiritual way. Of course there is matter everywhere; perceptions, actions and affections, but they are filled with a non-material, temporal and spiritual sense. Or rather, the spiritual and the material are two distinct yet indiscernible sides of the same fold (Bryden 2001: 241). In this section I will develop the temporal aspects of Medem's time-images. In the next, I will develop the spiritual aspects of his films. In the time-image the actual (as present that passes) and the virtual (as past that conserves itself) are both real and sometimes become indistinguishable, as if crystals of time come together. Especially in relation Angela, Angel's virtual side literally enters the picture. Three scenes in *Tierra* particularly illustrate this. In the first scene, Angel talks to Angela on the phone. Like at the beginning of the film, this scene starts with the camera moving from the cosmos to earth, while on the soundtrack we hear the voices of Angel and Angela in conversation. When the camera has entered Angela's house, we see her on the phone. When Angel (invisible on the other side of the phone line) tells her that he wants to imagine her, his virtual double suddenly moves from the left side of the screen into the image and kisses her face. Angela does not see him, although he does touch her with his voice and words. The second scene in which the virtual and the actual are both present, is again a scene in Angela's house, right after her father tries to kill himself because he cannot get over the loss of his wife. Angel saves him and he wants to console Angela. He stands behind her, while she is sitting at the kitchen table. He stares at her back and we hear his thoughts, expressing his profound love for her[10]. The camera movements suggest he is touching her with his look and thoughts, and just before he actually embraces her, his virtual self detaches from his body and puts his arms around her shoulders. The last scene takes place at the local bar, where Angel's virtual side seduces Angela, and Angela is again touched by Angel's angel-side, this time through his looks. But his man-side chooses to go and visit Mari. He leaves his virtual double angrily behind at the bar.

All these scenes show a doubling of the virtual and the actual, but they could still be considered as imaginations in Angel's head. The end of the film, however, clearly puts these moments in a very clear temporal perspective as well. In the one-but-last scene, Angel is in hospital after he has been hit by a stone on his head. He has just left both Angela and Mari. Nevertheless Mari comes to visit him and promises to leave the island with him. Then the camera moves into Angel's head. We see Angel walking behind Angela and her daughter while his virtual side says:

> Listen to me for the last time. I'm not going with you. If you ever need me, you'll find me here, beside Angela, under these skies we like so much. Never forget this island. Even if it's just a memory lost in the vastness like the woodlouse under the earth, like the earth in the midst of the cosmos, like a tiny particle in the depth of your imagination. I'll live here if you don't forget me.

Then the scene changes, the colours change from the dark red of the earth to the deep blue of the sea. Angel and Mari are driving along the coast, leaving the island. In these last scenes it becomes evident that we can see the split personality of Angel not just as a projection of his schizophrenic mind, but it could also be seen in a philosophical way, as a recollection-image, in which time is split up between a present that passes (Mari) and a past that preserves itself (Angela). Perhaps Angela died and Angel keeps her alive as a memory (like a tiny particle); or perhaps Angel did die from the blow on his head, and Angela still keeps him alive in her memory while Angel now meets Mari in heaven (the colour changes could indicate this). Or perhaps Angel and Mari do leave, and Angela will feel Angel's presence forever, like she did before. The point is, of course, that all these alternatives are possible, like the real illusions in the Necker cube. The alternatives between the actual and the virtual are distinct but have become inseparable, making the distinction between fiction and reality blurred and unimportant for the brain/mind.

Flash Five: Sensation and Spirituality as a Cold Choice

In his article, 'The Scattering of Time Crystals' Michael Goddard points to the relationship between (virtual) time and spirituality: "Like an iceberg, the majority of which remains submerged beneath the surface of the ocean, mystical experience gives rise to a form of temporality that crystallises powerful virtual forces, beyond the power of an individual body or discourse to actualise: the body plunges into the virtual or spiritual depths which exceed it, rather than containing the spiritual as a personal property" (2001: 226). Another scene in *Tierra* seems to address literally this kind of spirituality related to time. After Angela's father has tried to commit suicide, Angel asks him to look for his deceased wife in the following way:

> You're separated by an enormous distance. Your wife is 20 million years from here. That's how old the universe is. And as she has ceased to exist she's had to go back all that time.
> *They watch the sky. The camera sees them from a low angle at the back.*
> It's an enormous loss.
> *They turn to each other and look each other in the eye, framing still from below.*
> We live at our own eye level mid-way between the stars and the atoms. We can only move with our thoughts.
> *Angel looks at Angela who feels she's being watched.*
> Tomás, imagine a woodlouse. Do you see it? If your mind can reach the smallest thing it can reach the biggest. Then you can see the edge of the universe. You must do that with your wife. Ask her to come close.

Angel asks Tomás to travel in his mind and embrace the enormous vastness of time and cosmic spirituality. Spirituality is related to movement of the mind.

Throughout the whole film we see how cinema can become a spiritual tool, capable of facilitating "an experience of ecstatic subjectivation in which spectators experience cinema as a pure optical and sound situation, a vision and a voice, a scattering of time crystals that lead them beyond the boundaries of their static selves and into profound contact with the outside" (Goddard 2001: 249). Now, what is particularly important for cinema (and art in general) is that it operates through sensations. So what is sensation in the brain and in which ways does this relate to spirituality? In *What is Philosophy?*, Deleuze and Guattari discuss how sensation in art (cinema) responses to chaos by contracting 'the vibrations of the stimulant on a nervous surface or in a cerebral volume':

> Sensation itself vibrates because it contracts vibrations. It preserves itself because it preserves vibrations. Sensation is the contracted vibration that has become quality, variety. That is why the brain-subject is here called *soul* or *force*, since only the soul preserves by contracting that which matter dissipates, or radiates, furthers, reflects, refracts, or converts (1994: 211).

A sensation is therefore a contraction, a contemplation of elements of matter that preserves the before in the after. And Deleuze and Guattari relate this aspect of sensation not just to humans but to all kinds of organisms. Plants and rocks do not posses a nervous system, but they seem to share chemical affinities and physical causalities that constitute 'microbrains' or an 'inorganic life of things', as they put it (1994: 213).

In this vitalistic conception of spirituality, when speaking of the soul, or force of life that art can make us feel, it is interesting to inquire a little further into the nature of this force of life, that is so fundamental to the sensations that cinema can bring about. According to Deleuze, spirituality has nothing to do with dreams or fantasy, but it is rather 'the domain of cold decision, of absolute obstinacy, of the choice of existence' (Flaxman 2000: 366). The cold choice seems to contradict the sensations that go with it, but in fact it is completely logical from a vitalistic perspective that sees the universe full of microbrains that are constantly moving, acting and reacting, but in sensations find a moment of pause, where all options are still open, and a decision has to be made.

When in *The Movement-Image* Deleuze discusses the affection-image, the image category that creates sensations par excellence, he explains this idea of spiritual choice further: the alternatives are not between terms (such as 'good' or 'bad') but between modes of existence of the one who chooses (1986: 114). The true spiritual choice is choosing choice (choosing that you have a choice) or choosing that you have no choice. For instance choosing between the mode of existence where you choose to believe in God, or the mode of existence where you choose not to believe in God. Deleuze analyses all the different ways in which choice can manifest itself in the films of Bresson, Dreyer and Rohmer. Another more contemporary movie also presents us with this kind of spiritual choice, albeit not in the form of a time-image but rather in a Hollywood movement-image in which in the end the narrative leaves no ambiguities between crystals of time. *Signs* tells the story of a priest, Graham Hess (Mel Gibson), who looses his faith after his wife dies in a terrible coincidental accident, and finds it back after he and his family survive an invasion of aliens and through which all the previous events of his life make sense. The main question the film raises, however, is certainly a spiritual one because it is a question of choosing between modes of existence. In one scene, Graham and his brother Merril (Joaquin Phoenix) have just been watching television where unexplained signs and lights are reported as a possible alien invasion. Graham says that there are two groups of people: those who believe co-incidence does not exist, that everything is a sign of miracles and evidence of some higher power (be it cosmic or divine); or those who believe they're on their own. He asks Merril to which group he belongs. Relating to a rather silly incident in his youth, that he endows with much significance, Merril says he is a miracle man[11]. Graham refers to the last words of his dead wife, 'see' and 'swing away', and says that these words were just caused by a coincidental electric wiring of her brain (zigzag) caused by the accident she was involved in, that made her recall a random memory of her brother-in-law who as a baseball player. Her last words seem completely irrelevant and without any sense and therefore Graham does not believe in miracles or higher forces.

Even though it is not said in the exact same words we are here dealing with a spiritual choice between the mode of existence of choosing to believe (in God, in external forces), or choosing the mode of existence of choosing not to believe. When Mel Gibson asks his brother to which group of people he belongs, he actually asks him to which group he chooses to belong — because there is no hard evidence. Merril chooses to believe; Graham has chosen not to believe. In the end, the film (and the filmmaker) will make clear that the electric wire of Graham's wife's brain does make sense, and that her words provide clues to fight the aliens[12]. As if her brain, in a flash, could see into the future, or, from the far away place in the cosmos that she was already travelling to, she could look back in order to give her loved ones a sign that would become crucial in their future. But in the scene just described, all the options are still open, no evidence is given and a spiritual choice has to be made. Cinema gives us this experience of perpetually renewed spiritual decisions, every time a sensation on the brain gives us a flash of insight.

Flash Six: Spiritual Automaton — Restoring a Belief in the World

Deleuze ends his cinema books by concluding that cinema constitutes a whole psycho-mechanics, a spiritual automaton that can indicate the highest exercise of thought, but can also become possessed of automization of the masses ('Hitler as filmmaker') (1989: 266). Looking at the technological and social evolution of cinema, Deleuze sees that the spiritual automata are changing with the advent of the electronic and numerical image. Instead of motor action, characters in cinema are no longer psychologically motivated persons that act, but more like 'puppets', cartoon-like characters, mechanical automata that express speech acts, as if they receive these speech acts from a spiritual, non-personal dimension.

With computer animation that becomes increasingly realistic, many questions have been raised about the ontological status of the image.

Although it no longer seems to be grounded in reality, computer animation becomes increasingly realistic and indistinguishable from analogue images. But, as we have seen, for Deleuze and for biologists of the brain the distinction between 'real' and 'unreal' is not a very important problem in the first place. This is also the reason why already at the beginning of *The Movement-Image* Deleuze argues that animation fully belongs to cinema because the figures are always 'in the process of being formed or dissolving through the movement of lines and points taken at any-instant-whatevers of their course' (1986: 5). Like Eisenstein who was lyrical about Disney, Deleuze argues that because it moves, it's a life and has the potential quality and power to affect the brain.

The difference then between old animated forms and new animated forms is not a degree of realism, but it is a difference in spiritual automaton. This spiritual automaton is not in the first instance dependent on the technological possibilities, but on a will to art (1989: 266). The principles of cinema of the movement-image are defined by a brain and a spiritual automaton that is directed at sensory-motor action. In the time-image (and possibly in the new digital-image)[13] they are defined by a brain, which has a direct experience of time, in which the virtual and the actual are distinct but sometimes interchangeable or indistinguishable. And this is why the new spiritual automata, characters and films as a whole, become speech acts that create the reality of illusions that express the reality of the virtual.

As is known that Austin speech acts are performances of language that do something: by saying 'yes' at a wedding ceremony you actually change in civil status[14]. In a similar way Deleuze refers in *The Time-Image* to the performative quality of images (not only the language, but the whole image as creative storytelling) and to the power these performances have to actually change status since they become part of reality (1989: 268). This is of utmost importance for instance in political cinema that has as its goal fabulation, creative storytelling and performative filming that calls for a people to come into existence. But it is a characteristic of new spiritual automata in general.

The question of the spiritual choice is of great importance, says Deleuze, because "choosing to choose is supposed to restore everything to us" (1986: 116). What is regained is a belief in this world, because the modern fact is that the link between man and world is broken. And thus, Deleuze argues:

> ... this link must become an object of belief: it is the impossible which can only be restored with a faith. (...) Only belief in the world can reconnect

man to what he sees and hears. The cinema must film, not the world, but belief in this world, our only link. (...) Whether we are Christians or atheists, in our universal schizophrenia, we need reasons to believe in this world. (1989: 172)

Philosophy, art and science all seem to bring something from the outside, chaos into the world, into our brains. Like Angel who speaks half as a dead man from a virtual place in the cosmos, the philosopher, the scientist, and the artist also seem to return from death, the chaos and vastness of the universe (Deleuze and Guattari 1994: 202). But this should not be seen as a cult of death:

> Between the two sides of the absolute, between the two deaths — death from the inside or past, death from the outside or future — the internal sheets of memory and the external layers of reality will be mixed up, extended, short-circuited and will form a moving life, which is at once that of the cosmos and of the brain, which sends out flashes from one pole to another (Deleuze 1989: 209).

With these zigzagging movements, thunderbolts and strokes of lightening the last flash of insight is that the 'zed' is also the 'zed' of zombies. Philosophers, artists and scientist are zombies who are half-dead because they are overwhelmed by life[15].

Bibliography

Austin, J. L. 1962. *How to do Things with Words.* Cambridge, Massachusetts: Harvard University Press.

Boer, J. 2003. *Neurofilosofie. Hersenen, bewustzijn, vrije wil.* Amsterdam: Boom.

Deleuze, G. & Guattari, F. 1994. *What is Philosophy?* London & New York: Verso. (Trans. Graham Burchell and Hugh Tomlinson.)

Deleuze, G. 1986. 'The Brain is the Screen: An Interview with Gilles Deleuze. G. In Flaxman. (ed.) 2000. *The Brian is the Screen. Deleuze and the Philosophy of the Cinema.* Minneapolis & London: University of Minnesota Press. (Trans. Marie Therese Guiris)

Deleuze, G. 1995. *Negotiations.* New York: Columbia University Press. (Trans. Martin Joughin.)

Deleuze, G. 1986. *Cinema 1: The Movement-Image.* London: Athlone Press. (Trans. Hugh Tomlinson and Barabara Habberjan)

Anderson, J. 1997. *Reality of Illusion. An Ecological Approach to Cognitive Film Theory.* USA: Southern Illinois Press.

Damasio, A. 2003. *Looking for Spinoza. Joy, Sorrow and the Feeling Brain.* Amsterdam: Wereldbibliotheek.

Deleuze, G. 1989. *Cinema 2. The Time-Image.* London: Athlone Press. (Trans. Hugh Tomlinson and Robert Galeta.)

Goddard, M. 2001. 'The Scattering of Time Crystals. Deleuze, Mysticism and Cinema' in Bryden, M. (ed.) *Deleuze and Religion.* New York & London: Routledge.

Pisters, P. 2003. *The Matrix of Visual Culture. Working with Deleuze in Film Theory.* Stanford: Stanford University Press.

Sheldrake, R. 2003. *The Sense of Being Stared At: and other aspects of the extended mind.* New York: Crown Publishers.

Notes

[1] *L'Abécédaire de Gilles Deleuze* with Claire Parnet. Dir. Pierre-André Boutang. Video Editions Montparnasse, 1996. See for an english summary of this video http://www.langlab.wayne.edu/CStivale/D-G/ABC1.html .

[2] See Gilles Deleuze and Félix Guattari. *What is Philosophy?* Trans. Graham Burchell and Hugh Tomlinson. London and New York: Verso. 1994: 218.

[3] Gilles Deleuze. 'The Brain is the Screen. An Interview with Gilles Deleuze'. Trans. Marie Therese Guiris. In Gregory Flaxman (ed.). *The Brain is the Screen. Deleuze and the Philosophy of Cinema.* Minneapolis and London: University of Minnesota Press. 2000: 365-373.

[4] 'The Brain is the Screen', pp: 366.

[5] In the same way, by film philosophy or film theory Deleuze does not mean philosophy about cinema, but theorizing the thoughts and concepts that are raised by cinema by its own means.

[6] Since this is a first investigation in this transdisciplinary field, the issues here are not systematically mapped but rather meant as a starting point for further reflection. On a general note however, it should be noted that Deleuze's film philosophy could not be understood without contemporary scientific knowledge ranging from knowledge about the smallest molecular and atomic level of life (neurology, DNA, etc.), to the largest matters and measures in astronomy.

[7] See Antonio Damasio. *Looking for Spinoza. Joy, Sorrow and the Feeling Brain.* Trans. into Dutch by Marjolijn Stoltenkamp. *Het Gelijk van Spinoza. Vreugde, verdriet en het voelende brein.* Amsterdam: Wereldbibliotheek, 2003, pp. 107-108. And Johan den Boer. *Neurofilosofie. Hersenen, bewustzijn, vrije wil.* Amsterdam: Boom, 2003: 144.

[8] *Het Gelijk van Spinoza*: 177.

[9] See Pisters, Patricia. 2003. *The Matrix of Visual Culture. Working with Deleuze in Fim Theory.* Stanford: Stanford University Press.

[10] Here it is possible to make another transdisciplinary connection, namely to the work of Rupert Sheldrake. In *The Sense of Being Stared at and Other Aspects of the Extended Mind* (2003), Sheldrake describes many scientific experiments that prove that the human mind can reach out and touch something in the field of vision. See also http://www.sheldrake.org .

[11] Merril discusses a moment at a party where he is about to kiss a girl. Because he has a chewing gum in his mouth he just turns around to take it away. When he turns back the girl is throwing up. Without the chewing gum she would have vomited on him instead of on the floor. Merril sees this as a proof of higher forces.

[12] When an alien has captured Graham's son, Graham suddenly *sees* what his wife meant. He tells Merril to *swing away* with his base ball bat and hit the alien.

[13] In his conclusion of the cinema books, besides the new spiritual automaton, Deleuze gives three other characteristics of the new image: its space becomes omni-directional, it becomes an opaque surface inscribed with data, and sound and vision enter in new complex relationships. *The Time-Image*, p. 265-266.

[14] See Austin, J. L. 1962. *How to do Things with Words*. Cambridge, Massachusetts: Harvard University Press.

[15] Deleuze also refers to zombies. See *The Time-Image*: 209.

Cinema as Externalization of Consciousness

Pia Tikka

The approach of cinema as externalization of consciousness assumes that the mind reveals some of its functional structures in its products. This perspective is inspired by the film theorist Sergei Eisenstein's organic-dynamic synthesis of arts and sciences. Two recursive loops of cognition are assumed to constitute the fundamental cognitive dynamics of conscious acts, here referring to the particular area of authoring cinematic space. The inner loop corresponds to the dynamics for regulation of the body-brain homeostasis, and the outer loop refers to the body-environment interaction. These loops penetrate the social, perceptual, and neural levels of conscious mind. From the evolutionary survival-oriented point of view, it is proposed that Antti Revonsuo's theory of internal simulation of dream world could be applied to describe also cinematic immersion.

> These ideas are childishly obvious, but in them are contained the most complex problems of the structure of a work of art, for they touch on the most vital aspect of our work: the problem of representation and relationship to what is being represented (Eisenstein 1987: 3)

We all like to see films where beings like us do silly or dangerous things. We are vulnerable against the emotions elicited in the erotic or fearful situations of the fictional characters on the screen. These narratives become part of our personal experience in the psycho-physiological process of simulation, which is the main interest here. This chapter will review fundamental biological mechanisms that enable human cognitive processes. It makes an attempt to describe how the conscious mind is capable of producing artworks, which have the capability of affecting other minds, as films do.

The essay assumes that the higher-level conscious cognition emerges from mostly unconscious biological functions. This happens in a continuous interaction with the world, body and brain. The cultural domain shapes the biological domain and vice versa, in reciprocal manner. Similarly, the neural and experiential levels of the human organism shape the individual's needs and interests, and her further enactment in the world. The claim explicitly put out here is that the process of filmmaking and the mechanisms of emotive-cognitive complexity of the cinematic thinking may help in analysing the human mind within further generalized scope — consciousness as a biological organization critical for survival.

In order to cover the necessary range of interrelated trans-disciplinary issues, each of them is a subject of an entire chapter and the discussion will be limited to explicitly pointing out the main themes of future research. The reader who desires for more profound knowledge of the issues, may find the references provided at the end of the chapter useful. Perhaps, for example, the issue in the chapter on synaesthesia, i.e. the phenomenon of the subject experiencing visual objects or patterns as associated with certain taste or sound, may turn out to be an important field of study in connection with how people create and experience cinema. Or, if considering the involuntary reading of other peoples' facial expressions, assumed to form one of the basic mechanisms of the evolutionary survival game, the mind reading apparently can be named as one of the most important neural level functions of cinematic understanding.

The title *Cinema as Externalization of Consciousness* posits the view that the mind reveals its functional structures in its productive procedures. The process of making a film is an ideal object for empirical experiments on phenomena like emotions or meaningfulness. Even though cinematic expression is strictly framed, it manipulates all plausible elements of everyday life — both the visual and literal, spoken and written, conventional and emergent sign systems. In what follows, the Russian film theorist and filmmaker Sergei Eisenstein's cinematic thinking can serve as a model of how the *embodied* preconceptual schemata of being in the everyday world makes the imaginative and creative thinking possible, and how it appears in the process of cinematic categorization and generalization.

Eisenstein was haunted by the unified organic-dynamic synthesis between the arts and sciences; his mind working on a broad holistic scale[1]. He considered the multisensuous aspects of cinematic thought and feelings in a manner that could today be described as the embodied mind approach. Embodiment for Eisenstein meant inseparable bidirectional causality between the sensorimotor body functions and emotionally expressive behaviour, which, when guided by the author's vision, enabled the intellectual level of understanding, and further, the leap to the highest level of unity in ecstasy. When observing the bodily expressions of the actor, the spectator inevitably was injected by the mental condition assigned to the viewed body movements,[2] Eisenstein's ideas actually correspond to many contemporary views of embodiment, which consider an organism's unconscious and conscious micro- and macro scale activity as fundamentally based on the brain-body-world interaction, and manifesting in the interpersonal mimicry such as empathy, for example (Varela et al. 1991; Thompson and Varela 2001; Gallese 2003; Metzinger and Gallese 2003).

Eisenstein developed an exhaustive film montage theory, where "orchestral composition" of the perceptual elements leads the spectator to the *intellectual level* of experience, and further to the *conscious ecstasy* of organic-dynamic holism (Eisenstein 1987: 35-37). The structural formation of Eisenstein's montage theory, vertical levels composed on horizontal dynamics of simultaneously flowing independent but interrelated auditory and visual modalities, resembles the multilevel structures of mind presented here. The cinema is inseparably based on synchronization and timing throughout. The internal relations and properties of cinematic elements, which *are chosen to appear* or *happen to emerge* in the moment of image recording, are the constitutive mechanisms of cinematic experience. Eisenstein's belief in cinema's power over the human mind links his work to the contemporary science of consciousness. By *cinematic consciousness* I promote the notion of consciousness in relation to cinema. The purpose is, in Eisensteinian spirit, to scrutinize the recursive loops of cognition and perception as the basic structure of conscious enactment in authoring and sharing cinematic space.

Theoretical background

The notion of *cinematic consciousness* can be described as a 'miniature' consciousness, which is understood to emerge from the holistic interaction between an organism and her environment particularly framed by narrative aspects. By definition, cinema is about authored moving image representations that provoke in the viewer an experience of immersion — a conscious state that relates the emotive-cognitive experiences of the viewer to the stream of events of the film in such a manner that she momentarily can be claimed *not* to be fully conscious about the other events around her. In addition, 'cinematic' as such refers to the functional aspect of the representation, which integrates the history of moving image conventions, techniques, and genres (e.g. a romantic comedy, documentary, experimental film, etc.). Consciousness, in turn, escapes the definition[3]. Even if restricted under the scrutiny in relation to cinema only, it is far too complex a subject and the domains that the science of consciousness cuts through are far too many to be discussed here. In avoiding getting lost into the domains of philosophy, and in order to keep in mind the author's practice-based cinema research, this essay is framed around the experiential view of consciousness. In what follows, I will briefly define the main terminology applied.

Firstly, it is assumed, that consciousness or conscious mind is supervenient to *embodied cognition*, which is gained through continuous enactment in the world (Varela et al 1991; Maturana and Varela 1987). The other way around, cognition involves both conscious and unconscious functions of the brain-body system (Lakoff and Johnson 1999). It is notable that consciousness forms just the top of the iceberg of embodied cognition, as Lakoff and Johnson (1999) metaphorically formulate the relationship. Instead, the unconscious states are understood as remarkably excessive with regards to the amount of experiential information they supply to the brain. It is necessary to remind that all conscious cognition is founded on the emotional evaluation processes of unconscious cognition.

Secondly, the *recursive dynamic character of cognition* penetrates through all the levels of biological existence, i.e., social, perceptual, and neural levels. To the subject's interaction ecology[4] I assume two dynamical cognition circuits as critical for survival: the *inner loop* for regulation of the body-brain environment, and the *outer loop* for orienting and controlling the body-environment interaction, as proposed in Kaipainen (1996). The inner and outer loops serve for describing distinct but interrelated domains of subject-world dynamics ranging from emotions to technological extensions. By *being conscious* I mean *situatedness* in the world experienced from the unique egocentric perspective of the subject. From the evolutionary point of view[5], without the attentive perceptual consciousness continuously updating the environmental coordinates in relation to other entities or objects, the survival game would have ended short.

As the third point, I adopt the notion of *simulation* in a special meaning of mind's active extension. Accepting the recursive dynamics in the brain, the simulation's internal representations or recognition patterns in for example the processes of remembering, imagining or dreaming. The recently discovered brain's simulation mechanism involving the mirror neuron networks may correlate to the phenomenal level imitation, or mind reading, perhaps constituting all socio-emotional interaction[6]. The view presented here is parallel and overlaps to some extent with the approaches that are based on world simulation models (Revonsuo 2000; Gallese 2003; Metzinger 2004), on action-perception motor theories (e.g. Rizzolatti and Arbib 1998; Preston and de Waal 2002), and on dynamic systems (e.g. Varela et al. 1991; Port and van Gelder 1995; Thompson and Varela 2001). The dynamic systems approach generally rejects representations, focussing on the real-time adaptive activity of cognition (e.g. Port and van Gelder 1995)[7]. They claim to be in conflict with the representational view. In the present context this seems to be merely superficial. Here the conflict is resolved by assuming that representations are dynamic systems themselves.

Experiential world

Cinema grows from the author's experience and, vice versa, it manifests itself in the spectator's experience. Ideally, the spectator walks out the theatre emotionally moved, the fictional story presented on the screen recycling in her mind. It is due to understanding the situatedness of other people, which may manifest as a feeling of empathy, perhaps. In my view, embodied simulation is an inseparable continuation of an organism's enactment in the world, which provides the mind with an experiential updating system. Simulation is thus an experiential extension of cognition. In what follows, the cinematic narrative is in main focus. In addition it is noted that *all* conscious inferences like interpretation, imagination and evaluation, are understood as narrative.

Narrative is seen as an epiphenomenon of socio-emotional interaction; it always deals with the *other* and *otherness* (Tikka 2005: 103). The 'other', here, refers to the Husserl's (1859-1938) phenomenological inquiries on a subject's awareness of the intentions and acts of co-living things. The phenomenology of perception in Merleau-Ponty (1962) and the neurophenomenology of Francisco Varela (1991, 1999) have inspired views presented here. For Merleau-Ponty, the theory of the body schema is already the theory of perception, which enables rediscovery of the self as the subject of perception (Merleau-Ponty 1962: 206). Varela's methodological focus is on the first-person view to experience (Varela and Shear 1999), describing the neural temporality patterns as fundamental constituents of conscious experience (Varela 1999; Metzinger 1995, 2004, 2004a), in turn, proposes widely distributed bottom-up processes for enabling the undeniable indivisible experience of self, embedded in the world. This subject's *perspectivalness*, first discussed in Nagel (1974),[8] emerges from the *singularity of experiential holism* (Metzinger 1995, 2004, 2004a).

The following definitions owe to the study of consciousness in Metzinger (1995, 2004) and in Revonsuo (1995, 2005). The *phenomenal world* is understood as the real world, which is *a priori* given in the subject's psychophysical experience of the indivisible unchangeable environment. The phenomenal world becomes elaborated in the experiential domain of the apparently omniscient subject, and from there emerges the *representational world,* for example, childhood memory, or here cinematic narrative. The internal mediated representation of being-in-the-world as simulated *virtual reality* is discussed in Revonsuo (1995, 2005) and in Metzinger (2004).[9] Here I explicitly assume that in simulation of illusory virtual reality of the cinematic world, the conscious mind dominates the embodied representational resources of the simulation system in a different top-down manner than it would do when simulating the external environmental stimuli. This is because the narrative process involves primarily the representational level (e.g. conceptual metaphors, causalities, relationships), which, in turn, is based on the experiential level (e.g. embodied metaphors, causalities and relationships).

Embodiment of metaphors

In order to bridge the conceptual division between mind and its externalizations such as thoughts, acts, artistic processes, or technological extensions, I have adopted the approach of embodied and spatial metaphors as the mediating domain, as discussed in Lakoff and Johnson (1980,1999)[10]. Metaphors are both descriptions of the personal phenomenal world and the building blocks for interpersonal socio-emotional communication. Within metaphors, all embodied, unconscious and conscious knowledge of being-in-the-world is projected to the higher conceptual levels of cognition and enacted in the cultural life, e.g. philosophical arguments, scientific theories, interactive media, or other abstract model systems.

A conscious subject is automatically encaged into a situational dialogue within herself. In the field of psychology, William James (1890) applied introspection to explain the intrinsic aspects of the stream of thought,[11] which further inspired Damasio's (1999) metaphor of 'movie-in-the-brain' for describing mental imagery. Eisenstein, in turn, owes to James Joyce's method of inner speech applied in *Ulysseus*[12], when he notes that the flow is the simplest and most primitive method for realization of the unity of the whole, thus, preceding the cognitive analyses "that actively 'makes divisions' at higher stages of its development" (Eisenstein 1987: 249-50).

Drawing from Damasio's (2003) view on emotions as the basis for cognition, the three frames of emotive-cognitive simulation could be analysed as follows: a) the *subpersonal* frame of *homeostasis*, regulating the neurochemical body states and autonomic nervous system, for example breathing and heart rate; b) the *intrapersonal* frame, where *feelings* are perceptions, i.e. within the first-person experience only and not perceptually sharable; c) *interpersonal* frame, where emotional *expressions* of e.g. fear, anger, joy, or shame, constitute social patterns. These frames are only conceptual descriptions for embodied levelless phenomena emerging in interaction between the embodied subpersonal dynamics and the interpersonal cinematic space.

When the movie-reference of Damasio is turned the other way around, there are two metaphors of mental reflections often associated to cinema, the *mirror metaphor* and the *dream metaphor*. Here the public and private levels are present, respectively. As the dream metaphor describes the *intra*personal dimensions of experiential holism, the mirror metaphor describes the *inter*personal phenomena like empathy, imitation, character identification, or situated contextualization. In my view, the only available toolbox for understanding situatedness of the others is experiential knowledge via simulation, which manifests in the conceptual level of metaphors.

Here, I have in mind a description of holistic dynamics of cinematic simulation, which considers assumptions from both neurobiological and techno-cultural domains. The proponents of the *radical embodiment* suggest that consciousness cuts across the brain-body-world division (Thompson and Varela 2001: 418; Clark 2001). The biological, functional and operational structures of cognition are 'tuned', or adapted to the external artificial cognitive aids embedded in the environment (Clark 2001: 132). In my view, the brain is the biological niche of consciousness despite the fact that the cognitive data embraces the whole existing world, including the infinity of the living cellular body as well as the celestial space.

I will liberally apply the idea of *biological realism* as proposed in Revonsuo (2005). This, I claim, continues in accordance with the holism of autopoiesis, i.e. an organism interacts with the changing environment in continuous recursive loops of self-evaluation and self-

organization as seen by Maturana and Varela (1980). In addition, the
sensorimotor interaction loop between the organism and the environment is taken to modify the *qualitative* aspects of perception, and not
only the internal bidirectional pathways between the peripheral sense
organs and the brain (O'Regan and Noë 2002; Noë and Thompson
2004). It is necessary to note that without any experience of enactment
in the world there would exist no qualitative knowledge of that world.
Still, in imagination, i.e. internal simulation, any embodied knowledge
of any world can be qualitatively modified and reorganized in the
mind, even when momentarily physically disconnected from that
particular world. At least it *appears* to the mind that also qualitative
aspects of representation constitute a fundamental part of the internal
simulation resources. The author can manipulate things or events in
the mind, spatially, metaphorically and conceptually (visual phenomena like grading, saturation, or distortions, dissolves, movements of
turning objects, figure-background oscillations, etc.). If this internal
sensorimotor extension is turned the other way around, the authorship
of cinema extends to the domain of technological aids like script
writing programmes, digital cameras, computers and image compos-
ing tools, that are used for developing the coherent cinematic world.

Simulation as extended cognition

Fiction is composed in the holistic interaction between author's embodied knowledge gained in the real-life-situatedness and the modified representations of author's embodied knowledge gained therein.
Here it is suggested that narrative emerges, when mind recycles purposefully modified forms of the dynamic patterns or *'false' body-state
representations*. The data from inner and outer interaction environments feed the mind with perceptions, which, in cognitive recursive
loops involve simultaneous interaction of emotional systems, associa-
tive networks, long-term memory and the short-term memory. The recognition of the embodied knowledge happens in a complex dynamical manner in and between a multiplicity of bottom-up and top-down
processes, under the cognitive guidance of the author. When imagining any story, scene, event, or character's behaviour or desires, the
author utilizes the intentionally 'distorted' simulation in order to
manipulate the experiential self-referential resources of herself-as-
author.

The simulation view of Gallese and Goldman (1998) suggests that
phenomenal level mind-reading involves both 'pretend' and natural

'non-pretend' states of simulation routine. In my interpretation, the 'pretend' state would allow the fictional cognition. The simulation theory[13] suggests that mind-reading occurs when the other person's emotive-cognitive states 'resonate' with the mental states of one's own (Gallese and Goldman 1998: 493; Preston and de Waal 2002). How mind-reading is physiologically plausible and what are the biological mechanisms of this emotional resonance? The simulation-based view has gained evidence in the recent reading of neuroscience. The finding of the mirror neuron system in the brain suggests that sensorimotor imitation forms the physical basis for human-human interaction, e.g. language, and mediated images[14] (Rizzolatti and Arbib 1998; Metzinger and Gallese 2003). This neural level simulation, in turn, is understood as a functional mechanism of unconscious automatic control (Metzinger and Gallese 2003: 555-6). Thus, if constituted by the lower-level functional dynamics, the resonant states[15] in the experiential level of empathy[16], for example, could be considered to 'carry' similar 'meaningfulness' as the neural level activity.

With respect to experiential holism promoted in Metzinger (1995), I assume that any embodied activity, at any level of the biological organism occurring in the same temporal window, can be assumed to relate to the same phenomenal function. This leads to the view that low-level neural activation correlates with high-level representations of the mind, when they are *functionally synchronized*. In this manner, functional synchronization also shapes conceptual level descriptions of particular embodied phenomena, and may further be assumed to the human-human dimensions of the particular phenomenon. For example, functional synchronization enables to describe the macro-scale simulation such as behavioural imitation, or empathy, as manifestations of simultaneously active micro-scale simulation of the mirror neuron network.

Most neuroscientists agree on locating the cognitive speech production and conceptual categorization to the human brain's left hemisphere, mainly to Broca's area (speech production) and Wernicke's area (language comprehension) (Gazzaniga et al 2002: 386-387). Gazzaniga (1998) has gone further and claims for the left hemisphere position as 'the interpreter' between the embodied experience and the *socially coherent* descriptions about those experiences[17]. His innate interpreter has developed a language-related skill to fill up gaps if there are missing parts in the causal chain of events. It associates, invents metaphors, it tells lies to positively enhance its own first-person view, but also reads minds (Gazzaniga 1998: 24). Gazzaniga's interpreter appears as a storyteller, whose supplies of the narrative are embedded in brain.

In comparison to the left hemisphere, which is also associated with the approaching or outward tendencies, the right frontal cortex, in turn, is devoted to recognizing emotions and socially relevant information in the expressions of others (Adolphs et al. 2000). The right hemisphere, which is associated with the withdrawal or inward tendencies, seems to understand "anomalies via irony, jokes and other emotionally sophisticated strategies" (Baars 2003: 6). The right somatosensory cortices carry the task of creating the body state mapping. If damaged, the subject is not able to simulate the body states of other people properly, and no empathy in the phenomenal level of experience occurs (Damasio 2003: 117).

Consciousness contributes to the organism in *orientation*, responding to the concerns arising from the circuits of the body (Damasio 2003: 208). In turn, actions of approach or withdrawal correlate to embodied pain and pleasure perceptions, manifesting in the drives and motivations. Damasio (1994, 2003: 115-8) discusses his simulation equivalents for mirror neuron system as 'as-if-body-loops'. In my understanding, 'as-if' body states may partly constitute also the narrative ability of mind in similar manner as any causal or relational understanding demanded by the body-brain system. An interesting aspect in relation to narratives is provided by Damasio who describes 'as-if-body-loops' that have the capability to simulate *false* body states. (Damasio 2003: 115-8) The false body state occurs in a bottom-up manner, due to a physiological damage or neurochemical intoxicant because of which incoming signals are distorted, modified or filtered. This causes, for example hallucination, which, in turn, manifests in Gazzaniga's interpreter as a 'real', coherent description of experiencing, what it is like 'being a bat'. The other way around, narrative enters the brain-body system in a top-down manner. The low-level body data is purposefully modified in continuous interaction with the high-level cognition, involving long-term motor memory and emotional communication. This enables creating description of the false body state, e.g. the illusory experience of what it is like 'being a bat'.

The false body state would correspond to Metzinger's notion of "actuality of situated self-awareness as a *virtual* form of actuality" (Metzinger 2004: 41), or internalist presence-in-the-world simulation model in Revonsuo (1995, 2000a, 2005). In addition, as explicitly suggested by Ramachandran and Hubbard (2001: 17), metaphoric language may use the neural cross-activation basis of conceptual maps, which is analogous to the synaesthetes' cross-activation of perceptual maps. Synaesthesia manifests itself in people, who taste shapes, or hear colours, for example (Ramachandran and Hubbard 2003)[18]. The synaesthetes' hyperconnective use of language, for example in the arts, may eventually provoke heuristic interpersonal understanding. By simulating common things from radical perspectives or in novel contexts, synaesthetic activity perhaps elicits cultural 'mutations'.

The point here has been in showing that there is no emotive-cognitive expression or description available in the mind without embodied understanding of the constitutive experiential level of that particular phenomenon. The storyteller needs not to experience everything herself before being able to imagine. But imagining itself is based on complex neural level simulation of the potential events, threats, or desires in the domain of her own embodied understanding, cultivated within cultural conventions and cognitive technologies.

Method: Equating cinema and the dreaming mind

Aristotle analyses the perceptual reality that the dreaming state presents to the sleeping soul in a similar manner as one might analyse it today. The 'actual given' here can be interpreted in accordance with the sensory perceptions when awake, i.e. as immersion.

> Moreover, as we said that different men are subject to illusions, each according to the different emotion present in him, so it is that the sleeper, owing to sleep, and to the movements then going on in his sensory organs, as well as to the other facts of the sensory process, [is liable to illusion], so that the dream presentation, though but little like it, appears as some actual given thing[19].

The view of cinema as externalization of consciousness is motivated by Revonsuo's (1995, 2000, 2005) experimental approach to the dreaming mind as a model system for consciousness. I claim that the fictional cinema world reflects the multimodal experience in a similar way as the dream world. Cinema and dream share elements that relate to aspects like immersion, empathy, identification with the protagonists, visualization, framed or otherwise limited ability to determine the narrative, physical immobility in the viewing situation, darkness in the cinema theatres, etc. In short, the dream and the immersive cinematic experience exemplify characteristics of an emotionally situated consciousness.

When discussing immersion in relation to the conscious mind, one could claim that immersion falls outside of the scope of Consciousness Studies, because it actually describes a kind of unconscious phase of the human mind. In what follows, it is assumed that the neural level simulation connects the mirror metaphor and the dream metaphor to the phenomenon of immersion. The constituting mechanisms of immersion are assumed here in the neural mechanisms of *simulating the otherness,* as described in an earlier section of the text. All socio-emotional interaction might be based on unconscious subliminal processes of *mirroring the other.* It is reminded that the subject's embodied interaction is divided into the *inner body-brain loop* and the *outer body-environment loop* (Kaipainen 1996).

If sleep in psychology is considered as an unconscious state, from where all the connections to the external world are excluded, what does it indicate for the discussion here? Let us assume here, that in the Rapid Eye Movements (REM) phase when dreaming occurs, the outer interaction loop between the real world and conscious brain is disconnected, while the inner loop continues feeding the brain with the internal dynamic representation patterns. Revonsuo (1995, 2000) adds a dimension of internal consciousness into the simulated picture by claiming, that the dreamer, while unconscious of the external world, lives through vivid internal conscious experiences. Likewise, in an immersive cinematic experience, interaction with the real world and the conscious brain becomes disconnected at least partially, while the mirroring interaction between the brain and the cinematic representations can be regarded as an extended inner loop. The dynamic representation of the embodied world emerges due to the simulation mechanisms of the brain, be it in the act of dreaming a dream or viewing a narrative story.

The cinematic consciousness involves the widely discussed two-faceted problem of the viewer being conscious of the viewing situation (real world) vs. the cinematic immersion (fiction world). These psycho-physiological states seem to oscillate in a manner, where a dominating state discloses the alternative state completely out. The immersion in relation to cinema means a total emotional involvement with the fictionally contextualized events on the screen. Immersion disappears momentarily, if the viewer is disturbed, but can be gained again. The two-facet phenomenon of internal immersion vs. external reality exists also in the virtual realities provided with the technological extension. Revonsuo (1995, 2005) also suggests that the computer-driven virtual reality caves enable 'being-in-there' immersion as close to on-line world simulation in mind as technology today can provide.

My view, in contrast, is that visual consciousness and immersion is about experiencing embodiment as emotional situatedness, and not about the perfect image projection. It is also necessary to remind that visual consciousness here describes one sensory modality dimension of the embodied spatiality. Visual immersion, I claim, is not about 90-120° perspective, or identifying the point of view in Euclidian coordinates. The world may be projected as window — like (cinema screen), container-like (computer screen), world-like (VR cave), or life-like (dream). If the context of the perceived world — interpersonal relationships, causal events, nature's forces, or facial movements — is meaningful, it will enable immersion. And this is where cinematic immersion comes into play as a powerful extension of consciousness with all its distortions and grains, opposite to the perfect virtual reality without emotional devotion. Thus, it appears that visual immersion as described in Revonsuo (2005) is not identical with the embodied spatiality suggested here. It may describe some dimensions of it, similar to the physiological stimuli in the retina's visual receptors. The dynamic interaction of the constitutive sensory modalities and neuro-chemical reactions enable representation in the brain, but cannot be analysed reciprocally back to separate modalities or elements. In the fullest sense of immersion, the embodied spatiality integrates all senses.

How cinematic experience might correspond to simulation in the immersive experience of the dream? According to Revonsuo's (2000) evolutionary framing, the modern dreaming brain performs a survival simulation mechanism that evolved in the ancestral environment filled with dangers. Revonsuo and Valli's (2000a) analysis on the test group's dreams show a strong dominance of the scary or fearful dreams that involve escaping from natural forces, strange men, and wild animals, while the positively valued evolutionary elements appear less, e.g. emotional bonding and tendencies for care-taking of children. Instead of giving comfort or resolving some everyday family problems, dreams may have more survival value as a threat rehearsal programme that keeps instincts alert — hence the nightmares (Revonsuo 2000). One of the clues that leads to the threat simulation theory is the notion that the living situations in dreams seem to lack daily working routines such as reading, typing or writing. Revonsuo's explanation for this is that dreams mainly simulate situations that could be assumed to be present already in the ancestral environment.

Does the threat theory then suggest that dreams have not adapted to the modern environment? If so, wouldn't it also suggest that there must exist correlating temporal evolvement or adaptation gaps embedded in the brain, lets say between the earlier developed limbic system, and the neocortical regions of the brain such as prefrontal cortex. As shown by Revonsuo and others, the prefrontal area of the brain, which is mainly assigned with tasks of abstract organization, management and long-term planning in the mind, does not activate during REM phase. Instead, according to Revonsuo (2000) the amygdala-cortical network assigned to emotional evaluation[20] is activated, and indicates the threat recognition phase of REM-sleep while activation in the occipito-temporal region indicates visual recognition and projections from long-term memory. In turn, the threat avoidance phase primes the perceptual-emotional contents and activates the cortical motor programmes, which are inhibited by motor output paralysis (muscular atonia) characteristic for sleep (Revonsuo 2000)[21].

Now, if accepting the idea presented by MacLean (1993) that the physio-functional structure of the mammal brain corresponds to the brain's evolutionary development[22], which is similar to the view defended also by Damasio (1999), the following suggestion can be made. The dissociation of neocortical area in the dreaming phase may support the idea of parallel evolutionary hierarchies in the brain, the one manifesting when awake and the other when dreaming. The ancestral survivalist and the sci-fi techno-manager in the brain would further represent the differences between two simultaneous interaction loops of internal and external environments. In other words, in this respect human beings may still be living in the stone ages and try to survive according to the ancestral inference structures.

Cinematic consciousness as embodied spatiality

The phenomenon of cinema motivates two domains of scrutiny — towards internal and external structures of the emotive-cognitive self in the act of artistic production. In addition, the recursive character of experience is related to functional synchronization, which is assumed to penetrate all the levels of biological existence, here in particular the social, perceptual, and neural levels. In other words, the subjective dimensions of experiential holism are shown to manifest in the vertical intrapersonal and the horizontal interpersonal interaction dynamics spanning over the brain-body-world division. In my understanding, these elements have been present also in Eisenstein's organic-dynamic cinematic thinking.

In the latter part of the chapter I suggest an analogue between immersion in dream consciousness and cinematic consciousness, with the purpose of providing a novel perspective to the study of cinema, as well as of consciousness. This is a starting point for further inquiry about what does the cinematic experience allow to assume about consciousness, and, how do the conscious and unconscious states of embodied cognition interact in the cinematic experience? Visual consciousness is the most important sensory dimension for facilitating the feeling of presence in the virtual reality space of the fictional world similar to the visual landscape of the dreaming brain.

I have promoted the idea of simulation in the domain of authorship. This means suggesting that the author takes into consideration the potential participation of the spectator through reviewing or 'mirroring' the behaviour of the other in one's mind. The innate neural mechanisms of simulating otherness are equal to the recursive loops of constituting mechanisms of cinematic immersion. In addition, all socio-emotional interactions are proposed to be based on unconscious subliminal processes of *mirroring the other*. In this sense, narrative cognition appears as emotionally guided imitation of the intentions and actions of the other, merging continuous recognition dynamics, and emerging as an interpretation. During the design of interactive narrative spaces, the conscious and unconscious interaction experiences of the spectator-participant are simulated within an authored sphere characterized by multiple perspectives. In other words, the embodied structure of the author(s)' mind, or authorship, is based on continuous simulation of otherness, which, respectively, is embedded in the structure of the artwork. In the spirit of Eisenstein, these structures become interpersonally accessible and shared, because people apparently perceive and understand the world according to similar embodied structures of the mind.

If the scene is viewed from the holistic standpoint, the multiple levels presented here cut across the brain-body-world division in a descriptive manner. The author's process of structuring the cinematic space according to different levels of recursive loops of recognition and perception extends to the spectator's experience. Eisenstein writes about the method of *pathos*, the sense of organic unity, which reaches its peak when the mind makes a leap in ecstasy from one mode of existence to a new one in a similar manner as water becomes steam:

> Here, born out of the *pathos* of the theme, the compositional structure re-
> peats that single basic principle by which organic, social, and all other proc-
> esses of the formation of the universe are achieved, and cooperation with
> this principle (whose reflection is our consciousness, and the area of appli-
> cation — our whole being) cannot but fill us with the highest feeling experi-
> enced by man — pathos (Eisenstein 1987: 36).

Eisenstein develops further the idea of the highest organic unity in the process of art making, which is reached only if the whole work becomes "an organically inseparable whole with the thoughts, feelings, the very being and existence of the author" (Eisenstein 1987: 36). Then the spectator can experience the pathos through the structure of the artwork, when it is based on the pathos of the artist's experience.

The dream metaphor for Eisenstein describes cinema's ability to project individual and social goals: an artistic construction of inactive dream-like harmony should eventually lead to active construction of dream of social justice (Eisenstein 1939: 369). For tying together some empirical aspects of the complex dynamics of embodiment and cinematic consciousness, it is the future experiments within cinematic installations that may show, how embodied spatiality can be extended to a shared embodied space of interactive media script writing, and applied to other media environments.

Conclusion

The chapter has made an attempt on describing the fundamental biological mechanisms of why we are vulnerable against the emotions elicited in the erotic or fearful situations of the fictional characters on the screen. The focus here was on simulation, which enables the narratives to become part of our personal experience. Further, the chapter made an attempt to describe how the conscious mind is capable of producing artworks, which have the capability of affecting other minds, as films do. In the spirit of Eisensteinian organic-dynamic holism, recursive loops of cognition and perception have been shown to form the basic structure for conscious acts, and further, for authoring and sharing cinematic space.

I will conclude with a speculation that relates to the survival-based purposefulness intrinsically 'written' into the human evolutionary psychology: could cinema provide a survival-oriented simulation system, similar to Revonsuo's threatening dreams, for evolutionary purposes? This speculation becomes plausible, if considering cinema's apparent power over any human mind. The orientation to the survival game inherited in the biological organism, in my view, manifests explicitly in the domain of entertainment, in the survivalist aspect of game players and cinema-goers. Interactive video games may have gained popularity exactly because of the situated threat simulation they provide. In commercial cinema productions, as well as art house movies, sex and violence are the two dominating themes. How suppressed or open the themes are depends on the genre and target group of the film, but the survival game appears to be there with its merciless rule of 'eat or be eaten'. In this respect, cinema could be claimed to complement the same evolutionary task of threat simulation in the modern society as dreams, according to Revonsuo, may have had in the ancestral environment. Mind's extension to cognitive technology has made it possible to perform the assumedly evolution-related task of simulating potential danger in safe entertainment environments. Unlike most dreams, though, films tend to return the spectator to a happy ending with a positive socio-emotional message.

Bibliography

Adolphs, R., Damasio, H., Tranel, D., Cooper, G., & Damasio, A. 2000. 'A Role for Somatosensory Cortices in the Visual Recognition of Emotion as Revealed by Three-Dimensional Lesion Mapping' in *Journal of Neuroscience* 20 (7): 2683-2690.

Extract from Aristotle 350 B.C.E."On Dreams", Part 3, J. I. Beare (Transl.), provided by The Internet Classics Archive. On line at http://classics.mit.edu//Aristotle/dreams.html.

Avikainen, S. 2003. *Cortical Mechanisms of Action Observation, Imitation and Social Perception in Healthy and Autistic Subjects.* Academic dissertation in Brain Research Unit, Low Temperature Laboratory, Helsinki University of Technology.

Baars, B.J. 2003. 'The global brainweb: An update on global workspace theory', guest editorial in *Science and Consciousness Review;* on-line at http://cogweb.ucla.edu/CogSci/Baars-update_03.html

Barrett, L., Dunbar, R., & Lycett, J. 2002. *Human Evolutionary Psychology.* New York: Palgrave Publishers Ltd.

Clark, A. 2001. 'Reasons, Robots and the extended Mind' in *Mind & Language* 16(2): 121-145.

Dailey, A., Martindale, C., & Borkum, J. 1997. 'Creativity, synaesthesia and physiognomic perception' in *Creativity Research Journal* 10 (1):1–8.

Damasio, A. 2003. *Looking for Spinoza: Joy, Sorrow, and the Feeling Brain.* New York: Harcourt Inc.

— 1999. *The Feeling of What Happens: Body and Emotion in the Making of Consciousness.* New York: Harcourt Brace & Company.

— 1994. *Emotion, Reason, and the Human Brain.* New York: Harper Collins.

Davies, M. & Stone, T. (eds.) 1995. *Mental Simulation: Evaluations and Applications.* Oxford: Blackwell Publishers.

Dennett, D. 2001. 'Are We Explaining Consciousness Yet?' in *Cognition* 79(1-2): 221-237.

di Pellegrino, G., Fadiga, L., Fogassi, L., Gallese, V. & Rizzolatti, G. 1992. 'Understanding Motor Events: A Neurophysiological Study' in: *Experimental Brain Research* 91: 176-180.

Domino, G. 1989. 'Synaesthesia and creativity in fine arts students: An empirical look' in *Creativity Research Journal* 2(1-2): 17-29.

Eisenstein, S. 1987 (1939). 'On the Structure of Things' in Marshall, H. (trans.) *Nonindifferent Nature: Film and the Structure of the Things.* Cambridge: Cambridge University Press.

Eisenstein, S. 1998 (1924). 'The Montage of Film Attractions' in Taylor, R. (ed.) *The Eisenstein Reader.* London: BFI Publishing.

Fadiga, L.; Fogassi, L.; Pavesi, G. & Rizzolatti, G. 1995. 'Motor facilitation during action observation: a magnetic stimulation study' in *Journal of Neurophysiology* 73: 2608–2611.

Gallese,V. 2003. 'The Roots of Empathy: The Shared Manifold Hypothesis and the Neural Basis of Intersubjectivity' in *Psychopathology* 36: 171-180.

Gallese,V.; Fadiga, L.; Fogassi, L. & Rizzolatti, G. 1996. 'Action Recognition in the Premotor Cortex' in *Brain* 119: 593-609.

Gallese, V. & Goldman, A. 1998. 'Mirror Neurons and the Simulation Theory of Mind-Reading' in *Trends in Cognitive Sciences* 2(12): 493-501.

Gazzaniga, M. 1998. *The Mind's Past.* Berkeley: University of California Press.

Gazzaniga, M. S.; Bogen, J. E. & Sperry, R. W. 1965. 'Observations on Visual Perception after Disconnexion of the Cerebral Hemispheres in Man' in *Brain* 88(2): 221-236.

Gazzaniga, M.S., Ivry, R.B. & Mangun, G. R. 2002. *Cognitive Neuroscience: The Biology of the Mind.* New York and London: W.W. Norton & Company Inc.

Gibson, J. J. (1950). *The Perception of the Visual World.* Boston: Houghton Mifflin.

Gibson, J. J. 1979. *The Ecological Approach to Visual Perception.* Boston: Houghton Mifflin.

Grodal, T. 1997. *Moving Pictures: A New Theory of Film Genres, Feelings and Cognition.* Oxford: Oxford University Press.

Hasson, U.; Nir, Y.; Fuhrmann, G. & Malach, R. 2004. 'Intersubjective Synchronization of Cortical Activity During Natural Vision' in *Science* 303: 1634-1640.

Hobson, J. A. 1999. *Consciousness.* New York: Scientific American Library.

James, W. 1890. *The Principles of Psychology.* In: Classics in the History of Psychology. An internet resource developed by Christopher D. Green, York University, Toronto, Ontario.

James, W. 1912. 'Does Consciousness Exist?' in *Essays in Radical Empiricism.* New York: Longman Green & Co. 1-38. [Originally appeared in *Journal of Philosophy, Psychology and Scientific Methods* I(18)].

Järveläinen, J.; Schürmann, M.; Avikainen, S. & Hari, R. 2001. 'Stronger Reactivity of the Human Primary Motor Cortex During Observation of Live Rather than Video Motor Acts' in *Neuroreport* 12: 3493-3495.

Johnson, M. 1987. *The Body in the Mind: The Bodily Basis of Meaning, Imagination, and Reason.* Chicago: University of Chicago Press.

Kaipainen, M. 1996. 'Prospects for Ecomusicology: Inner and Outer Loops of the Musical Mind-Environment System' in Pylkkänen, P.; Pylkkö, P. & Hautamäki, A. (eds.) *Brain, Mind and Physics.* Amsterdam: IOS Press.

Lakoff, G. 1987.*Women, fire, and dangerous things: What categories reveal about the mind.* Chicago: University of Chicago Press.

Lakoff, G. & Johnson, M. 1980. *Metaphors We Live By.* Chicago: University of Chicago Press.

Lakoff, G. & Johnson, M. 1999. *Philosophy in the Flesh: The Embodied Mind and its Challenge to Western Thought.* New York: Basic Books.

Lang, P.J. 1988. 'What are the data of emotion?' in V.Hamilton, G.H.Bower & Frijda, N. (eds.) *Cognitive perspectives on emotion and motivation.* NATO ASI Series D, 44. Dortrecht: Kluwer: 173-191.

LeDoux, J. 1998. *The Emotional Brain.* New York: Touchstone.

Leslie, K.R, Johnson-Frey, S.H. & Grafton, S.T. 2004. 'Functional imaging of face and hand imitation: towards a motor theory of empathy' in *NeuroImage* 21(2): 601-607.

MacLean, P.D. 1993. 'Cerebral evolution of emotion' in Lewis, M. & Haviland, J.M. (eds.) *Handbook of Emotions.* New York: Guilford. Maturana, H. & Varela, F. 1980. *Autopoiesis and Cognition: The Realization of the Living.* Vol. 42: Boston Studies in the Philosophy of Science. Dordrecht: D. Reidel.

Maturana, H. & Varela, F. 1987. *The Tree of Knowledge: The Biological Roots of Human Understanding.* Boston: New Science Library.

Merleau-Ponty, M. 1962 (1945). *Phenomenology of Perception.* London: Routledge & Kegan Paul.

Metzinger, T. 1995. 'Faster than Thought: Holism, Homogeneity and Temporal Coding' in Metzinger, T. (ed.) *Conscious experience.* Thorverton, UK: Imprint Academic.

Metzinger, T. 2004. 'The Subjectivity of Subjective Experience: A Representationalist Analysis of the First-Person Perspective' in *Networks* 3(4): 33-64. [A revised edition of the chapter first appeared in — (ed.) 2000. *Neural Correlates of Consciousness — Empirical and Conceptual Questions.* Cambridge, MA: MIT Press.]

— 2004a. 'Appearance is not knowledge: the incoherent straw man, content-content confusion and mindless conscious subjects. Commentary for Noë, A. and Thompson, E., 'Are there neural correlates of consciousness?' In: *Journal of Consciousness Studies.* Vol 11(1).

Metzinger, T. & Gallese, V. 2003. 'The Emergence of a Shared Action Ontology: Building Blocks for a Theory' in *Consciousness and Cognition* 12: 549-571.

Meyerhold, V. 1981 (1922). *Teatterin lokakuu.* Helsinki: Love Kirjat. (For English translation see for eg. Brown, E. *A Revolution in the theatre*).

Nagel, T. 1974. 'What Is It Like to Be a Bat?' in *Philosophical Review* 83: 435-450.

Neisser, U. 1976. *Cognition and Reality: Principles and Implications of Cognitive Psychology*. New York: W. H. Freeman.

Nishitani, N. & Hari, R. 2000. 'Temporal Dynamics of Cortical Representation for Action' in *Proceedings of National Academy of Sciences of the USA* 97(2): 913-918.

Noë, A. & Thompson, E. 2004. 'Are there neural correlates of consciousness?' in *Journal of Consciousness Studies* 11(1): 3-28.

Oatley, K. & Jenkins, J.M. 1996. *Understanding Emotions*. Cambridge, MA: Blackwell Publishers.

O'Regan, J.K. & Noë, A. 2002. 'On the brain-basis of visual consciousness: A sensorimotor account' in Noë, A. & Thompson, E. (eds.) *Vision and Mind: Selected Readings in the Philosophy of Perception*. Cambridge, MA: MIT Press.

Port, R. & van Gelder, T. 1995. *Mind as Motion: Explorations in the dynamics of cognition*. Cambridge, MA: MIT Press.

Preston, S. D. & de Waal, F. B. M. 2002. 'Empathy: Its Ultimate and Proximate Bases' in *Behavioural and Brain Sciences* 25: 1-72.

Ramachandran, V. S. & Hubbard, E. M. 2001. 'Synaesthesia — a window into perception, thought and language' in *Journal of Consciousness Studies* 8(12): 3-34.

— 2003. 'Hearing Colours, Tasting Shapes' in *Scientific American* 288(5): 42-49.

Revonsuo A. 1995. 'Consciousness, Dreams, and Virtual Realities' in *Philosophical Psychology* 8(1): 35-58.

Revonsuo, A. 2000. 'The Reinterpretation of Dreams: An evolutionary hypothesis of the function of dreaming' in *Behavioural and Brain Sciences* 23(6): 877-901.

— 2005. *Inner Presence*. Cambridge, MA: MIT Press.

Revonsuo, A. & Valli, K. 2000a. 'Dreaming and Consciousness: Testing the Threat Simulation Theory of the Function of Dreaming' in *Psyche* 6(8).

Rizzolatti, G.; Fadiga, L.; Gallese, V. & Fogassi, L. 1996a. 'Premotor Cortex and the Recognition of Motor Actions' in *Cognitive Brain Research* 3: 131–141.

Rizzolatti, G.; Fadiga, L.; Matelli, M.; Bettinardi, V.; Paulesu, E.; Perani, D. & Fazio, F. 1996b. 'Localization of Grasp Representations in Humans by PET: 1. Observation versus execution' in *Experimental Brain Research* 111: 246–252.

Rizzolatti, G and Arbib, M.A. 1998. 'Language within Our Grasp' in *Trends in Neurosciences* 21: 188-194.

Root-Bernstein, R. & Root-Bernstein, M. 1999. *Sparks of Genius: The Thirteen Thinking Tools of the World's Most Creative People.* Boston: Houghton Mifflin.

Tikka, P. 2002. 'Sergei Eisensteinian kuvakieli dynaamisen mielen näkökulmasta' ('The Visual Language of Sergei Eisenstein from the Point of View of an Embodied Mind') in *Lähikuva* 2(2): 26-41.

— 2003. 'Cinema (interativo) como modelo para a mente' ('[Interactive] Cinema as a Model of Mind') in Maciel, K. & Parente, A. (eds.) *Redes sensoriais: arte, ciência, tecnologia.* Rio de Janeiro: Contra Capa Livraria: 45-50.

— 2005. 'Dynamic emotion ecologies in cinema' in *Integrated Media Machine.* Helsinki: Edita & Rovaniemi: University of Lapland: 103-126.

Thompson, E. & Varela, F.J. 2001. 'The radical embodiment: neural dynamics and consciousness' in *Trends in Cognitive Sciences* 5(10): 418-425.

Varela, F. 1999. 'The Specious present: The Neurophenomenology of Time Consciousness' in Petitot, J.; Varela, F.J.; Pachoud, B. & Roy, J.M. (eds.) *Naturalizing Phenomenology.* USA: Stanford University Press: 266-314.

Varela, F. & Shear, J. 1999. 'First-person Methologies: What, Why, How?' in Varela & Shear (eds.) *The View from Within: First Person Approaches to the Study of Consciousness.* UK: Imprint Academic:1-14.

Varela, F., Thompson, E., & Rosch, E. 1991. *Embodied Mind: Cognitive Science and Human Experience.* Cambridge, MA: MIT Press.

Notes

[1] My claim presented in Tikka (2002, 2003) is similar to the note of translator and researcher Herbert Marshall on Eisenstein's interest of the creative process and his attempt on establishing; "a link between the most general aesthetic laws and the laws of developing human consciousness" (Eisenstein 1987: 408 &150).

[2] In his early work, Eisenstein (1924) applied the scientific ideas of human body kinaesthesia and actor's training techniques, known as *biomechanics,* of theatre director Vsevolod Meyerhold into his early montage theory of film attractions (Eisenstein 1998 refers to a definition of biomechanics in Meyerhold 1922: 103-106).

[3] An option would be to deny the physiological existence of consciousness, and treat it as a culturally constructed functional phenomenon like 'fame in the brain', as discussed in Dennett (2001).

[4] The notion of ecology here refers to the psychological exploration and perception circuit that enables the subject to adapt to the changes in the environment, as discussed in Ulrich Neisser (1976). Originally the term was coined by J.J. Gibson as the concept of 'stimulus ecology'. See Gibson 1950, 1979. He introduced the term for describing how an organism's perceptual system continuously adapts to the visual cues afforded in the environment, which happen in an unmediated direct manner. The question about direct perception divides the views of the ecological approach. The view defended in this contribution holds that perception is mediated in both the low-level and the high-level cognitive processes.

[5] See Barrett et al. (2002).

[6] The mirror neuron system discovered in frontal cortex of monkeys (di Pellegrino et al. 1992; Gallese et al. 1996; Rizzolatti et al. 1996a) and of humans (Fadiga et al. 1995; Rizzolatti et al. 1996b; Nishitani and Hari 2000)[6] is assumed to function as a motor-based *simulation system* for learning from the others as well as understanding one's relation to the embodied and emotive space of the others. (Avikainen 2003)

[7] The proponents of dynamic systems theory generally describe their view to cognition as noncomputational and non-representational. Instead, the dynamic systems are characterized by state-determinism, complexity, low dimensionality, and, are fundamentally described in relation to independent variables of time (eg. Port and van Gelder 1995: 5).

[8] The organism bound to a perspectivalness, which means experiencing the world from the first-person-perspective, is discussed in Nagel, T. (1974). Metzinger (1995, 2004) has adopted the concept, which will also be applied here. In my idea, perspectivalness appears as a continuously variable self-modifying figure or dynamic pattern coupled with the background of multiple potentialities.

[9] Metzinger (2004) explicitly notes that his views on 'full immersion' and the self-model of human being as 'the virtual reality' converge strongly with those of Revonsuo (1995).

[10] See also individual contributions in Johnson (1987); Lakoff (1987).

[11] James suggests abandoning the notion of consciousness and replaces it with the pragmatic equivalent in realities of experience (William James 1912: Chp.1).

[12] Several witnesses have reported that James Joyce discussed with Eisenstein about filming *Ulysses* in late 1929, but that did not lead to further cooperation.

[13] See Davies and Stone (1995) for approaches on the simulation theory.

[14] See comparative neuroimaging research between 'direct' perception and 'mediated audiovisual image' perception in Järveläinen et al. (2001).

[15] Mental simulation as resonant states in the phenomenal level could be considered to have same functional meaning as synchronization in the neural level. Hasson et al. (2004) have provided evidence of intersubject correlation in an experiment, where the tested viewers showed the tendency for reacting in a similar way at the same moments of film action. The researchers recorded intersubject emotional synchronization of different human brains, in correlation to the same events or moments in a film viewing situation involving images with high attention value that maybe critical for

survival and dominated by eg. hand movements, close-ups of emotional facial expressions, or abrupt loud sounds.

[16] In addition to the widely discussed mirror neuron network involved in imitation of the hand movements, i.e. grasping, the mirroring may extend to explain mental phenomena, such as empathy; eg. Leslie et al. (2004) assume the right hemisphere mirror neuron network for enabling empathy, especially via recognizing facial emotional expressions. See also about 'motor resonance system' that links perception-action system to emotions in Preston and de Waal (2002).

[17] Gazzaniga's research is based on experiments with split brain patients, who have the left and right hemispheres disconnected due to, for eg. a brain infarct. See Gazzaniga et al. (1965). See exhaustive research on emotion theories in Oatley and Jenkins (1996).

[18] Many of the synaesthetes are artists or poets, as noted by Ramachandran and Hubbard (2001, 2003). For research on artists and poets, see also Dailey et al. (1997); Domino (1989); and Root-Bernstein & Root-Bernstein (1999).

[19] Extract from Aristotle "On Dreams", Part 3, J. I. Beare (Transl.), provided by The Internet Classics Archive. Available online at http://classics.mit.edu//Aristotle/dreams.html

[20] LeDoux (1998) discusses the evidence that the amygdala receives auditory and visual data directly via the thalamus. In dream, when neocortex is not activated, the amygdala may assign the significance and meanings to the dream events.

[21] The PGO signals that stimulate the brain both when awake and asleep, link to the threat recognition/avoidance response, thus indicating the 'flight or fight' evaluation critical for survival (Revonsuo 2000). See also Hobson (1999: 169), whose view is based on the idea that dreams are random noise without any purpose, and emerge from the neural patterns of motor experience.

[22] MacLean is inspired by a research of Papez (1939), who assumed three pathways to the brain: the stream of movement goes to the striatal region, the stream of feeling to the limbic system connected to the hypothalamus, and the stream of thought to the neocortex. MacLean (1993) suggests that these pathways developed in distinct phases of brain evolution, which are reptilian, Paleo-mammalian and Neo-mammalian phases. See in Oatley and Jenkins (1996: 137).

Extended Body, Extended Mind: The Self as Prosthesis

Susan Stuart

What we call the 'self', the object of our self-consciousness, is neither solely the mind nor the body, nor is it some amalgam of the two. The self is a prosthesis. It is the result of an agent's action within its complex and changing world. It is an extension of the agent as an embodied system embedded within its world; adaptable and technological, able to enhance and reconfigure itself to replace and augment its capabilities. This thesis adopts an active externalism — because of the role the environment plays in driving and directing cognitive processes — in the claim that the limits of the self are not the limits of the body.

According to Kant (1929) the most we can say about ourselves is that we are logical subjects of thoughts, necessary for the very possibility of coherent cognition. We look for the self, we reflect, and we find no thing, nothing that is the bearer of properties, and we try to conjure it up in the concept of a soul or mental thing (Descartes 1968), or a bundle of discrete perceptions (Hume 1739). But we are looking in the wrong direction and must reorient ourselves. Self-consciousness requires the existence of a perceiving and conceiving being that acts and interacts with other objects and organisms in, what must at least appear to be, an objective world. It requires embodiment and embeddedness within its world; it is 'fallen' (Heidegger 1962), necessarily adaptable, necessarily technological, extending itself through the use of tools, restoring lost functions and replacing lost organs and limbs. But also enhancing and reconfiguring itself, augmenting its capabilities and pushing itself further into its world and away from the first place we look. The self is not the body. The self is not the mind. The self is active agency within the world; it is prosthesis.

In speaking of self-consciousness we seem to specify some thing or object that is being conscious. I will argue that there is no such object, that the self is neither mind nor body, nor some alchemic amalgama-

tion of the two that manages to satisfy the hard problem of consciousness and bridges the explanatory gap (Chalmers 1995; Shear 1997). I
will argue that the self is active agency within a dynamically changing, experienced world, and that that world is not especially privileged
because it is assumed to be physical, for a virtual world or virtual
reality would just as well serve the purpose of providing us with a
sense of self. Thus, complex selves are inventions which provide a
locus for mental states, and which enable us to identify thoughts and
ideas as coming from this, rather than that, point of view. Selves are
things that can form 'depictions' and, so, have a sense of being out
there in their world. The term 'self' is just shorthand for a set of
relations between the senses, actions and objects; it is nothing more
than an artefact of engagement with the world.

I am not arguing that having a body, or at least thinking we have a
body, is unimportant. On the contrary, it is crucial that we have perceptual and conceptual abilities that enable us to get to the stage where
we can bring such an extraordinary thing as a self into existence —
even if it is illusory — and it is the body that makes this possible.
After all, it could be argued that, it is the activity of the body that
shapes the mind (*Viz.* Gallese 2005). We must, and this 'must' has a
nomological force, be 'embodied', whatever we may later turn out to
mean by that term, for we need to experience our world and we need a
point of view from which, as distinct from other entities, we can
develop a body image and a body schema (Meijsing 2000). We must
also be embedded within our world, for it is the sensation of being and
acting in our world that presents us with the stimuli, afferent and
efferent impulses that we need for thought, will and action. Without
sensation we would cease to function. Our existence as unitary selves
would dissolve with the impossibility of content-free thought.

The necessary and, together, sufficient criteria for this complex,
self-generating embeddedness can be stated as follows:

> 1. we must be situated and embodied;
> 2. we must have multiple goals;
> 3. our environment must be sufficiently complex and challenging for us to
> be capable of complex responses;
> 4. we must sense our world through a rich sensory interface;
> 5. we must be capable of having inner representations of our world;
> 6. we must have a rich repertoire of possible interactions with our environ-
> ment, continuously manipulating its world in ways that bring about signifi-
> cant changes (Stuart 2002; Dobbyn & Stuart 2003).

From a Heideggerian perspective we are fallen, essentially social, interacting with animate and inanimate things, and with things that exhibit mentality and others which do not, that is, with *Dasein* and non-*Dasein*. Within this complex environment we are adaptable, using tools to change our relationship with the world, using technology to extend ourselves and augment our capabilities but also to restore lost functions, replace damaged parts and even replace or alter our physical features. It is, as Heidegger (1962) suggests, *contra* Aristotle, that our potentiality precedes our actuality; we are, but we become ourselves. The actuality that emerges is our being, our immersed engagement with our world. Our self is what we do and how we do it. It requires a sensing and actuating body, a thinking and conceiving mind, but together or alone they are insufficient; we need a world as well. It is as Merleau-Ponty argues that; "there is no inner man, man is in the world, and only in the world does he know himself" (2002: xii).

How the self was lost: Descartes and Kant

For many of us there remains a strong temptation to follow Descartes in his methodical reflections and bring to mind some idea of the self that is a persisting, purely immaterial, non-composite, thinking thing, the thing referred to by each of us as 'I'. After all, Descartes's conception provides us with that essential element of ourselves that is not reducible to physics and some kind of physical explanation. It is pure in its being the antithesis of the physically vulnerable, ultimately decaying physical body. But this is the very thing refuted, almost completely successfully, by Kant in his attack on rational psychology in the *Paralogisms of Pure Reason* (Kant 1929: A341/ B399 — A405/ B432)[1].

Descartes falls into error according to Kant because he conflates the meaning of the term 'subject of thought' in the following argument:

1. All that is thought as subject is substance.
2. The 'I' is thought as subject.
3. The 'I' is substance.

Having now found himself with substance in his hands that is unlike any empirical substance, and giving a great deal of thought to what its nature must be, Descartes concludes that this 'I' or self must be mental or conscious, indivisible and immortal, with all that these characteristics imply. But Kant's objection seems certain: the 'thought as

subject' in the first premise refers to empirical objects, the things that
we think of as physically substantial and divisible, and which are the
'subjects' of our thoughts; the 'thought as subject' in the second
premise refers to the subject having the thoughts, the 'I' or self, about
which nothing more can be said, except that which Kant has said
already in the *Transcendental Analytic* (Kant 1929: A65/ B90 —
A292/ B349).

The self negated, then reinstated

Kant's account of the mind has two essential elements that we might
think of individually as reception and ordering; they are:

1. perceptual awareness or *intuition* of our world;
2. conceptualisation of the perceptual experience of our world through *categories* or
   concepts.

And we can say exactly what Kant means by looking at two of his
most famous phrases: 'Thoughts without content are empty, intuitions
without concepts are blind' (Kant 1929: A52/B76). If we have no
content, no experiential or perceptual input, our thoughts will be no
thoughts at all for they will be empty. If we have perceptions or experience without any understanding to guide us in our organisation of
the data of that experience, we will be as good as blind, for all we will
experience is chaos. So what makes our experience unchaotic — well,
the concepts in our understanding that make possible the synthesis of
our experience, drawing together the unity of self-consciousness and
the unity of objective experience. The revelation of a self is only
possible in simultaneous relation to the revelation of a world. Let us
unpack this just a little.

Experience is only possible if it refers to an objective world, that is,
if we are embedded in an experientially rich and changing environment. This is as true of human beings as it is of animals and even of
artificially constructed animated agents.

If, for a moment, we suppose that Descartes is right that I can
determine my consciousness in time without granting the existence of
a physical world, then we must ask how can this be so. In judging my
own existence in time, I need to be able to perceive myself in relation
to other things, some of which will be moving and some of which will
not, for it is only in this state that I am able to perceive change. If
everything was moving or if everything was still, I would be unable to
measure the passage of time in any ordered way. We need order and

regularity against which change can be perceived. This is most clearly demonstrated if we look at a simple analogue watch. The face remains static whilst the hands move. If we, our entire world, consisted only of ourselves in relation to the watch, and the face and the hands either both moved or both stood still, we would have chaos or nothingness[2]. Either way no coherent notion of a self would emerge, or continue for very long, for no relationship would exist. It is only in the sensing of motion, that change is conceived, and it is only through the conceptualisation of change that a distinction between self and other is made possible. Self is not possible without other. They are not simply inter-related; they are interdependent. Thus Kant concludes that inner experience cannot be all there is for inner experience requires outer experience, and outer experience brings content through the sensing of motion and the conceptualisation of change.

Kant says of the self that "it must be possible for the 'I think' to accompany all my representations" (Kant 1929: B131), and what he means is simply this: when I have an experience it must be possible for me to be self-consciously aware of it, but it is not necessary for me to be so. Thus, the 'I think' is only, after all this, the 'vehicle of all concepts' (Kant 1929: A341/ B399) awaiting content from the sensory system (B421), and once we have some content to make up a thought we have the means, on reflection, of inventing a complex self that must be having it. As Walsh says, "what is being sought is presupposed in the seeking" (Walsh 1975: 179). What we cannot then do is conclude that what is presupposed is known in some other way. "The 'I think' expresses the act of determining my existence', but does not itself amount to a form of self-intuition" (Ibid.). The 'I think' or 'I' is not an expression of an experience, it is merely the form that an experience can take.

So what remains of our traditional view of the self? On the one hand, it has become a Cartesian non-entity, and on the other it is merely the form that a thought must take. But Kant's theory bears more fruit than most, for in uncovering the necessary unity of self-consciousness we first require sensations, understanding and the employment of a cognitive imagination that makes it possible for us to recognise our thoughts as our own; and none of this is possible without an 'external' world with which we must engage if we are to have even the illusory sense we have of a continuing self (Hume 1739; Brook 1994; Strawson 1997 & 1999).

The Kantian subject posits a world, but, in order to be able to assert a truth, the actual subject must in the first place have a world to be in the world, that is, sustain round about it a system of meanings whose reciprocities, relationships and involvements do not require to be made explicit in order to be exploited (Merleau-Ponty 1962: 149). Our picture now is of cognition as an embedded process with the mind, body and world interacting to such an extent that the traditional boundaries between world and mind no longer exist (Clark & Chalmers 1998). What appears to be a separate world of distinct objects is not. Boundaries appear but in reality we are only conceivable as selves in dynamic conjunction with our world, and the roles that technology plays in that conjunction alter irrevocably our perception of our location, our extension and our limitation.

In a similar vein to Clark & Chalmers (1998) I am advocating 'an active externalism, based on the active role of the environment in driving cognitive processes'[3], but where they say simply that 'human reasoners... lean heavily on environmental supports' it needs to be emphasised that 'leaning' is not optional. It is a necessary part of conscious being in the world, the part that makes possible the creation and, thus, conception of distance and proximity, of otherness and separateness, and which presents us with a locus for thought, a point of view. The element of choice arises only in the individual instances of reliance, so I might count on my fingers, or keep in my pocket a notebook of names I frequently forget, or use 'pen and paper to perform long multiplication' (McClelland et al. 1986; Clark 1989). To this list we might easily add the use of all kinds of instruments such as logarithmic tables and astrolabes, and we might think further of how our idea of ourselves has changed through the shift from an oral tradition, through writing, to the printing press, the telegraph, telephone, networked computer, and on to SMS texting with, and without, images. In extending my mind into the world, I demonstrate my role as an embodied and embedded, active cognitive system. I have skills but they are merely a part of my self in their manifestation. I might say that I am a pianist, but unless I play the piano, unless I demonstrate my skill, I am not a pianist. Being a pianist is not part of me, my self, if I cannot play the piano — though wanting to be a pianist might be[4]. I am what I sense, think, and do; not merely what I say, though saying in certain circumstances can be doing.

So, we are sensing and cognising systems who have an intricate neuroanatomy and physiology, which requires stimulus from outside if we are to function effectively in responding safely to our world in real time. The 'we', spoken of here, is not a collection of stories constituting a narrative self (Dennett 1992, and exemplified in the film

Rashômon, 1950), nor is it some Lockean feat of memory (Locke 1690), of the kind favoured by films as diverse as *Total Recall* (1990), *Dark City* (1998), and *Memento* (2000)[5]; it is intentional agency with our perceived environment playing an active part in the orchestration of our behaviour.

Our conception of our perceived environment as a physical, mind-independent reality has been constructed over many years of interacting with our world through a complex network of sensors, transducers, and actuators; more technically through a system of afferent and efferent impulses conditioned by action-feedback mechanisms. It is a framework that led Descartes, and many others both before and after him, to believe that the mind and body are, not only, separable, but also separate. In Descartes's case consciousness, self-consciousness, and the mind are all one and the same thing, and only possessed by human beings. All other organisms are mechanical in nature and, therefore, non-conscious[6].

But we know Descartes to be mistaken. We have established a necessary link between the perceiver and the perceived, and while it is possible that only human beings are conscious of their environment, it is unlikely that consciousness is a phenomenon limited only to them. Consciousness imparts an evolutionary advantage to those that possess it, and given that it is explicitly linked to neurophysiology, those animals that have qualitatively similar neurophysiologies to our own are likely to be conscious (Griffin 1981, 2001). Many animals use a language of some kind to communicate, and in humans and other animals tools are devised to conquer tasks for which bodies by themselves are insufficient. In this way our tools come to embody some aspect of our mind, the need for something to be achieved and an abstracted way in which it could be seen to be possible.

But, a note of caution must be sounded. This complex system of relations between senses, actions and objects — the self, presents us with only sense data, whether it is through our outer senses, in actively perceiving and bringing about changes in our world, or through our proprioceptive sense. This complex relationship has, at its core, phenomenology and it is a phenomenology that is revealed because of the rich and lively interplay of the body and world. So, two pathways open up. Firstly, we might accept the world as a given but be inclined to jettison the idea of ever being able to talk about it in a mind-independent way. In this instance a correspondence theory of truth — by which we can confirm that the world is how it seems to be — is doomed to failure, for there is nothing we have access to other than our sense data against which we can do our 'check' of reality. Secondly, we might admit that with the rapid progress being made in virtual reality interface technology, we are, all too quickly, beginning to ask the sorts of question Bostrom (2003) asks in: 'Are You Living In a Computer Simulation?', and the answer is neither obvious nor straightforward. The sense of realness we currently have can be reproduced — and we deceived — by good simulacra of the kind found in virtual reality simulators. It is, as Pepperell argues in the following chapter, and Bradley (1893) that: 'everyday conceptions of the world contain hidden contradictions which appear, fatally when we try to think out their consequences'.

Technology: location, extension, limitation

Stern (1985) suggests that in the early months of life the human child begins to form a distinction between itself and its world. The ability to make such a distinction must be a precondition of self-consciousness and the formation of a self, for without it the development of a point of view and the ability to locate, identify and interact with objects relative to your current spatio-temporal position would be impossible. This further confirms the need for a body, separable from but not independent of the environment, with a sensed boundary between it and the wider world. The defining features of a body seem to be a set of sensory channels through which information about the environment can be gleaned, an actuator system enabling manipulation of the world, and proprioceptive mechanisms that enable the evolution of an inner 'egocentric' space (Brewer 1992). It is as a result of these mechanisms that we are able to update and maintain our body schema, which is the very thing we need for locating the position of a touch to our skin or the region of our body in which a pain is felt[7]. Our body schema provides us with; "continually updated, non-conceptual, non-conscious information about [our] body... [providing] the necessary feedback for the execution of... gross motor programmes and their fine-tuning" (Meijsing 2000: 39). Gross motor functions can determine lifting and holding, and we need accurate input if we are going to be able to fine-tune our actions to distinguish between holding a glass, holding a marshmallow and holding a child. Without the ability to fine-tune your haptic sensing and actuating mechanisms we might crush the child or smash the glass.

In human beings the dominant sense is vision with the other senses playing a subservient, though often corroboratory, role[8]. If your dominant sense is impaired to such an extent that it alters your experience of depth and proximity, then it is expedient to have your eyes tested and wear spectacles with correcting lenses. Without this technology you would be different, tentative in movement, and more reliant on your other senses, most specifically on touch and hearing. With your spectacles your unimpaired functionality is restored and your sensory system extends you once more out into your world, a world that, once again, consists of distinguishable objects in spatio-temporal relations to you and to one another. In more extreme cases where the visual sense is seriously impaired, or lost altogether, depth and distance perception might come through using a stick, especially in non-local, unfamiliar environments. No visual feedback is available about the distance to the edge of the kerb, or how deep the kerb is, so the stick supplies the afferent input through the tactile and muscular feedback system in the hand and arm; it is a haptic device for touching and feeling the world and responding appropriately. The active perceiving person, now plus stick, with its world and its processing and acting, constitutes the self.

The emphasis in this case is on the interplay between vision and touch, and on touch when vision is lost or impaired. But a curious reversal of sensory emphasis is present in those people who have lost their proprioceptive sense, and thus the ability to create or maintain their body schema. Cases of this kind reveal, as Gibson (1979) thought, that the visual sense is crucial for their retaining a sense of self. Meijsing says of a patient, IW, that; "In the dark he did not know where his hand was; and even if he knew, he would not have been able to move it towards the bedside table without visual feedback" (Meijsing 2000: 42). IW felt disembodied, absent, even 'dead', and his sense of self returned only when he had learned once again, and with a great deal of visual concentration, to move in a controlled manner. Here we find again that self-directed movement is crucial for self-identity, and that a sensory system is only necessary in organisms that move, because organisms that do not move require no capacity to avoid or manipulate objects. Being informed that there are environmental changes is not enough, there needs to be a rich interplay between this information we are receiving and our active self-movement, for it is this; "that places the self firmly at the centre of the environment. Active self-movement gives a sense of agency, as the perceived environment changes as a result of the purposive action" (Meijsing 2000: 46).

IW had to work hard to recover this sense of selfhood and agency. One of his greatest breakthroughs came when using the DART robot — a teleoperations device that extends an individual's sensing and manipulation abilities — at NASA's Johnson Space Center, Houston.

This robot has arms and joints isomorphic to the human arm. In other words it has a shoulder, elbow and wrist joints that move as ours do. Its hands consist of a thumb and two opposing fingers... Its arms are looked down on from its head by two cameras that allow stereo-vision. This is the 'slave'.

The 'master' is a human subject rigged up with sensors on the head and arms with special gloves that sense joint angles and movements. When [the subject moves], the robot moves, after a short delay. Finally the subject wears a virtual reality set on the head that gives him a view of the robot's arms. It also precludes vision of the subject's own arms or hands. Then the game, and it is extraordinary fun and easy to do, is to move the robot's arms by moving one's own with the feedback coming from vision. "The human master can make the slave robot pick up a drink, tie knots, pass a wrench hand to hand... Within a few minutes of moving and seeing the robot's arms we experienced our corporeal selves occupying the robot's body" (Cole 2000: 51).

IW, who had no proprioceptive sense but was used to acting on visual feedback, very quickly became 'reasonably proficient at a task of robot manual dexterity'. The simplest explanation for this is that his body schema is dependent upon visual feedback and not shared between visual and tactile feedback, as is usually the case, or based on tactile feedback alone as with someone with a serious visual impairment. IW's case works in completely the opposite way from the blind person who uses a stick to gain extended haptic feedback about their world; he cannot use touch, so he must use vision.

The illusion of occupying the robot's body, of it being your body, your interface with the world, and not just part of you, is clearly possible, but there is still something clunky and exoskeletal about the experience. It may 'feel' real but we can see it is not; we know we can be separated from it. Like riding a horse, when you are working well together, the gait is right, and you and the horse are in harmony; or when driving a car and the gear change is smooth, the cornering is controlled and you feel as though you are one entity. In both cases your experience of your self has been extended to include the horse or the car as part of your world, as part of you. Yet in each case you can get off or out, and distinguish yourself from the horse or car by increasing the distance or otherwise altering the relationship between you and it.

The sensation of unity we can have with the robot, horse, or car, is made possible not simply — with the exception of I W's unusual case — by the visual sense which is only one-way, but by the tactile sense which is two-way or co-dependent, providing a sensation of resistance, or force-feedback, to the pressure of our touch. Salisbury says of feeling a cup that:

> ... we grasp and manipulate the object, running our fingers across its shape and surfaces in order to build a mental image of a cup. This co-dependence between sensing and manipulation is at the heart of understanding how humans can so deftly interact with their physical world (1995).

But the sense of realness that is presented to us in this way is no more reliable as an indicator of a mind-independent physical world than the visual input we receive, or even the unified input from our combined sense experiences. The experiences are real, possibly even verifiably so, but their objects existing in a mind-independent reality are not. Perhaps Bradley is right that; "Feeling, thought and volition... are all the material of existence and there is no other material, actual or even possible' (1930: Chp. XIV). It is certainly true that our worlds need to be there, for otherwise our thoughts would have no content and we, ourselves, would not exist, but it is also true that we cannot speak about these worlds independently of ourselves. But, even though our worlds may be a given in our experience, there is no compelling reason why either they or our embodiment need be physical. Claims of this kind can be fortified by an examination of the impressive but illusory sense of 'realness' offered by haptics technology in the form of haptic devices that provide rich and self-consistent sensory feedback (Hannaford 2002).

Haptics, the science of touch, lets computer users interact with virtual worlds by feeling. Scientists use computers to simulate not only the impact of a golf club hitting the ball, but also the springiness of a kidney under forceps, the push of an individual carbon nanotube in an atomic force microscope, and the texture of clothing for sale on the internet (Ruvinsky 2003). The home page of the Immersion Corporation offers these kinds of experiences for sale.

> Feel your light saber hum or your shot gun blast and reload with Immersion's force-feedback sensations through your mouse, joystick, game pad or steering wheel. Easily add a new dimension of realism to gaming! Allow your medical professionals to practice difficult procedures in a risk-free en-

vironment with Immersion Medical's force-feedback surgical training simulators and improve your quality of medical care.
(http://www.immersion.com)

The sensory and kinaesthetic feedback provided in haptic technology is the same kind of force-feedback we get in our experience of every day objects, and in a virtual environment those things which might start off feeling artificial quickly begin to feel real. Advances in telepresence systems, which make use of a head-mounted display along with body-operated remote actuators and sensors to control, for example, distant machinery or a weapon in a game, reveal how easy it is for the virtual environment to feel real, and with transparent telepresence it is possible to have the experience of being fully present in another part of the world, geographically remote from one's own physical location. As Stone says, developers aim to create;

> the ideal of sensing sufficient information about the teleoperator and task environment, and communicating this to the human operator in a sufficiently natural way, that the operator feels physically present at the remote site (2000:1).

Virtual reality environments are not particularly new; we have had simulators that enable a golfer to practice her swing, or an airline pilot to learn to deal with landing safely in inclement conditions for quite a few years, and new, small-scale environments are being developed all the time[9]. But these are not the fully immersed environments of the kind with which we are only now becoming familiar. Fully immersed environments are those in which we can feel ourselves walking around and manipulating objects, while at the same time feeling the warmth of the sun on our face, smelling the newly mown grass, and hearing the dog next door barking. Our immersion in these virtual environments will be so complete; the integration of our array of sensory input will be so seamless, that we will feel as though we are there, that the objects and experiences are real (Kurzweil 1999 and Hayles 1999). Telepresence will have been achieved and to such an extent that we will be unable to tell the difference between the virtual world and the one we once assumed to be physically real and separable from us. In the context of a medical training environment Salisbury says:

> People will really begin to feel like they're holding the tissue and they're tearing it... And they'll feel bad about it because they squeezed too hard.
> (Salisbury in Ruvinsky 2003)

In the film *The Matrix* (1999) Neo, Morpheus and Trinity discover that the world that has appeared to them to be real is only a facade created by a malevolent cyber-intelligence known as the 'Matrix' that is sapping human beings of their life-force. It is a fascinating film[10] and the subject of more than one undergraduate dissertation, but it is based on an implausible premise that some powerful and nasty artifice — a Cartesian *malin genie* (Descartes 1968, First Meditation) — is employed in controlling all of our sensory input. Why go to such extremes, except to make a good film, when full-body haptic suits are being developed as we write and speak (Washburn 2004); and over a decade ago Youngblut, Johnson, Nash, Wienclaw and Will were specifying what would be needed for a fully-functioning body suit that would present the wearer with a complete experience of a virtual environment[11].

The role of visual interfaces is obvious and needs no discussion except to point out that humans are strongly oriented to their visual sense... While tracking is a type of interface that is largely transparent to the user, it is critical in keeping the VE system informed about user movements so that sensory inputs can be correlated to the user's position. Auditory interfaces can play a key role in providing informational inputs to the user, increasing the realism of a simulated environment and promoting a user's sense of presence in a VE. Haptic interfaces provide the tactile and kinaesthetic feedback arising from user contact with objects in the environment. Full-body motion interfaces fall into two categories. Active self-motion interfaces allow a user to move freely through an environment, for example, walking over various types of surfaces or climbing stairs as necessary. Passive motion interfaces reflect the use of some type of vehicle to move a user through the environment. The final interface technology... is that of olfaction, where odours are used to provide the user with additional sensory cues about his environment (Youngblut et al. 1995).

It takes very little stretch of the imagination to see that once the military releases the unclassified technology, it will spin down into our economy for commercial use. In a few years full immersion virtual reality suits will be readily available to the public in some shrink-to-fit synthetic skin, tempting us with all manner of experiences that can be had without our actually going anywhere. The range of experiential opportunities is limitless from walking holidays in the Apennine mountains and snorkelling off the coast of Borneo, to taking up an apprenticeship in stonemasonry, and learning how to cloud hop. And, if we don't have to be restricted by the laws that hold in what we take to be our physical world, then why should we be restricted to 'travelling' in only this current time period. The traditional school trip could become a lot more exciting as we learn our history by being taken to some virtual version of it. Our experiences will, all the time, be feeding back into the construction of what we think of as ourselves, and there will be little, perhaps nothing to tell them apart from those we have — up until now — been calling real experiences. The phenomenology at the heart of our being, at the heart of our self-consciousness, will remain the same.

Following many thinkers before us we have dismantled the artificially constructed division between mind and body. Our selves remain, but as a complex set of relations between sensings, thinkings, actions and objects; and a virtual world is as successful as a real world in providing the interplay and content we need to make these *relata* possible. What we think of as our selves turn out to be nothing more than artefacts of these integrated experiences; they are, after all, very simply creations of the interplay between mind and world; they are prostheses.

Bibliography

Bostrom, N. 2003 'Are You Living In a Computer Simulation?' in *Philosophical Quarterly* 53 (211): 243-255.

Bradley, F. H. 1930 (2nd edn., original 1893) *Appearance and reality: a metaphysical essay*. Oxford: Clarendon Press.

Brewer, B. 1992 'Self-location and agency' in *Mind* 101: 17-34.

Brook, A. 1994. *Kant and the Mind*. UK: Cambridge University Press.

Chalmers, D. 1995. 'Facing Up to the Hard Problem of Consciousness' in *Journal of Consciousness Studies* 2(3): 200-19.

Clark, A. 1989. *Microcognition*. Cambridge, MA: MIT Press.

Clark, A. &Chalmers, D. J. 1998. 'The Extended Mind' in *Analysis* 58(1): 7-19.

Cole, J. 2000. 'Commentary' (on Meijsing, M.) in *Journal of Consciousness Studies*. 7(6):50-2.

Cottingham, J. 1998. *Descartes*. Oxford: Oxford University Press.

Dennett, Daniel C. 1992. 'The Self as a Center of Narrative Gravity' in Kessel, F. Cole, P. & Johnson, D. (eds.) *Self and Consciousness: Multiple Perspectives*. Hillsdale, NJ: Erlbaum.

Descartes, R. 1968. *Discourse on method, and the Meditations* (translated with an introduction by F.E. Sutcliffe). Harmondsworth: Penguin.

Dobbyn, C. & Stuart, S. 2003. 'The Self as an Embedded Agent' in *Minds and Machines* 13 (2): 187-201.

Duke-Elder, S. 1958-1976 (ed.). *System of Ophthalmology*. London: Kimpton.

Gallese, V. 2005. 'Embodied simulation: From neurons to phenomenal experience' in *Phenomenology and the Cognitive Sciences* 4(1): 23- 48

Gibson, J. J. 1979. *The Ecological Approach to Visual Perception*. Boston: Houghton Mifflin

Griffin, D. 1981. *The Question of Animal Awareness*. Los Altos: William Kaufman Inc.

— 2001. *Animal minds: beyond cognition to consciousness*. Chicago & London: University of Chicago Press.

Hannaford, B. 2002. 'Haptic Research — Teleoperation'. On line at: http://haptic.mech.nwu.edu/Teleoperation.html   (consulted 25.01.2005) Hayles, N. K. 1999. *How We Became Posthuman: Virtual Bodies in Cybernetics, Literature, and Informatics*. Chicago: University of Chicago Press.

Head, H. & Holmes, G. 1911 — 1912. 'Sensory disturbances from cerebral lesions' in *Brain* 34:102–254.

Heidegger, M. 1962. *Being and time* (translated by John Macquarrie and Edward Robinson). London: SCM Press.

Hume, D. 1739. *A Treatise of Human Nature* (edited, with an analytical index by L.A. Selby-Bigge). Oxford: Oxford University Press.

Kant, I. 1929 (1781/87). *The Critique of Pure Reason* (trans. Norman Kemp Smith. UK: Macmillan (A edition 1781, B edition 1787)

Kurzweil, R. 1999. *The Age of Spiritual Machines: When Computers Exceed Human Intelligence*. New York: Penguin.

Locke, J. 1690. *An Essay Concerning Human Understanding*. UK: Collins Fount Paperbacks

McClelland, J.L; Rumelhart, D.E. & Hinton, G.E. 1986. 'The appeal of parallel distributed processing' in McClelland & Rumelhart, D.E. (eds.) *Parallel Distributed Processing*, Volume 2. Cambridge, MA: MIT Press.

Merleau-Ponty, M. 2002 (1962). *Phenomenology of Perception* (translated by Colin Smith) London: Routledge.

Meijsing, M. 2000. 'Self-Consciousness and the Body' in *Journal of Consciousness Studies* 7(6): 34-50.

Ramachandran, V.S. & Blakeslee, S. 1998. *Phantoms in the Brain: Probing the Mysteries of the Human Mind.* New York: William Morrow.

Ramachandran, V.S. 2003. *The Emerging Mind.* London: BBC in association with Profile Books Ltd.

Reed, C.L. 2002. 'What is the body schema?' in Printz, W. & Meltzoff, A. (eds.) *The Imitative Mind: Development, Evolution, and Brain Bases.* Cambridge, UK: Cambridge University Press: 233-43.

Ruvinsky, J. 2003. 'Haptic technology simulates the sense of touch — via computer'. On line at: http://news-service.stanford.edu/news/2003/april2/haptics-42.html (consulted 26.01.2005).

Salisbury, K. 1995. 'Haptics: The Technology of Touch' in *HPCwire Special to HPCwire.*

Shear, J. 1997. *Explaining Consciousness: The Hard Problem.* Cambridge, MA: MIT Press.

Stern, D. 1985. *The Interpersonal World of the Infant: A View from Psychoanalysis and Developmental Psychology.* New York: Basic Books.

Stone, R.J. (2000) 'Haptic Feedback: A Potted History, From Telepresence to Virtual Reality', *First International Workshop on Haptic Human-Computer Interaction,* Glasgow, August 31-September 1.

Strawson, G. 1997. 'The Self' in *Journal of Consciousness Studies* 4(5/6): 405–428.

— 1999. 'The Self and the SESMET' in *Journal of Consciousness Studies* 6(4): 99–135.

Stuart, S. 2002. 'A Radical Notion of Embeddedness: A Logically Necessary Precondition for Agency and Self-Awareness' in *The Journal of Metaphilosophy* 33(1/2): 98-109.

Walsh, W. H. 1975. *Kant's Criticism of Metaphysics.* UK: Edinburgh University Press.

Washburn, D. 2004. 'Haptic Applications for Multi-Modal Environments Research (HAMMER) Laboratory'. On line at: www.ist.ucf.edu/pdfs/Haptics.pdf (consulted January 2005).

Youngblut, C.; Johnson, R.E.; Nash, S.H.; Wienclaw, R. A. & Will, C.A. 1996. 'Review of Virtual Environment Interface Technology', IDA Paper P-3186, Final, March 1996.

Notes

[1] I say 'almost completely' because Kant fails to give Descartes credit for his insight that there is a necessary referent for a thought, or even for a depiction, even if Descartes does then go on to over-develop the 'I' or *cogito* as a *sum res cogitans*. It would seem that if the judgement 'I think' is a transcendental judgement, the 'vehicle of all concepts'; it is the vehicle of transcendental concepts in particular, and this ought to be compatible with its implying existence, which it seems Kant is not prepared to admit. The 'I' is not just a vehicle, there is some referent having the thought. If Kant resists this existential implication, how much of the Cartesian programme is left? Surely it is possible for Kant to accept the *cogito* without being committed to the *sum res cogitans* doctrine, but he discards both.

If Descartes had not claimed that knowledge of the experiencing subject was possible *a priori*, and had not then tried to move from the *cogito* doctrine to the *sum res cogitans*, he would have been left with the interesting and informative thesis that the 'I' is guaranteed a referent, but he attempts too much. None of this is in dispute, but Kant's own attack is incoherent. He has said, in his arguments for a transcendental unity of apperception, that there is an 'I' that can accompany my representations, it is an 'I' whose existence is implied, yet in the paralogisms he speaks as though we cannot even go this far. The Cartesian point seems good because existence is implied, regardless of the truth-value of the statement 'I think', and the 'I' is guaranteed a referent. Kant should not attack the *cogito*. The 'I' is more than a vehicle, some referent is disclosed by the use of 'I', and Kant suggests as much in his introduction of the transcendental subject.

The 'I' needs a referent and the Cartesian insight in the *cogito* is secure. Kant should shift his attack on rational psychology more decisively to the *sum res cogitans* where he can acknowledge the partial success of the Cartesian programme while bringing to a halt its further excesses. After all we find that the Cartesian 'illusion cannot be avoided', though a direct attack on the *sum res cogitans* doctrine can render it 'harmless'.

[2] One might think here about solitary confinement or sensory deprivation, both of which create in the experiencer feelings of dislocation and disorientation.

[3] Externalists hold that mental events do not supervene merely on physical events internal to the agent's body, but supervene on environmental events as well.

[4] It is arguable that I might be a pianist but only play very badly, but I think that in our conception of 'a pianist' there is the implicit assumption that the pianist plays, at least, moderately well!

[5] Information about these films can be found at *The Internet Movie database:* http://www.imdb.com/

[6] Descartes's position is complicated but the basis for his division is possession of a soul. Only human beings possess souls, so only human beings have minds and are conscious. We know of their self-consciousness because they have a language with which they report their thoughts and feelings, and no other animal has language. Indeed Descartes takes the absence of language to be *a priori* proof of the absence of consciousness. For more information read, for example, *Descartes*, edited by John Cottingham (1998).

[7] The neurologists Head and Holmes (1912) coined the term 'body schema' from their examination of patients with lesions of the nervous system. For contemporary work

on body schema and its role in defining our sense of self from a neurological point of view based on research into phantom limbs, paralyses and mirror neurons see, for example, Ramachandran 1998 & 2003, and Reed 2002: 233-243.

[8] Duke-Elder states that; "the most salient factor in the evolution of man was the ousting of smell as the dominant sense and its replacement by the infinitely more useful and effective faculty of vision".

[9] One excellent example is the 'haptic cow' being designed by Sarah Baillie at the University of Glasgow. On line at: http://www.dcs.gla.ac.uk/~sarah/brpsX.html

[10] Once again, *Viz.* Nick Bostrom (2003).

[11] Technology of a much more limited kind is already employed to extend the perception of self to correspond with the inner sense of self and the best example to date is Ramachandran's mirror box with which he treats patients with phantom limb pain (1998, 2003, pp 10-20).

Where's the screen? The paradoxical relationship between mind and world

Robert Pepperell

In this chapter I will consider recent philosophical proposals about the extended mind, and link them to wider epistemological arguments about extensionism, and boundaries in general. I will argue that evidence from neuropsychology, recent developments in paraconsistent logic, and certain tendencies in the development of technology suggest that the human experience of reality might be regarded as essentially paradoxical. This, I suggest, adds further support for the notion of an extended mind.

> One of the most dangerous of ideas for a philosopher is, oddly enough, that we think with our heads or in our heads. The idea of thinking as a process in the head, in a completely enclosed space, gives him something occult.
> *Ludwig Wittgenstein, Zettel.*

Introduction

The recent scientific study of consciousness has been largely driven by the assumption that, whatever it is, consciousness is located in the human head. Some cognitive neuroscientists have claimed that very specific parts of the brain are responsible for certain conscious states, and for many the holy grail of neurological research is to identify the so-called 'neural correlates of consciousness', or those precise biological structures that sustain our lived, aware experience[1]. What this amounts to, it could be argued, is a perpetuation of the long-theorized split between thinking substance (internally located) and non-thinking substance (externally located), which has been a perennial problem for the philosophy of mind from at least the time of Descartes. For cognitive neuroscientists, and some philosophers, there is in effect a distinction between the conscious mind located in the brain and the non-conscious objective world in the extended space beyond[2].

The belief that consciousness, mind and in fact all perceptual and cognitive activity resides in the head — sometimes called 'internalism' — has been challenged in recent years. There are growing numbers of philosophers, psychologists and biologists who claim that the conscious mind extends in one way or another beyond the neurological fabric of the brain. They propose 'distributed' or 'externalist' models of mind that locate consciousness more widely in the body, in environmental objects, and even the far reaches of the cosmos[3]. Although internalism has dominated contemporary science and humanities, externalist models are increasingly being applied in areas like robotics and cultural anthropology[4].

The purpose of this chapter is to consider some of the arguments in favour of the internalist and externalist models of mind and to show that while they seem diametrically opposed, in fact, we have good reasons for holding to both. Not only does this obviously make it very hard to choose between them, it may point to a deeper epistemological crisis in which the very assumption that there can be a choice is thrown into doubt.

To help ground the discussion I will consider internalism and externalism with reference to a specific case that exemplifies many of the issues involved, namely the perception of screen-based moving images. Despite the numerous differences between formats (DVD, video, film, etc.), screen-based media have certain attributes in common, not least the capacity to command our visual attention and sustain a compelling illusion. This investigation will focus, therefore, on theories and evidence about visual perception and cognition, which is not to deny the importance of other sensory modalities.

Considering how the mind relates to images on a screen is an unavoidably transdisciplinary undertaking that implicates a range of overlapping fields, some of which will be mentioned here, but none of which can account for the totality of the experience alone. Indeed it is unclear whether even a transdisciplinary approach combining knowledge from the arts, sciences and humanities would be able to fully account for the deepest epistemological and metaphysical problems that a foundational consideration of this perceptual act entails. Even a question that might appear prima facie to have a stupendously obvious answer — 'Where is the screen located in relation to the viewer who perceives it?' — may turn out to be impossible to resolve unambiguously. Nevertheless, I will refer to this question while sketching a tentative transdisciplinary response, drawing on some recent ideas in the philosophy of mind, Consciousness Studies and non-classical logic.

Internalism

There is much theoretical and empirical evidence to support a distinction between internal subjective experience and external objective reality, and hence an internalist model of mind. Because this model requires an indirect relationship between mind and reality, where reality is represented rather than directly accessed in the exterior world, it can be understood as a form of 'representationalism'. In representationalism we perceive things differently from what they are. Take a common visual illusion like the Necker cube:

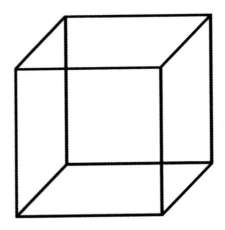

Figure 1. The Necker cube

Figure 1. consists a number of black lines arranged on a white surface. The image is flat, having no three-dimensional attributes; this much is almost too obvious to state. Yet despite being fully aware of these facts, I see a three-dimensional cube where there is none[5]. With some concentration I am able to judge it for what it is: a perspective-less pattern of lines and shapes, interlocking triangles and trapezoids. But it insists on reverting to a depth illusion as soon as my will falters. Moreover, the depth illusion flips between upward and downward orientations, sometimes at my volition, sometimes not. Strange to say, the picture does not change, but what I see changes. True to say, the illusory cube is oriented *both* downward and upward.

In psychology, this effect is often taken as evidence that retinal apprehension is subject to perceptual processing before becoming available to consciousness. In other words, I am seeing with my mind as much as, if not more than with my eyes, where 'seeing' means not just sensing light but interpreting visual data according to memory, experience or imagination. I am bound to cognize the arrangement of lines such that I misrepresent what is there, even when I am aware of the misrepresentation[6].

The Necker cube illusion illustrates the discrepancy between subjective experience (what is seen) and objective reality (what is there), a distinction that has long been recognised in philosophy, and more recently in psychology. One of the leading figures in early experimental psychophysiology, Hermann von Helmholtz (1821-94), was instrumental in establishing the scientific basis of this distinction, which had previously been maintained on philosophical grounds by figures such as John Locke and Immanuel Kant. Helmholtz (Cahan 1995) argued that we are mistaken when we assume a veridical connection between quantitative physical stimuli, e.g. certain electromagnetic frequencies, and their qualitative apprehension in the mind, e.g. certain colours:

> ... the objects at hand in space seem to us clothed with the qualities of our sensations. They appear to us as red or green, cold or warm, to have smell or taste, etc., although these qualities of sensation belong to our nervous system alone and do not at all reach beyond into external space. Yet even when we know this, the appearance does not end, because this appearance is, in fact, the *original truth*...(1995: 352, my emphasis)

For Helmholtz, we unconsciously infer a holistic representation of visual reality through fragmentary clues gathered from the external environment by our senses; thus the world we see is not objective or direct, but a subjective and indirect representation constructed internally by the nervous system.

Helmholtz's death at the end of the nineteenth century coincided with the birth of an illusionistic medium that provided an enduring example of this 'original truth' about perception. The technology of cinema requires an involuntary projection of subjective qualities into objective reality in order to sustain what became known as 'motion pictures', an inappropriate term given that the cinema audience sees no images move at all. Each frame is held still in the gate of the projector for a fraction of a second before being blacked out by a shutter as the film reel shunts to the next frame. The oft-cited belief that the appearance of motion is due to the 'persistence of vision' in the eye is now almost entirely discredited[7]. Instead, it seems that illusory motion in cinema is attributable more to neurology than ocularity. Although the precise psychological and neurological mechanisms at play are still not understood, we do have mounting evidence that given the right cues the brain can perceive motion where none exists objectively.

Work undertaken by neurobiologist Semir Zeki (1993 et al.) shows how even unchanging images (such as Isia Leviant's *Enigma* painting[8]) can give rise to perceptions of movement that can be detected in areas of the brain active during objective, that is, real motion; so the sensation of motion can occur quite independently of whether any actual motion is present before the eyes. This fact, combined with the determination that motion consciousness is most likely consequent on a specific portion of the brain, damage to which can cause a condition known as *akinetopsia* which leaves subjects unable to see things that move (Zihl et al. 1980), implies that whatever may be happening 'out there' the appearance of motion is a construction of the brain 'in here'.

Helmholtz's views and the evidence from neurobiology tend to support a 'representationalist' approach to human consciousness and perception. Put very simply, this means that what we know of the world is not garnered directly from external stimuli but construed from internal representations of reality in our minds[9]. For the representationalist and the internalist, the screen we see is not the 'real' screen but an internal representation of a screen. The degree to which the internal representation coincides with external reality is, as one would expect, the subject of vigorous debate; but they are nevertheless regarded as distinct. This of course connotes a tension between what we see and what is there — that what appears to us in our conscious mind is to some degree independent from what exists in the world.

Externalism

Despite the predominance of internalist models there is also strong evidence to suggest a contrary view: that the development and operation of perception, at least in the case of visual cognition, is entirely dependent on direct engagement with the external world[10].

In his book on art and the brain, *Inner Vision,* Semir Zeki (1999) cites the work of an early twentieth-century French surgeon, Moreau, who perfected a technique for removing congenital cataracts in children. Since the late-seventeenth century, philosophers like John Locke had speculated as to how a person blind from birth would see the world if their sight could be repaired. Rather than the glorious revelation of an elaborate spectacle, as Biblical miracles might lead us to expect, Moreau's patients reported extreme difficulty in making out anything at all, and he concluded:

> It would be an error to suppose that a patient whose sight has been restored to him by surgical intervention can thereafter see the external world (Zeki 1999: 92).

Moreau concluded, and more recent evidence has confirmed, that without appropriate sensory stimulation the visual components of the brain fail to develop the capacity for instantaneous object recognition that sighted people take for granted. In cases where sight has been repaired, it usually takes years for the necessary adaptations to occur in the patient's perceptual system before visual data can become a useful source of information about the world, and even then most prefer to trust the tactile cues they have been most familiar with since birth.

In fact there are numerous sad reports of once confident and assured individuals becoming deeply depressed and insecure shortly after having acquired vision. In a seminal study, the psychologist Richard Gregory (1963), working with Jean Wallace, wrote of the case of S.B., a middle-aged man whose vision was restored after nearly a lifetime of almost complete blindness. The subject had been a cheerful and dominant person before the operations through which his sight was restored.

> But talking to him now he seemed dispirited, and we formed a strong impression that his sight was to him almost entirely disappointing... He described the world as rather drab; he still to a great extent lived the life of a blind man, sometimes not bothering to put on the light at night, and he still made little of the normal visual occupations of the cinema or television (Gregory & Wallace 1963: 33).

Without early and continual stimulation from the world, the capacity for visual perception is severely impoverished, even obliterated, although alternative modes of perception can develop to compensate. Despite his lifelong handicap and the deficiencies of his post-operative vision, S.B. showed a remarkably immediate grasp of certain visual forms after the restoration of sight. According to Gregory, this was because he was able to translate across modalities, that is, to project his tactile knowledge into the visual world.

Perhaps the most important outcome of our study is the evidence it provides for transfer from early touch experience to vision many years later. The fact that our patient was able, certainly with a minimum of training — and perhaps with none at all — to recognise by vision upper case letters which he had learned by touch, and that he was unable to recognise by vision lower case letters which he had not learned by touch, provides strong evidence for cross-modal transfer (Gregory & Wallace 1963: 37).

The case of S.B. confirms that we need direct contact with reality to build up any cognitive map of our environment. But it also demonstrates that the information we gather through each different sense need not necessarily be restricted to that specific modality. Through the process of physically exploring the world during early development we synthesise all our senses — sight, smell, touch, etc.; building up a 'cross-modal' account of our environment that allows us, for example, to 'see' roughness from a visible texture, 'feel' shininess by the gloss of a material or 'hear' different kinds of space. It is this capacity that enables people deficient in one sense to develop compensatory abilities in others[11].

Gathering information about the world by a combination of sensations and bodily actions requires co-ordinated 'sensorimotor' activity — integrating sensory data with bodily and spatial awareness — and is of fundamental importance to the way we interact with the environment. Although psychologists generally recognise this, it is given differing weight according to the model of perception that is favoured. One model that strongly emphasises sensorimotor integration is the so-called 'enactive' approach to visual cognition.

In an important and controversial paper, *A sensorimotor account of vision and visual consciousness*, experimental psychologist Kevin O'Regan and philosopher Alva Noë (2001) argue that the world we see is really 'out there' and not 'in here', drawing on empirical evidence from perceptual phenomena like change blindness to support their case. Change blindness[12] is a remarkable phenomenon, discovered by O'Regan and colleagues, in which quite large changes between images will usually not be perceived if there is a brief interruption, like a blank or a flash, between one image and the next. O'Regan claims that we do not hold a detailed representation of the visual world in our brain, but continually access the real detail 'out there' through active engagement with the world. One way of demonstrating what O'Regan and Noë call 'the world as an outside memory' is to look at any scene for a few seconds, then close your eyes, and try to visualise it in as much detail as you can. Unless you have a photographic memory, it is very likely you will have only the haziest picture of what was in front of your eyes but a few seconds ago.

Unlike the internalists, O'Regan and Noë's approach stresses the externality of perception as conditioned by the active engagement of the body and senses with the world.

> ... seeing is a way of acting. It is a particular way of exploring the environment. Activity in internal representations does not generate the experience of seeing. The outside world serves as its own, external, representation. The experience of seeing occurs when the organism masters what we call the governing laws of sensorimotor contingency (O'Regan & Noë 2001: 939).

For the enactive theorist the screen and the viewer's perception of it are (at least in part) 'out there', an external presence sustaining our memory and cognition. The technical apparatus and the objects it represents are yoked, as it were, to the sensory apparatus of the viewer in a way that extends the perceptual domain far beyond the immediate locality of the brain and its store of memories and experiences.

Double reality

The ideas and evidence presented so far paint a rather two-sided picture of the relationship between mind and world. One might call it, to borrow a phrase from Richard Gregory, a 'double reality'. First, it seems the subjective operation of visual perception is to a great extent independent of what exists objectively; the mind operates internally within the confines of a 'sensory horizon'. One might also refer to dreams and vivid hallucinations as examples of veridical perceptual experiences that (as far as we know) are internally generated rather than derived from direct sensory data. Second, it seems that without early and continuous sensory contact with the external world, visual perception can barely develop at all. And even then, according to the enactivists, we need to actively maintain direct continuity between mind and world if we are to enjoy rich, detailed knowledge of what is around us.

This leaves us with opposing responses to the question of where the screen might be located, and how it relates to the mind that perceives it. Put bluntly, for those defending internalism the screen is perceived in the mind, and for the externalists the screen is perceived in the world. Hence, we are faced not just with a technical contradiction about the location of the screen, but a metaphysical contradiction about the relationship between mind and world.

Contradiction, paradox and circularity in mind-world relations

The question of how a perceiving subject relates to a perceived object is inextricably bound to the more general question of how the mind relates to the world. Is the mind an independent realm that remains distinct from external reality; or is the mental realm an extension or continuation of reality? Without an adequate response we can never definitely choose between internalism and externalism, and will never know exactly how the screen stands in relation to the viewer.

The uncertain relationship between mind and world has of course generated countless finely nuanced philosophical arguments. But, put starkly, it seems there are three options:

> That the mind and world are distinct.
> That the mind and world are unified.
> That the mind and world are both distinct and unified[13].

Depending on which of these mutually inconsistent claims one holds, one will arrive at a different solution to the question of where the screen is located. While there are many powerful arguments in favour of the first two options, it is the third I will explore here, and the one I will suggest is most plausible. It seems sensible to embark on the discussion by reference to the thinker who inaugurated the modern philosophical debate on the relationship between mind and world.

René Descartes (1596-1650) is often credited with formalising the dualist distinction between thinking substance (*res cogitans*) and material substance (*res extensa*); that is, between ideas attributable to the mind on the one hand and the material world of bodies and objects on the other[14]. He made some very elegant arguments in favour of this distinction, one of the most famous is found in Meditation VI of his *Meditations on First Philosophy*:

> ... there is a vast difference between mind and body, in respect that body, from its nature, is always divisible, and that mind is entirely indivisible. For in truth, when I consider the mind, that is, when I consider myself in so far only as I am a thinking thing, I can distinguish in myself no parts, but I very clearly discern that I am somewhat absolutely one and entire... But quite the opposite holds in corporeal or extended things; for I cannot imagine any one of them (how small so ever it may be), which I cannot easily sunder in thought, and which, therefore, I do not know to be divisible (1912: 139).

For Descartes, the indivisible conscious mind has the unique quality of being certain — we can't be deceived into believing we have a mind without first having a mind to be deceived. The divisible material world, by contrast, might be entirely illusory, or put another way, what we know about the physical world may not in fact accord with what is *really* there, since our senses are imperfect and prone to deceive us[15]. The force and simplicity of Descartes' arguments are such that they are difficult to overturn to this day, and remain the subject of voluminous scholarship.

Descartes' reputation as the prototypical dualist, however, does not fairly convey the complexity, some say confusion, of his view on the distinction between mind and world. In the synopsis of the *Meditations*, we read:

> ... the human mind is shown to be really distinct from the body, and, nevertheless, to be so closely conjoined therewith, as together to form, as it were, a unity (1912: 78).

And again in Meditation VI itself:

> Nature teaches me... that I am not only lodged in my body as a pilot in a vessel, but that I am besides so intimately conjoined, as it were intermixed with it, that my mind and body compose a certain unity (1912: 135).

Despite the hint of qualification, Descartes is quite explicit: The mind and body are *both* 'really distinct' *and* united — they are two and one. Indeed, his later writings confirm an increasing commitment to the 'substantial union' of mind and body, while at the same time never retracting his belief in their distinctiveness. In his last book, *The Passions of the Soul* (1649), Descartes argues that the union of mind and body is an empirical fact deducible from lived experience. This appeared self-contradictory to those who regarded him as the most prominent advocate of dualism[16].

On the face of it, Descartes' position is not only inconsistent but potentially paradoxical and circular. One of the main pillars of his argument for the distinction between mind and material bodies is that the mind, unlike the body, is indivisible — whatever is in thought consists in one entity. But, in order to claim my mind is (in Descartes' words) 'really distinct' from my body I have to think about two conceptual categories, namely 'mind' and 'body'. Since both these categories are bound together in a single thought concerning the relation between the two, they are both part of my mind and so not really divisible or distinct. The notion of 'body', then, is ultimately mental.

We are indeed faced with paradox and circularity: First, to make the distinction between mind and body Descartes has to deny the possibility of making the distinction; the body cannot be conceived separately from the mind that conceives it. Second, if the notion of 'mind' is a conceptual category attributable to the mind, how can it be a distinction of itself?[17]

True contradictions

Like many before who have considered how mind and world relate, we are being sucked into the jaws of contradiction, paradox and circularity. And the natural temptation is to kick and fight our way out.

Philosophers are sometimes led by the force of argument to contradictory and paradoxical conclusions and, finding themselves staring at these vicious teeth, look for another way out. For instance, discussing the existence or non-existence of mind-independent reality in *Realism and Anitrealism* (Alston 2002), Mark S. McLeod recognises that the compelling nature of the arguments on both sides suggests each might be equally valid. That is, the 'realist' view that there is a world which exists irrespective of whether we are there to think about it is just as compelling as the 'anti-realist' view that the world is dependent on our minds for its existence. Hence, a contradiction: realism is true and anti-realism is true. But he rules out this conclusion on the grounds that "there is no pair of contradictory statements both of which we *must* admit is true" (Alston 2002: 29). And so McLeod's interim solution is to posit two worlds, one in which the realist position holds and one in which the antirealist position holds. This is his way out.

Whether the 'two worlds' solution is any less fantastical or illogical than the one it seeks to avoid should be judged by the reader after having consulted McLeod's argument in full. It is mentioned here only to illustrate the reluctance on the part of some contemporary philosophers to countenance the possibility of contradictory conclusions. As the rather cruel jibe attributed to Kierkegaard has it, "Take away paradox from the thinker and you have a professor."

But there have been a number of recent thinkers willing to countenance contradictory solutions and construct plausible logical and philosophical systems to accommodate them. Prominent among these are Stéphane Lupasco (1987), George Melhuish (1973), and more recently, Graham Priest, whose book *Beyond the Limits of Thought* (2002) rigorously sets out arguments in favour of what he calls 'dialethic' logic (literally — 'two truths') in which 'true contradictions' become unavoidable when we contemplate the ultimate limits of thought and reality.

> I claim that reality is, in a certain sense, contradictory... What I mean is that there are certain contradictory statements (propositions, sentences — take your pick) about limits that are true (2002: 295).

For example, when we try to conceive the limits of thought and what might lie beyond, we encounter the following: The unknowable is precisely that which we can know nothing about, and in knowing we can know nothing about it we know something about it, which is contradictory, not to say paradoxical.

For Priest, such contradictions are not logical aberrations, nor the result of fundamental errors of conception; they are a part of the fabric of human experience. Even the doctrine of dialethism itself is not immune to the same conclusion. He says: "... it may... be rational to accept that dialetheism is both true and false. In a sense, this is what I do accept" (Priest 2002: 275). A visual case of dialethia occurs in the shape of the Necker cube discussed earlier, for which it is just as true to say it appears oriented upwards as downwards.

Since, as Priest shows, certain aspects of our conception of reality and existence are inherently contradictory, there are valid logical precedents for making the following claims: that mind and world are *both* distinct and unified; that visual perception occurs *both* internally and externally.

This is bad news for those seeking a clear-cut answer to the question of where the screen is located and where it is perceived. Were the mind and world distinct we could more justifiably defend the internalist view that the screen is perceived somewhere inside the perceptual apparatus of the brain. Were the mind and world unified we would tend towards the externalist position that the perception of the screen occurs as much in the world as it does inside the mind, since the two are continuous. But on the third count, that of simultaneous distinction and unity, we encounter a dialethic state — the screen is perceived 'in here' and 'out there' *at the same time.*

A dialethic model of the viewer-screen relationship

The case put so far is this: both internalist and externalist models of mind are plausible that leads to a contradiction. But as I have suggested, attempts to rationalise the relationship between mind and world seem bound to lead to contradiction, not to say paradox and circularity. This does not necessarily negate the possibility of knowing how mind and world relate, although it may expose what Graham Priest calls the 'limits of thought'. Consequently, questions such as 'Where is the screen located in relation to the viewer?', cannot be answered in any non-contradictory sense; the best that can be said is that the screen exists in some Schrödingerian state of indeterminacy, being both distinct from and unified with the audience, experienced both inside the viewer's head and outside it. What might the implications be for our understanding of the viewer-screen relationship?

First, when considering the relationship of mind to screen, we can no longer conceive of two distinct sets of apparatus, one sentient and the other insentient, one internal and the other external to the viewer. Further theoretical and practical investigations of how mind and screen relate may need to take this into account. Second, the peculiarly compelling nature of the illusion of moving images and the oft-drawn analogies between film and mind, have tempted us to think of either 'the screen in the mind' or the 'mind on the screen'; that is to say, either phenomenal experience is played out through some internal projection — a Cartesian theatre of the kind critiqued by Dennett (1991) — or the screen stands as a prosthetic mind-extension which displaces our mental experience into the technological world. Given the present considerations, neither of these can be complete as a self-standing model, although a combination of both may be viable. Third, the dialethic logic applied here may help to account for the efficacy of the illusion in which we simultaneously believe in and do not believe in what the screen affords — the so-called 'Paradox of Fiction'. For the characters, objects and events that appear neither in the mind nor on the screen alone are, being representations, *simultaneously* present and absent. As viewers we are trapped in a perceptual vice between opposing forces, transfixed (in the sense of both pierced and fastened) by the pincers of an immaculate contradiction between two sets of belief. Finally, the possibility of a 'conscious cinema' — an enhanced cinema that deploys prospective artificially conscious technology — cannot be discounted. Given the increasing proximity of artificial intelligence and interactive entertainment, we can expect a great deal of theorisation to emerge on the subject of mind-technology integration in the field of sentient entertainment systems, with an extension of current debates in AI about the degree to which cognition can be understood as an internalised or an externalised process[18]. It is precisely here that a dialethic model offers a way of managing these divergent tendencies, although clearly not to the satisfaction of those wedded to a purely classical logic.

Transdisciplinary approaches

A dialethic model of the viewer-screen relationship, which condones contradiction, paradox and circularity, and renders the relationship between viewer and screen with a high degree of indeterminacy, may prove useful in subsequent analyses, if only because it offers hope of a reconciliation between internalism and externalism without neutralising either. The dominance of internalism has receded in recent years as scholars pay greater heed to notions of the world as extended mind or external memory and explore alternative models of ecological cognition, intersubjective relations and distributed consciousness[19]. Some examples are presented in this volume. But the model offered here could be regarded as creating more problems than it resolves. It may, for instance, lead to doubt about the validity of 'internal' and 'external' as epistemological descriptors, that the distinction itself is invalid, or at least unhelpful.

The question of how mind and world relate is ultimately a metaphysical one that may never be definitively resolved. But it is a question that nevertheless remains central to all epistemological and ontological debates, and upon which all solutions will finally depend. In our quest to respond productively to these debates we will turn increasingly, I believe, to transdisciplinary modes of inquiry, seeking insights from all branches of the humanities, sciences and arts, and perhaps more esoteric forms of knowledge that are as yet to be academically sanctioned. In seeking to orchestrate knowledge from across several disciplinary fields this chapter is a microscopically small contribution to this larger project.

Bibliography

Alston, W. P. 2002. *Realism & Antirealism*. New York: Cornell University Press.

Anderson, J. & B. 1993. 'The Myth of Persistence of Vision Revisited' in *Journal of Film and Video* 45(1): 3-12.

Anderson, J. 1998. *The Reality of Illusion: An Ecological Approach to Cognitive Film Theory*. Carbondale: Southern Illinois University Press.

Cahan, D. (ed.) 1995. *Herman Von Helmholtz: Science and culture.* Chicago: Chicago University Press.

Chalmers, D. & Clark, A. 1998. 'The Extended Mind' in *Analysis* 58: 10-23.

Clark, A. 2004. 'Embodiment and the Philosophy of Mind' in Peruzzi, A. (ed.). *Mind and Causality.* Philadelpia: John Benjamins.

— 1997. *Being There: Putting Brain, Body and World Together Again.* Cambridge, MA: MIT Press.

Crick, F. & Koch, C. 1998. 'Consciousness and Neuroscience' in *Cerebral Cortex* 8: 97-107.

Dennett, D. 1991. *Consciousness Explained.* New York: Little, Brown & Company.

Deregowski, J. B. 1980. *Illusions, Patterns and Pictures: A Cross-Cultural Perspective.* London: Academic Press.

Descartes, R. (tr. J. Veitch 1912). *A Discourse on Method: Meditations and Principles.* London: J.M. Dent & Sons.

Garber, D. 2003. 'Descartes, René' in Craig, E. (ed.). *Routledge Encyclopedia of Philosophy.* London: Routledge. On line at: http://www.rep.routledge.com/article/DA026SECT8 (consulted 23.12.04).

Gell, A. 1998. *Art and Agency: An Anthropological Theory.* Oxford: Oxford University Press.

Giambattista della Porta. 1584. *Magia Naturalis.* (English translation 1658).

Gregory, R. and Wallace, J. 1963. 'Recovery from Early Blindness: A Case Study' in *Experimental Psychology Society Monograph* No. 2. On line at http://.www.richardgregory.org (consulted 23.12.04).

Gribbin, J. 1992. *In Search of Schrödinger's Cat.* London: Black Swan.

Houghton, D. 1997. 'Mental Content and External Representations' in *The Philosophical Quarterly* 47(187): 159-177.

Lupasco, S. 1987. *Le Principe D'Antagonisme et la Logique de L'Énergie (L'Espirit at la Matière).* Paris: Le Rocher.

Melhuish, G. 1973. *The Paradoxical Nature of Reality.* Bristol: St Vincent's Press.

O'Regan, J. K.; Rensink, R. A.; & Clark, J. J. 1999. 'Change-blindness as a result of 'mudsplashes' in *Nature* 398: 34.

O'Regan, J. K. & Noë, A. 2001. 'A Sensorimotor Account of Vision and Visual Consciousness' in *Behavioural and Brain Sciences* 24: 939-1031.

Pepperell, R. 2003. 'Towards a Conscious Art' in *Technoetic Arts.* Volume 1 (2).

Putnam. H. 1975. 'The Meaning of 'Meaning' in *Mind, Language and Reality: Philosophical Papers.* Vol. II. Cambridge: Cambridge University Press.

Priest, G. 2002. *Beyond the Limits of Thought.* Oxford: Oxford University Press.

Russell, B. 1987. *A History of Western Philosophy.* London: Unwin.

Searle, J. 1983. *Intentionality.* Cambridge: Cambridge University Press.

Sheldrake, R. 2003. *The Sense of Being Stared At, and Other Aspects of the Extended Mind.* London: Crown.

Sobchack, V. 1991. *The Address of the Eye: A Phenomenology of Film Experience.* USA: Princeton University Press.

Watson, R. 1995. *Representational Ideas: From Plato to Patricia Churchland.* London: Kluwer.

Zeki et al. 1993. 'Going beyond the information given: the relation of illusory visual motion to brain activity' in *Proc. R. Soc. Lond. B.,* 252, 215-22.

Zeki, S. 1999. *Inner Vision: An Exploration of Art and the Brain.* Oxford: Oxford University Press.

Zihl, J. et al. 1980. 'Selective disturbance of movement vision after bilateral brain damage' in *Brain* 106: 313-40.

Notes

[1] For an important contribution to this work see Crick and Koch (1998).

[2] The philosopher John Searle (1983), for example, claims; "the brain is all we have for the purpose of representing the world to ourselves and everything we can use must be inside the brain." David Houghton (1997) makes an interesting counter argument.

[3] See for examples the work of Putnam (1975), Clark (1997) and Sheldrake (2003).

[4] See Clark (2004) and Gell (1998).

[5] I refer to my own perceptual experience here in order to avoid making assumptions about what others might experience. See note 6.

[6] Spatial readings of this kind are, however, not necessarily universal. In Jan Deregowski's (1980) studies on cross-cultural perception of illusions, for example, certain African subjects failed to see perspectival drawings as representations of depth.

[7] For an authoritative survey of the issue of persistence of vision in film theory see Anderson (1993).

[8] The image can be seen at
http://www.michaelbach.de/ot/mot_enigma/enigma780.gif.

[9] For an overview of representationalist thought see Watson (1995).

10 There are now many strands of externalist thought, some in disagreement with others. In addition to those already mentioned is the important paper by Chalmers and Clark (1998), which contributed to the wider discussion of the notion of 'extended mind' in recent philosophical debate.

11 See, for example, the extraordinary capacity some blind people have for 'facial vision', the ability to detect objects by their proximity to the face (O'Regan and Noë 2001: 959).

12 See O'Regan et al. (1999) and numerous examples on line, e.g. http://eyelab.msu.edu/VisualCognition/flicker.html.

13 There is another — that the mind and world are neither distinct nor unified — but since it is a variation on the third, we will not consider it here.

14 While not its originator, in *A History of Western Philosophy* Bertrand Russell says Descartes; "brought to completion, or very near completion, the dualism of mind and matter which began with Plato…" (1987: 550)

15 This is not to say that Descartes disputes the existence of the physical world, but he believes it to be of a different substance than the mental, which is what makes him, in the philosophical jargon, a dualist rather than an idealist.

16 For a discussion see Garber (2003).

17 The point here is not to undermine Descartes, or engage in detailed rebuttal and counter-rebuttal of the multiple interpretations of his philosophy. Rather it is to demonstrate that such considerations of the mind-body problem quickly test the bounds of rational thought.

18 For a discussion on internal vs. external theories of mind in contemporary AI, see Clark (2004).

19 See, for example, Anderson (1993) and Sobchack (1991).

INDEX

Printed in the United Kingdom
by Lightning Source UK Ltd.
114669UKS00001B/138